Praise for
Forever Flying

"Hardly any aviation buff will not have heard of Bob Hoover, and none will fail to be fascinated by his autobiography. . . . He has also met most of the other important aviators of the last sixty years, which well enables him to offer vivid portraits of the flyers as well as the machines. Thoroughly enthralling from beginning to end, this should be considered a mandatory addition to any self-respecting aviation collection."

— Roland Green, *Booklist*

"Entertaining anecdotes and insights that span the fifty-year career of the man General Jimmy Doolittle called 'the greatest stick and rudder pilot who ever lived.' . . . FOREVER FLYING is a work that should be on everyone's bookshelf."

— Daryl Murphy, *General Aviation News & Flyer*

"Hoover describes fully the maneuvers that make his air-show performances among the best in the world . . . a quick short course in all the spectacular stunts."

— *Abilene Reporter-News* (TX)

"Writing with the swagger he has justly earned, Hoover breezes past the mundane details . . . in favor of an unending series of flying stories and reminiscences that are full of nifty details. Casual readers as well as airplane buffs will be fascinated."

— *Library Journal*

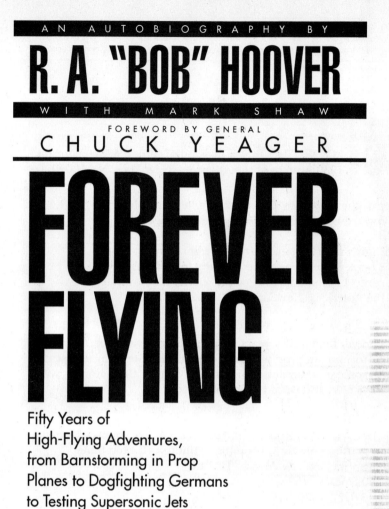

AN AUTOBIOGRAPHY BY

R. A. "BOB" HOOVER

WITH MARK SHAW

FOREWORD BY GENERAL
CHUCK YEAGER

FOREVER FLYING

Fifty Years of
High-Flying Adventures,
from Barnstorming in Prop
Planes to Dogfighting Germans
to Testing Supersonic Jets

POCKET BOOKS
New York   London   Toronto   Sydney   Tokyo   Singapore

POCKET BOOKS, a division of Simon & Schuster Inc.
1230 Avenue of the Americas, New York, NY 10020

Copyright © 1996 by Bob Hoover and Mark Shaw
Foreword copyright © 1996 by Chuck Yeager

Hoover, R. A. (Robert A.), 1922–
   Forever flying: fifty years of high-flying adventures, from
barnstorming in prop planes to dogfighting Germans to testing
supersonic jets : an autobiography / by R. A. "Bob" Hoover with
Mark Shaw : foreword by Chuck Yeager.
   p.   cm.
   ISBN 0-671-53761-X (pb)
   1. Hoover, R. A. (Robert A.), 1922–   .   2. Test pilots—United
States—Biography.   3. Air pilots, Military—United States—
Biography.   I. Shaw, Mark.   II. Title.
TL540.H66A3   1996
629.13'092—dc20
[B]   96-23017
                                                                 CIP

First Pocket Books trade paperback printing August 1997

10 9 8 7 6 5 4

POCKET and colophon are registered trademarks of
Simon & Schuster Inc.

Cover design by Joseph Perez; front cover photo by Robert
DeGroat; back cover photos by Rockwell International

Printed in the U.S.A.

*This book is dedicated
to my wife, Colleen,
and my children, Rob and Anita.*

ACKNOWLEDGMENTS

The authors wish to thank Richard Pine, the mercurial wonder of a literary agent who made this book possible. He is the very best at what he does and a valued friend. And Paul McCarthy, the gifted editor at Pocket Books, whose talent for the language and ability to inspire are unparalleled. No author could find two finer men with whom to work.

Additional thanks go to Wayne Smith and F. Lee Bailey, who brought the authors together, and to Jim Driskell, who contributed his aviation expertise to the manuscript.

Bob Hoover thanks his wife, Colleen, his son, Rob, and his daughter, Anita, for their continuing love and support. Also his good friend Chuck Yeager for writing the foreword to the book.

Mark Shaw thanks his colleague and friend Donna Stouder, whose ability to edit and write will one day make her a great author. He also thanks his beautiful wife, Chris Roark Shaw, and their children, Kimberly, Kyle, Kent, and Kevin, for their love and inspiration. And his six dogs, Bach, Snickers, White Sox, Peanut Butter, Shadow, and Reggie Miller, for their companionship and affection.

The authors also thank Wally Schirra, Jim McDivitt, Barron Hilton, Corwin Denny, Bob Cattoi, Tony LeVier, Ralph Albright, Dave Bingham, Fred Roark, and Denny McClendon for their contributions to the book.

Ladies and gentlemen, let me introduce to you Bob Hoover, the greatest stick-and-rudder pilot alive today. . . . No, that's wrong, let me introduce to you Bob Hoover, the greatest stick-and-rudder pilot who ever lived.

—Gen. James Doolittle, Retired
Monterey County Air Show, 1988

Suddenly, a P-38 prop fighter dove in on me. . . . I couldn't believe it. None of the other test pilots had ever started a dogfight, but this guy seemed determined to bounce on me.

I whipped the [Bell P-59] jet around and pulled up in a vertical climb . . . and I stalled going straight up. I was spinning down and that damn P-38 was spinning up, both airplanes out of control. . . . When we went by each other, not ten feet apart, my eyes were like saucers and so were the other pilot's.

We both fell out of the sky . . . smoking and wide-open. Finally, he said, "Hey, man, we'd better knock it off before we bust our asses."

I didn't know who *he* was. We landed, and I went over to meet this tall, lanky lieutenant. His name was Bob Hoover.

—Gen. Charles "Chuck" Yeager
From *Yeager: An Autobiography*

Awards Presented to Bob Hoover

MILITARY

Distinguished Flying Cross
Soldier's Medal for Valor
Air Medal with Clusters
Purple Heart
French Croix de Guerre

CIVILIAN

National Aviation Hall of Fame
Lindbergh Medal
International Council of Air Shows Hall of Fame
Society of Experimental Test Pilots
Kitty Hawk Award
Arthur Godfrey Aviation Award for Flight Testing
Wilkinson Silver Sword of Excellence
Aviation Pioneer Award
Aerospace Hall of Fame
International Aerobatic Pilot of the Year
Flying Tiger Pilot Award
Lloyd P. Nolen Lifetime Achievement in Aviation Award
Cliff Henderson National Aircraft Exposition Award
Godfrey L. Cabot Outstanding Contributions to the Science of
    Aerospace Award
Bill Barber Award for Showmanship
ICAS Art Scholl Award for Showmanship
Honorary Member—Original Eagle Squadron
Award of Merit—American Fighter Pilots Association
Honorary Member—American Fighter Aces Association
Honorary Member—Thunderbirds, Blue Angels

CONTENTS

Part IV

TEST-PILOT TERROR

Part V

FLYING OVER KOREA

Part VI

RETURN TO THE FRIENDLY SKIES

Part VII

AIR-SHOW MAGIC

FOREWORD

I simply call him Pard. That's my name for longtime friend Bob Hoover, the greatest pilot I ever saw.

I first met Bob at Wright Field in Dayton, Ohio, in 1945. We had just returned from the war, and I was assigned there as a maintenance officer.

I welcomed the challenge of flying with Bob since he was a former fighter pilot. Most of the test pilots at Wright Field didn't have that experience, but Bob's training made him a topflight aviator in any plane he flew.

The key to Bob's capability was his preparation. Whether he was test-flying experimental aircraft or blazing across the sky at air shows in P-51s, P-38s, and P-80s, Bob never tried any maneuver that he hadn't practiced over and over.

When we flew air shows together, Bob would go up above an overcast and use the top of it to simulate his baseline for the ground. He would practice every routine we were planning to do until it was as familiar as lacing his boots.

Bob was a true professional when it came to testing new aircraft. Flight engineers loved him because he would follow the "test card" orders to a T. Bob was also meticulous in gathering data, and if Bob Hoover told them something about a plane's capability or lack thereof, they knew they could count on it.

Other test pilots respected Bob because he could fly an airplane right on the feathered edge. He never expected a plane to do more than it was capable of, but he stretched the damn envelope as far as possible.

My dogfighting experiences with Bob still bring a smile to my face. There may be nothing I've ever done, including breaking the sound barrier, that gave me more pleasure.

That's in spite of the fact that when we battled, neither one of us could wax the other. We had many a dogfight in old AT-6s, but all we ever did was make each other sick by weaving all over the sky trying to gain the advantage.

We used to take a special AT-6 we'd rigged up and "smoke system."

Sometimes Bob and I took that plane up to Indian Lake north of the base. We'd try to write our wives' names in the sky, but we always got carried away and wrote some god-awful-looking words nobody could ever read.

Besides being a great pilot, Bob Hoover is about as good a friend as a man could have. He used to fly me down to see my wife, Glennis, in West Virginia in an old BT-13. Bob would land on a dime-sized dirt airstrip on the side of the hill, and I'd just meander over to my house. He would then take off downhill and drop into a hollow. I could hear the BT-13 grinding and whining away, but Pard would come back over that dirt strip upside down and then fly off toward Wright Field.

Flying together had its exciting moments as well. When we entered the X-1 program in an attempt to break the sound barrier, Bob and I flew up to the David Clark Company in Massachusetts to get fitted for pressurized suits. On the way back, our B-25 got hit by lightning and the blast nearly blinded us. All the Plexiglas was knocked out of the nose, and Bob and I gave each other that who's-going-to-bail-out-first look, but neither of us did.

Bob Hoover was never one to pass on a chance to unnerve me. I was hanging in the X-1 under the B-29 during one of the early nonpowered flights, going through my checklist and so forth. All at once my X-1 went blooey and jumped three feet in the air.

I looked out. There was ol' Pard zooming by in his P-80 chase plane rocking and rolling that X-1 so that he nearly shook it out of the sky. The words I yelled at him are unprintable, but I did get even later when I busted his tail in a dogfight during the final approach on a powered flight in that record-breaking plane.

While Bob and I had some great moments in the sky, many of my fondest memories came during cross-country road trips with him. The very day Bob got married to Colleen in Dayton, my six-month-old boy, Mickey, and I climbed in my Ford coupe with them for a "honeymoon" trip out to Muroc Air Force Base.

Since I was just a captain and Bob a first lieutenant, we weren't flush with money. We never rented a hotel or anything, just drove all day and night before Bob pulled off the road somewhere in the wilds of Oklahoma.

We gathered up some blankets and slept out in a graveyard. Bob was famous for having nightmares. I remember waking up and seeing poor Colleen chasing Bob around and through the gravestones trying to calm him down.

Bob and I also drove his 1947 Buick Roadmaster cross country from Wright Field to Muroc. I recall lying scrunched up in the backseat, half-asleep, hoping we weren't going to crash since Bob had that Buick wide open all the way. We actually covered the long distance in forty-three hours, stopping only to eat, go to the bathroom along the side of the road, and jump into a river here and there to cool off.

Through the years, watching Bob Hoover pilot a plane at air shows and exhibitions has been a thing of beauty. He's very disciplined and never flies in a dangerous manner. Bob's also a true perfectionist. If there's a risk involved, he knows it's a calculated one before he ever attempts those aerobatic routines that have made him famous.

Bob's distinguished career and his contributions to aviation speak for themselves. I've known him as a friend and fellow pilot for over fifty years, and I'm just one of many who truly love the man.

That's why it's indeed a privilege to write the foreword for Bob's book. His life is filled with wondrous adventures that seem almost unbelievable, and I guarantee that you'll be spellbound reading about one of history's greatest aviators.

CHUCK YEAGER
Brigadier General,
_United States Air Force, Retired

INTRODUCTION

Chuck Yeager calls him the "greatest pilot I ever saw" and "a magician in the cockpit." Jimmy Doolittle said, "He's the greatest stick-and-rudder man who ever lived."

Bob Hoover is truly an American hero. Revered by fellow pilots, respected by those who design aircraft, and worshiped by air show fans around the world, Bob has contributed to the evolution of aviation like no other before him. His distinguished career spans more than half a century, and he's still going strong at age seventy-four.

Bob's been a balls-out barnstormer, a decorated World War II fighter pilot, a test pilot extraordinaire, and an aerobatic pilot without equal. He started flying at age fifteen, taught himself aerobatic maneuvers before he learned to drive, and then entered the war determined to shoot down every German who challenged him.

During his days in Africa and Italy, he was a whirling dervish combination of Waldo Pepper and the Red Baron. His exploits in the sky made him a mythical hero, but when anyone challenged his prowess in a dogfight, Bob quickly lived up to his top-gun reputation.

While trying to help a friend fend off a pack of German fighters over the Mediterranean, a Focke-Wulf 190 caught him with a high-angle deflection shot. He became a prisoner of war and, despite several courageous attempts to escape, spent sixteen months in the dreaded Stalag Luft I prison camp.

Near the end of the war, Bob finally did escape. He sidestepped the barbaric Russian infantry, commandeered an FW-190, and flew a life-or-death flight across the German border to freedom in Holland.

At Wright-Patterson Air Force Base in 1945, Bob linked up with Chuck Yeager. They flew captured German and Japanese aircraft, and both the P-59 and P-80A, our country's first jets. The tandem also provided fireworks in the sky with their dueling dogfights over Dayton and gained national notoriety at air shows around the country.

When Yeager broke the sound barrier, Bob was right next door in a chase plane. Their friendship has lasted a lifetime, each having a deep respect for the other's aviation accomplishments.

After leaving the military, Bob joined North American Aviation, the premier aircraft manufacturer in the world. There he became an experimental test pilot and rocketed across the sky in such innovative aircraft as the FJ-2, the AJ-1, and the famed F-86 and F-100. His knowledge of aircraft design also earned respect and admiration from the engineers who worked alongside him.

In the mid-1950s, Bob stepped up his career as an aerobatic pilot. Before long, air show fans began their love affair with him.

Hopscotching the globe, he has continued to perform his magical mystery tour through the sky for millions of starry-eyed spectators. Precision maneuvers (explained in the glossary at the end of book) in his famed P-51 became his trademark, as did the wide-brimmed straw hat and business suit he wore when flying.

Over the past four decades, his electrifying performances have dazzled all who have watched him glide across the sky. To fellow aerobatic great Leo Loudenslager, a seven-time national champion, and world champion, Bob is the "standard of excellence. The best there ever was." To air show fans like former World War II combat pilot Dave Bingham, Bob flies routines "that would be difficult for Christ to perform."

Longtime friend and announcer Jim Driskell says Bob's secret is that "planes are afraid not to do what Bob tells them." Former test pilot Joe Lynch said Bob's ability to twist and turn an airplane in perfect synchronization was due to his being "the eagerist bastard I ever met."

Barron Hilton, who has honored Bob with a life-size mural at his hotel sports facility in Reno, told me Bob is "a master of his craft. To watch him fly is poetry in motion." Wally Schirra labeled him "the finest aerobatic pilot we've seen in our lifetime" and added, "It's like Bob's wearing the airplane, instead of the other way around."

The list of awards that Bob Hoover has won is astounding. They include the Lindbergh Medal, the Kitty Hawk Award, the Distinguished Flying Cross, the Purple Heart, and the Soldier's Medal for Valor. Bob is also a member of the National Aviation Hall of Fame and was the first inductee into the Aerobatic Hall of Fame.

Along the way, Bob has known nearly every great aviator in the twentieth century. They include Orville Wright, the first American to achieve powered flight; Charles Lindbergh, the first man to cross the Atlantic; Chuck Yeager, the first man to break the sound barrier; Yuri Gagarin, the first man to fly in space; and Neil Armstrong, the first man to land on the moon. He also has cherished friendships with such outstanding aviators as Eddie Rickenbacker, Jimmy Doolittle, Jackie Cochran, Eric Hartman, Scott Crossfield, Wally Schirra, and Jim McDivitt.

Friendship has always been important to Bob Hoover. Time and time again, people interviewed for this book told me of their love for Bob. "He's the best friend one could have," air show promoter Dave Fink said, "and one of the most ethical men I've ever known." Another colleague noted, "Bob Hoover is very special. He can charm the birds out of the trees. A more loyal friend and gentleman I have never met."

When Bob ran into a furious dogfight with the FAA in 1993 over his capability to fly, friends flocked to his side. Thousands of letters supporting his crusade were written, and at the Oshkosh Fly-In and Air Show "Let Bob Fly" posters were displayed everywhere.

That effort and Bob's tenacity resulted in his being reinstated. In late 1994, Bob Hoover took to the skies solo once again. The reception was overwhelming. Half a million fans rose to their feet to welcome back their hero.

To work with Bob on this book has been an honor. My only experience with noncommercial aircraft had been a shaky flight in an F-4 fighter jet. I became dizzy and threw up all over the pilot. Despite that fiasco and my lack of knowledge of his profession, Bob chose me for this assignment. I am very grateful.

My own impressions of Bob bring to mind two words, *humble* and *patriotic*. Far and above, he is the most humble man I've ever known. I have had to pull information out of him about his accomplishments. He was always concerned that elaborating on his exploits would seem too boastful. Fellow pilots were right when they told me, "Hoover never talks about flying. He just lets it speak for itself."

I doubt whether our country has ever witnessed a more patriotic man than Bob Hoover. Time and time again he has put his life on the line for the United States of America. In addition to his contributions in World War II and Korea, Bob's experimental flying aided the development of many of the military aircraft that have protected America in this century.

When Bob was awarded the Wright Brothers Memorial Trophy, the speaker noted that "Bob's promotion of aviation progress in the military world is unparalleled by any other person in the United States." The committee that awarded him the Lindbergh Medal called Bob the "ambassador for aviation."

Bob's love for his country is exemplified by a story Jim Driskell tells. It seems Bob was at Oshkosh getting ready to perform. His trademark straw hat came off as the national anthem was announced. Off to the side, Bob spied two youngsters sitting on the ground. "Get up," he told them, "show some respect for your country. Freedom is very precious and you don't know what it's like not to have it." Later, the boy's father thanked Bob for his comments.

To help tell Bob's story in the following pages has not been easy.

The text could be twice as long. Hopefully, a sense of where he came from, what influenced his incredible passion for flying, and how certain developments in aviation led him to become such a phenomenal pilot shine through.

So come take to the skies with Bob Hoover, in my mind the greatest aviator who ever lived. I promise you it'll be the adventure of a lifetime.

MARK SHAW

PROLOGUE

Russian Roulette

Strapped securely in the cockpit of the supersleek Yak-18, I glanced out at the Soviet dignitaries standing on the ramp. They were celebrating their overwhelming victory over the United States in the 1966 International Aerobatic Competition. "I've got a little surprise for you, Ivan," I thought as I checked out the instrument panel in the unique Soviet plane.

Despite my years of experience as an accomplished aerobatic pilot, I'd never participated in a formal aerobatic competition. That had made it even more of an honor to be named the nonflying captain of our team.

Unfortunately, I'd experienced ten days of frustration watching the power-packed Yak outduel our nation's finest aerobatic pilots. We'd come out the big loser in this Cold War propaganda battle. Now that the competition was over, the pompous Soviets had agreed to let me, as a courtesy, fly their crown jewel.

Over a million Soviets, and reporters from around the world, were positioned at Tushino Airport in Moscow for the closing ceremonies. I was sure they all expected me to taxi out and take off in a normal fashion. Instead I added full power for takeoff and held the plane close to the ground.

The Yak had plenty of airspeed. I lifted the plane off and raised the nose slightly until the landing gear was up.

Rolling the aerobatic plane, I leveled off upside down and aimed dead center for the thirty-foot-high dike surrounding the airport. It looked as if I were going to blast right through it, but an instant before reaching the dike, I raised the nose of the Yak, leapfrogged the dike, and flew out of sight still upside down.

A smile came to my face. I knew I'd caused confusion on the ground. To stay low and out of sight of the crowd, I rolled the Yak rightside up and headed back around the airfield alongside the Moscow River below the height of the dike. I was sure everyone would be looking for a fifty-foot-high fireball to blossom somewhere on the other side of the dike from where I had disappeared from sight.

I remained at ground level out of sight until I reached the other side of the airport. Then I turned back toward the dike and rolled the plane upside down again. I could feel the adrenaline rush as I flew down directly in front of the crowd. Then I put the Yak-18 through the same series of pinpoint aerobatic maneuvers that I had demonstrated for so many years at air shows all over the world. It was a delight to fly. No wonder our pilots never had a chance.

The Yak split the afternoon sky and danced through the ether. Its power-to-weight ratio provided outstanding maneuverability, permitting a tight performance of the four-, eight-, and sixteen-point rolls, a Cuban eight (figure-eight routine), and a series of perfect loops similar to the ones I had perfected in the legendary P-51 Mustang.

I was performing at near ground level even though I was aware that Soviet pilots were not permitted to fly aerobatic maneuvers below three hundred feet.

Watching the performance closely was our military attaché to the American embassy, Ralph Albright. "I heard someone next to me yell, 'Ach ty, bozhe moy,'" he recalls. "Translated it meant, 'Oh, my God.' Those fans were mesmerized. They couldn't believe what the American was doing."

After a touchdown on one wheel, an aileron roll, and a touchdown on the other wheel, I landed the Yak. I was a little nervous about the reception I'd receive from the Soviets, but I'd proven my point. Now everyone would know the American pilots were just as capable as the Russians and that the plane had made the difference in the competition.

Taxiing the Yak toward the grandstand, I was surprised at the change in the crowd. During the closing ceremonies, the huge throng of people had been controlled and well-mannered. Even during the presentation of the championship trophy, the Soviet pilots had received only polite applause, a vase of flowers, and a few handshakes.

When I rolled up in front of that same crowd, people were waving their hands in the air, cheering loudly, and rushing toward the aircraft. I was shocked. My dramatic flight over the dike and back around the airfield had somehow electrified them.

Complete chaos erupted when hundreds of spectators descended upon the Yak. By the time I finally stood up to get out of the cockpit, they had completely surrounded the plane. The noise was deafening, and I had to stand up on the canopy rails and hold on to the windshield. The airplane was shaking violently back and forth. I was terrified because I didn't know the nature of their enthusiasm. The crowd was underneath the Yak, all over it, everywhere.

While I was worried about my own safety, I was also concerned about the aircraft. The Soviets were pounding on the sides of the plane, threatening to overturn it.

Soviet police and uniformed soldiers started beating a path toward the plane. They hit people with their gun butts. Injured and stunned spectators fell by the wayside. It was a cruel display of Soviet authority. I wanted to stop their brute force, but I was powerless.

I climbed out on the wing of the Yak and two Soviet soldiers signaled me to jump down. They whisked me across the taxiway and toward a staff car. I was shoved into the backseat.

Ralph Albright remembers that one Soviet official yelled, "If you were a Russian, you'd be in Siberia." But, I never saw Ralph, only the assigned interpreter, who slid into the seat next to me.

"Mr. Hoover, you're in very serious trouble," he bellowed.

"May I contact the American embassy?" I asked, certain I could gain some protection.

"That will not be possible. At this point you must consider yourself to be under arrest."

Charlie Hillard, later four-time national aerobatic champion and world champion and member of the famed Eagles Aerobatic Team, was part of the U.S. team, as were Bob Herrenden, Hal Krier, and Art Scholl. All were killed in flying accidents.

The International Competition was held every year. In 1966, seventeen countries gathered to compete. Most experts believed the challengers for the championship would be the Soviet Union and the United States, providing yet another quest for superiority between the feuding Cold War countries.

The International Competition at the Moscow Air Show was a face-to-face duel between the most famous aerobatic pilots in the world. Preset boundaries in the sky framed the competition. They were set at a thousand meters by a thousand meters by a thousand meters. The "box in the sky" stretched upward from three hundred feet above the ground.

Just as in Olympic diving and ice-skating competition, a group of international judges observed the competitors in both compulsory and freestyle maneuvers.

Compulsory routines included a vertical four-point roll, one-turn spin, an outside loop, three-quarter roll, a pull-up and then down, and a three-quarter vertical snap.

In the freestyle competition, judges were looking for flamboyant maneuvers performed flawlessly. A rating device called the K factor dictated point totals, with the large-K maneuvers being worth the most.

Competitors were also required to perform a routine called the Unknown Maneuver. Once the judges assigned that maneuver, pilots had twenty-four hours in which to study and master it. No practice was permitted, and even though the secret maneuver was chosen from a standard catalog, many times the pilot had never flown the routine before.

The U.S. aerobatic team could compete with any others in the world, but they were participating in the competition in privately owned planes not specifically designed for winning aerobatic competition.

In the Soviet Union, however, private individuals were not allowed to own airplanes. The Soviet pilots worked for the government. They practiced full-time for the aerobatic competition. As Albright described it, "The Soviets put their very best pilots in the finest aerobatic planes ever built." Our pilots, on the other hand, were part-time performers. All were from the private sector.

The power-packed Yak-18 was a single-engine, low-wing, tandem-seating (fore and aft) plane with retractable landing gear. It was designed specifically for aerobatics and not for any other purpose.

Besides the competition with the Yak, other matters were vying for my attention in Moscow.

Our government's military intelligence believed that Gen. Sergie Mikoyan, whose father, Anastas, was president of the Soviet Presidium, might possibly defect if given the opportunity to do so. Since I had struck up a friendship with him at the Paris Air Show the year before, our Central Intelligence Agency asked if I could determine if General Mikoyan was indeed interested in defecting.

My wife, Colleen, was not at home when two CIA agents came to discuss their scheme.

They told me General Mikoyan, a highly respected test pilot, was a primary CIA target because he had flown the supersecret E-266, later to be known as the MiG-21. That experimental jet fighter was believed to be far superior to anything we were flying at the time. Our government wanted to know everything they could about it. Mikoyan had all the answers.

The CIA believed that General Mikoyan was influential enough to get me a ride in the E-266. If need be, I could try to gain his favor by offering what would seem to be confidential information about our country's X-15 and XB-70 projects. Actually that material was available in published articles.

If I couldn't get a ride in the E-266, I was to accept flight time in any of the Soviet aircraft. I was to be a human surveillance camera and bring back any top-secret information I could gather.

Mike Murphy, a former U.S. aerobatic champion and the organizer of our country's entry in the Moscow competition, knew about my mission. Besides the CIA agents, he and a retired Air Force major general named Brook Allen were involved in the plans.

I flew to Washington, D.C., and was briefed at CIA headquarters about the trip to Moscow. Two agents briefed me about such James Bond–like communications devices as minuscule cameras and listening devices that were often hidden in watches or jewelry. It was real cloak-and-dagger stuff.

Those men also scared the hell out of me when one of the agents showed me a picture of a conservative businessman dressed in Brooks Brothers' finest. In the next photo, the head of that same man had been superimposed onto a man dressed in a black leather jacket and pants. He was cradled up with a sultry woman in a wildly incriminating pose.

"The man in the picture is a legitimate communications-industry businessman from New York," the agent explained. "The Soviet KGB threatened to expose this completely false picture to his wife, family, and business associates if he didn't cooperate with them."

After that and several other disturbing revelations I flew back to California, wondering why I had agreed to become involved in the first place. Patriotism was one thing, putting my head into a noose quite another.

I was under surveillance from the moment I landed in Moscow. An interpreter was assigned to our team, and we were rarely out of Soviet KGB agents' sight.

Being watched wasn't something I was used to. It made me feel uncomfortable, as if an unfriendly supervisor were scrutinizing every move I made.

At our hotel, a Soviet soldier stood guard outside in the hall. I found several "bugs" in my room. Every word I spoke was being recorded. Even in the bathroom, I sensed that I was being observed through peepholes. I had no privacy. That made me a bit paranoid.

General Mikoyan and I did have an opportunity to speak briefly at a dining-hall luncheon. He had been warm and cheerful with me in

Paris in 1965, but that was not the case now. Under such tight surveillance he wanted to distance himself from me.

The general's flight test of the E-266 or potential defection to the West was never discussed. I was not sure how I would have approached the subject anyway.

Even though I didn't meet with General Mikoyan, I was not impoverished for adventures. I had Ralph Albright to thank for that.

Since the CIA wanted me to take a look at Soviet aircraft parked at selected airports around the city, they needed to spring me from the hotel. Ralph and I were able to slip away from the guards in spite of sophisticated surveillance systems. It was exciting stuff. I felt like an amateur James Bond.

Once we hit the road, Albright showed me how he could evade the KGB, who were following us in another car. Now I felt like a sidekick to a leading character in a spy mystery novel.

After losing our "tail," Ralph took me out to the nearby airfields to see the latest aircraft. Like an enthusiastic tourist, I snapped several pictures of their airplanes and helicopters.

I kept waiting for the KGB to nab us. Ralph was cool. "You're going to get out of this all right," he told me. "Don't worry." I never believed him. I kept having visions of spending my remaining years in a Soviet hard-labor camp.

The International Competition followed. The Soviets easily won. Their propaganda machine was in full throttle, spreading the word about Soviet aviation superiority.

For ten days I seethed as the Soviets wiped out every competitor. Then I learned my request to fly the Yak-18 had been granted. The evening before I lay awake late into the night planning the repertoire of routines I wanted to perform. Nothing would be left to chance. That plane and I would perform as one.

The next day, the Yak-18 was parked in front of all of the dignitaries. I'd already been given a cockpit and systems checkout in the airplane, but I'd never flown it.

After some preliminary words from Soviet officials, I was introduced. Mild applause followed, and I headed for the plane.

When I had been informed by an American official that I would be permitted to fly the Soviet plane, we had discussed the extent of my performance. Since no restrictions had been placed on me, everyone agreed that I ought to make the flight as spectacular as possible. I was convinced that I had done so.

Now as I sat frozen in fear in the backseat of the Soviet staff car, it was time to find out what the consequences of my irreverent behavior would be.

* * *

After a few minutes of racing through Moscow streets, I was deposited back at the hotel and assigned two different rock-ribbed guards to stand outside my door. Holed up all alone, I wondered what was going to happen to me. The isolation brought back memories of being in prison camp during War II. It was that same disturbing sense of having no control, of utter and complete loss of freedom.

What seemed like hours went by before there was a knock on the door. The two original guards and the interpreter were there along with two other guards, all heavily armed. The interpreter said, "Come with us, Mr. Hoover." When I asked where they were taking me, he briskly stated, "We're not at liberty to tell you."

I felt like a recalcitrant schoolboy as they marched me down a hall-way next to a ballroom on the way to the lobby and front entrance of the hotel. Since this was the night of the big celebration banquet after the competition, cosmonaut Yuri Gagarin, the first man in space, was onstage speaking to the crowd in a large hall. I had also met Yuri at the Paris Air Show a year earlier. I leaned away from my captors to catch a glimpse of him. Fortunately, he saw me as well.

Even though Gagarin seemed a bit unsteady from perhaps one too many vodkas, he left the stage and came racing toward me. After a few words with the guards, Gagarin grabbed my arm and pulled me away. Since he was the biggest hero in the Soviet Union at that time, they didn't interfere. Before long I was onstage standing beside the first man to orbit the earth. It was a scene unlike any other I've ever experienced.

Gagarin spoke for a few minutes and the audience interrupted him with cheers. Later, I learned that he'd said, "What in the world are the guards doing? Mr. Hoover is a great aviator. What's going on here? What are they going to do with him?"

His efforts on my behalf only added to the confusion. But to his credit, he wouldn't let the guards take me away. Finally, he was so insistent that the officials appeared to just give up and bow to his wishes. For the first time I thought I might make it out of this mess without punishment.

One of the Soviet government officials finally seized the micro-phone and addressed the audience. Later I learned the essence of his comments: "Mr. Hoover has violated every rule and regulation that we have in our country. He has jeopardized one of our finest airplanes. He has made a mockery of our safety system. However, we have decided that no one pilot could ever conduct two flights of this type. We think that maybe now he has learned that he's lucky to be alive after flying like that."

While the crowd roared its approval, Gagarin grabbed me and gave me an awkward, good-bye bear hug. I was startled but hugged him back. I was then whisked away. I still wasn't quite sure of my fate, but instead of heading out the door of the hotel, our little group made a left turn toward my room.

With the guards still standing at the door, I barely slept that night because I was so apprehensive over my fate. Somehow I had to talk to someone at our embassy. I also wondered if Gagarin's efforts to save me would prove successful or whether he'd be ignored as an unruly drunk.

Early the next morning, my interpreter entered my room. I held my breath as I awaited his words.

"Are you happy to be going home, Mr. Hoover?" he said. "Home sounds good," I replied, "very good."

I was still a bit anxious on the drive to the airport. The interpreter and the guards stayed with me until I climbed aboard a commercial airliner. I headed for the safety of Norway. I never relaxed until I climbed off the Aeroflot plane and stood on friendly soil. I blinked back tears as I thought of my wife, Colleen, and my family. I couldn't wait to get back to the United States.

I have no doubt that Yuri Gagarin saved me from a Soviet prison camp. The experience reminded me of how fortunate and proud I was to be an American, where due process of law would have afforded me liberties not possible in the Soviet Union.

Even though I experienced a close call with the Soviets, I knew my counterpunching in the Yak worked since it diverted attention away from the Soviet victory in the International Competition. Even though I could very well have been punished for flying in violation of Soviet regulations, the extraordinary adventure over Moscow was one of the most satisfying I have had in my nearly sixty years as an aviator.

Over that time, I have experienced flight as a barnstormer, a fighter pilot in both World War II and Korea, a military and civilian experimental test pilot in such prestigious aircraft as the F-86 and F-100, and an aerobatic pilot performing in air shows all over the world in many different aircraft including the P-51, the Aero Commander Shrike, and the Sabreliner.

To date, I have flown over three hundred types of aircraft and logged nearly thirty thousand hours in the air. My travels have permitted me to know personally nearly all of the great aviators of the twentieth century. I have also witnessed a whirlwind of events that have affected the course of aviation. In my career, I have seen the development of the legendary P-51 Mustang and the first American flights in jet aircraft. I played an active role in the breaking of the sound barrier and the development of supersonic aircraft. I knew the men who first orbited the earth, and those who finally landed on the moon.

For the better part of the century, I have found myself positioned directly in the eye of the storm as aviation has triggered a miraculous revolution in the way human beings take to the sky and beyond. In spite of all those experiences, it's truly ironic that the very same aerobatic maneuvers that almost landed me in prison in Moscow in 1966 were the same ones I'd learned as a young boy in the late 1930s near my hometown of Nashville, Tennessee.

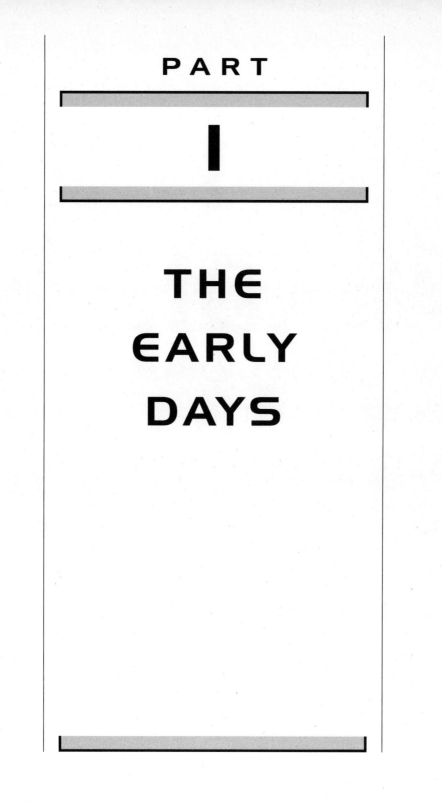

PART

I

THE
EARLY
DAYS

Flying Lessons

Contrary to myth, I was not born in a nest, nor have I felt the urge to migrate with seasonal changes. In fact, my parents swear they saw no wings sprouting when I came into the world on January 24, 1922, in Nashville, Tennessee.

I was the youngest of three children, pecking in behind Leroy Jr. and Sarah. My father, Leroy Sr., a soft-spoken, medium-built man, with a quiet, unassuming dignity, worked as an office manager/bookkeeper at the local American Paper and Twine Company. He also sported a rather large nose, a characteristic I inherited from him.

Bessie, my loving mother, ran the house. Rules were strict but fair.

We were a close-knit, religious family, and that extended to aunts, uncles, and cousins. At Christmas, they would all gather at our house and sleep on beds, cots, or mattresses on the floor, anywhere there was room.

Christmas dinner crowned the celebration. I can still remember the scent of buttery cinnamon, yeast, and sage drifting from the steamy kitchen as my mother, grandmother, and aunt prepared a feast for more than thirty relatives.

As I entered my teen years, the independence and daring that would dominate my adult life were already obvious. For example, my parents did not permit me to swim in the nearby Cumberland River because they thought it was dangerous.

One day we went across the river on the ferryboat, and I was in the backseat of the car. The ferryboat captain came over, shook his head, and said to my parents, "That boy of yours, I never saw anything like him in my life. I must have counted . . . he swam this river twenty times. . . . I've never seen anything like it." I was caught, but since the captain had been so impressed, my parents weren't too tough on me.

I loved to fiddle with anything mechanical. I had a paper route when I was thirteen, and somebody living along that route had the chassis of an old Model T Ford in the backyard. I bought it for seven dollars.

Since it didn't have a battery, I used long extension cords and connected it to the transformer from my electric train to get it started. I learned to drive in that old Ford. Being behind the wheel gave me a feeling of independence.

After a neighbor provided me with a battery, I sneaked off and drove the car around a local golf course. I discovered I could get airborne if I hit some of the bumps just right. That's when the fun began. It ended when someone told my parents about my golf-course joyride. I had to turn my attention elsewhere.

My infatuation with aviation began with Charles Lindbergh's transatlantic flight in 1927. Even though I was too young to witness the event, I learned about Lindbergh's achievement at an early age. His flight was truly remarkable. I envisioned myself in the *Spirit of St. Louis*, all alone over the Atlantic. I could feel Lindbergh's excitement.

My dad did not share my obsession with aviation, but he understood my infatuation with model airplanes. I would sit for hours and put together models of World War I planes such as the SE-5, the Nieuport, and the Spad.

I'd study the model planes and imagine what it would be like to fly real ones. When I cracked a plane or broke some part while playing, it was devastating.

In high school, I read everything I could find about aviation. I even memorized the handbook for the Alexander Eaglerock airplane.

The aviation heroes of the day were Lindbergh, Roscoe Turner, Eddie Rickenbacker, and Jimmy Doolittle. Even though I was captivated by all of them, it was Doolittle who first drew my attention.

General Doolittle, who may have put more high-water marks on aviation than anyone else, was one of our country's most intelligent pilots. He started out as a daredevil and later obtained his Ph.D. in aeronautical engineering. During World War II, he was a fearless pilot who led a devastating raid against Japan that inspired the book *Thirty Seconds Over Tokyo*.

General Doolittle was also responsible for the early high-altitude tests, setting speed records, and making the first blind instrument flights. I once described the great aviator in a speech as "a pioneer with the courage of a lion." He was my true idol. I wanted to be just like him.

Besides learning about these great heroes, I also read a remarkable book by an aviator named Bernie Ley, with whom I became good friends many years later. The book introduced me to the world of aerobatics. It detailed the aerodynamics involved and how each routine was performed with precision timing. I studied the maneuvers until I knew every one by heart.

Berry Field was fifteen miles from our home in Nashville. Even though it was a long haul, I'd ride my bicycle there just to be around the airplanes.

The Tennessee Air National Guard flew the Douglas O-38 there. It was a biplane used for observation, and I'd watch them for hours and dream of flying them someday.

I saw the great Roscoe Turner perform at Berry Field. He was one of the most famous aviators of the time. He had appeared in films and traveled with a magnificent mountain lion, Gilmore, named after his sponsor, the Gilmore Oil Company. It was one of the most beautiful animals I've ever seen.

Turner's flamboyance really impressed me. He flew a sleek Turner Laird, and he always wore an immaculately tailored, bright British officer's uniform, spit-polished black cavalry boots, a flashy tunic with gold buttons, sharply creased riding breeches, and a smart military officer's cap. He once said, "If you look like a tramp or a grease monkey, people won't have confidence in you. A uniform commands respect—aviation needs it."

Those words really impressed me. Later in life I flew in my military uniform, a flight suit, or a business suit. I always tried to look sharp.

Roscoe Turner was the closest thing to a hero that I had ever seen. With his thick, perfectly waxed handlebar mustache, he was the quintessential aviator, complete with the flowing white scarf.

One day at Berry Field I created an opportunity to meet him by approaching the gleaming Laird when his back was turned. Using a hand towel, I wiped the windshield free of oil spots and bug stains.

When the task was completed, I turned around to find the great Turner's handlebar mustache less than six inches from my nose. His look spelled trouble and I expected to be reprimanded. Instead a smile came to his face and Mr. Turner said he appreciated my simple gesture. He even let me sit in the cockpit of the plane. I was very nervous, but I tried to appear as casual as possible. I told my friends about that moment for weeks.

Sitting in the Turner Laird that day only reinforced what I already knew. The only thing I ever wanted to do was fly airplanes.

* * *

At fifteen, I began sacking groceries at Hill's Grocery Store downtown. I worked sixteen hours a day, earning two dollars. Instead of taking girlfriends to the movies, I spent the money at Berry Field on flying lessons.

I made the trip to Berry Field as often as I could. An hour's worth of flying lessons cost eight dollars, so my sixteen-hour workdays produced only fifteen minutes' worth of lessons. It was worth every penny.

My first instructor was Louie Gasser, a dark-complexioned man of Italian descent in his early thirties. I don't think he ever expected me to be a good pilot since from day one I suffered from chronic motion sickness. Many of my early lessons in the Piper Cub, which had a small forty-horsepower Continental engine but had been a great training airplane for thousands of aviators, were uncomfortable flights.

I *had* to overcome airsickness. I not only wanted to be an aviator but a fighter pilot like Eddie Rickenbacker. I knew that my dream of flying combat would never come true if I couldn't get over my uneasiness in the air.

The only way to overcome my malady was to make my brain not believe what my eyes were telling it. That took extreme concentration and focus, especially when the plane was twisting and turning in the sky. Riding with Louie Gasser behind the controls made me quite nauseated, but I stuck it out. My stomach never completely settled down, but I still enjoyed being in the air.

It took me almost a year to build up the eight hours in the air needed to qualify for solo flight, and I remember clearly the day I flew the plane by myself for the first time. Louie took me up and we did four takeoffs and touchdowns before he said, "It's all yours."

I was so excited that I didn't have time to get nervous. Away I went, solo for the first time at sixteen years old.

What I remember most about that flight is how different the plane flew without Louie's weight. It flew better, and I could maneuver the airplane with ease. I experienced another dimension of existence, no longer tied to the earth. I felt free, free of gravity, free of everything.

To lick the motion sickness, I pushed myself to the limit by doing wingovers and stalls and spins. Every time I found I could handle one maneuver, I went on to the next one until I conquered the airsickness. Each time it got easier, and finally I could perform all of the routines without much discomfort. I didn't have aerobatic training, but I had read about and memorized how to execute the maneuvers.

Whenever possible, I would go out of sight of the airport and practice loops and spins and different maneuvers. Nobody was around, and only my closest buddies at school knew what I was up to in the skies near Berry Field.

Shortly after I soloed, I decided to display my new skills for my family. I headed southeast in a Piper Cub out toward "The Camp," a beautiful spot on the Stones River where my relatives and some of their close friends had refurbished an old log cabin. With a full audience on hand, I decided to impress them by flying between two huge oak trees.

Having carefully measured the distance between the trees, I was certain I could easily fly the airplane between the trunks and beneath the limbs of the overlapping branches. There wasn't a lot of room to spare, but I was supremely confident.

It was a calm, clear day. I performed loops and rolls and finally got ready to fly between the trees. Unfortunately, I had not anticipated a sudden updraft, and it lifted the plane just enough to catch a wingtip on one of the branches. The plane jerked abruptly upon contact, but I quickly got it under control and made it out of there and back to a safe landing. Predictably, my parents were too concerned for my safety to be amused. I was embarrassed, but most of the relatives seemed to enjoy my little demonstration. One of my cousins, Warren Link, was a great one for practical jokes, and he poured some ice tea just behind where my mother had been standing. He then yelled, "Hey, ol' Bob scared the tinkle out of Aunt Bessie!"

While the spins and rolls were all part of my plan to defeat airsickness, I found I loved to perform the routines over and over again. I even took my dad up one time. He really enjoyed the flight. I felt great about that since he had never been in an airplane before.

I began attempting more precise loops and rolls in the Cub. Soon I was working on Cuban eights, Immelmanns, and hesitation rolls (see glossary for descriptions).

I was eighteen years old when I graduated from high school in 1940, but college was never a consideration since I didn't realize the importance of further education. All I knew was that I wanted a career in aviation, and the Tennessee Air National Guard provided me the opportunity to be in the air as a tail-gunner trainee in the 105th Observation Squadron.

Even though I wasn't getting pilot training, some of the hometown officers let me fly the Douglas O-38s that had dual controls. At that time, I wasn't eligible to go to the Air Corps flying school since I hadn't turned twenty-one and didn't have the requisite two years of college.

I was still living at home. My parents were very supportive of my efforts to become an aviator. With the few dollars I earned in the Guard as a weekend warrior, I continued buying flying time.

The war in Europe had broken out. Although the United States had not officially entered the conflict, the Tennessee National Guard went on active duty in September 1940.

Tennessee was known as the Volunteer State after those who fought at the Alamo. Our squadron was the first to volunteer for active duty and transferred to Columbia, South Carolina.

There I became acquainted with a buck private by the name of Denny McClendon, who was a member of our squadron.

Denny and I shared a real love for flying. He was a natural. Most people were required to complete at least eight hours in the air to be allowed to fly solo. Denny was cleared after an hour and a half!

We had a lieutenant in our squadron by the name of Buzwell, and he took a liking to both Denny and me. He had been a crop duster. When I flew with him, he scared me to death. He'd take me down so low we'd fly underneath the tree branches.

When Denny started learning to fly, Buzwell told me, "Denny's really good. Tell him what to do and he does it. He's ready to solo right now. He's only going to need an hour or so up there with an instructor."

That wouldn't be possible these days, but back then people taught themselves to fly. They could buy what would be known now as kit planes, assemble them, learn to fly, and solo in a month.

That type of flying was known as seat-of-the-pants flying. People with natural ability just used their instincts. There wasn't much mechanical about what they did, they just winged it and used trial and error until they soloed and got their license.

Denny's recollection about our first meeting and a subsequent barnstorming tour brings back a lot of memories.

> Bob Hoover was my tent corporal when I first met up with him. We'd pitched tents at the Municipal Airport there in Columbia, and Bob and I struck up a friendship.
>
> We were both interested in finding a plane to fly. As luck would have it, there was an old E-2 Taylor Cub that had been severely damaged when the pilot tried to fly it out of a farmer's field. Apparently, he had a 250-pound passenger with him, and that thirty-seven-horsepower engine couldn't get them over the fence. The wheels caught it and flipped the plane inverted, resulting in severe damage.
>
> In all, we'd end up spending about fifty bucks to fix up the plane. An old master sergeant who was an engine mechanic under the Civil Aeronautics Administration (now FAA—Federal Aviation Administration) supervised us. We were able to patch the plane back together so it passed CAA muster.
>
> At the time, neither Bob nor I were making more than forty-five dollars a month, so we had to watch our pennies. To keep ourselves from going into town and wasting the money we needed to fix up the plane, we shaved our heads. We were so unattractive that we were embarrassed to spend much time socializing.
>
> We allowed ourselves an allotment of five dollars a month for inci-

dentals such as beer and chewing gum. The rest went to repairing the plane.

When the Cub passed the CAA test, we decided to take it on a barnstorming tour. That's a trip we'll never forget, especially since we were never certain we had enough fuel.

We had a little nine-gallon gasoline tank that had as a gauge a metal wire stuck in a cork. The wire stuck up through the filler cap of the gas tank, which was right in front of the windshield. We could tell when the metal wire got all the way down that we were out of gas. That was the extent of our gas gauge.

The E-2 only cruised at sixty miles an hour and we couldn't get very far because it burned three gallons an hour. We only had three hours of flying before we were out of gas completely, so we had to land before then and refuel. We carried an extra one-gallon gas can that had a rubber hose in it, and just before we ran out of gas, Bob, crazy fool that he was, would climb out of the side (there were no Plexiglas windows on the open sides) and put his feet on the wing strut. He'd take that can of gas, holding on somehow or the other, and unscrew the gas cap in front of the windshield, get the rubber hose out of the extra gallon of gas, and pour it into the tank. I was stuck with the task of holding complete opposite controls because the wind against him was forcing the plane to the right. I just barely could keep the thing level while he was doing his sky-gassing routine. He did this two or three times on the trip, and of course, there was no parachute.

We'd taken a two-week leave of absence to take the tour. Our first stop was to visit my father in Decatur, Alabama, but we almost never made it there.

There is a ridge of mountains on the south side of Birmingham, and the E-2 almost didn't make it. We were trying to get there to refuel, but we couldn't seem to gain enough altitude to climb over the 1,200-foot-high ridge.

That ridge is known as Red Mountain, and it has a statue on it known as Vulcan, the god of metalworking. It was made of steel since Birmingham is known as the Steel City.

We looked that immortal Vulcan square in the eye several times before our thirty-seven-horsepower engine gasped and grunted us over the ridge. After refueling, we made it to Decatur, where Bob was kind enough to take my mother for her very first plane ride.

After visiting Denny's parents, I remember flying to a little town just north of Decatur called Athens. We located a field where we could land and then proceeded to circle the courthouse several times at less than a hundred feet. Startled passersby were greeted with Denny's deep voice amplified through a megaphone, "Plane rides. One dollar. Field south of town." That was great fun. We were young kids at heart.

It was illegal for me to take passengers up and charge them for the ride because I still didn't have a commercial pilot's license. Denny and I devised a scheme to fix that problem. We'd sell gold-plated wings to the passengers in exchange for a ride. Fuel and maintenance costs probably totaled at least ninety cents a ride, so we made no more than ten cents of profit per passenger.

The Cub was certainly no speedster. Denny remembers when we tried to keep up with a Pan American train.

> The Pan American was headed south on the Louisville-Nashville railroad track. We flew down just opposite the engineer's window and waggled our wings, and the engineer acknowledged us by blowing his whistle. The only reason we could stay up with the train is because it was slowing down going into Birmingham. Its top speed was probably eighty, ours all of sixty-five.

In all, I'd say Denny and I traveled nearly two thousand miles on that barnstorming trip. We'd get a farmer's permission to use his field and then try to find customers to go up with me in the Cub. Since there were no aviation rules to go by, I could give my guests the full treatment for their five minutes in the sky. Some were more adventurous than others, and watching their reactions to the more flamboyant maneuvers was the best part of all.

Most times, Denny and I slept under the wings of the plane. Denny alternated flying with me from town to town to build up his flight time.

The time spent with Denny was the beginning of a lifelong friendship. He would later become a respected aviation historian and would author two books, *The Lady Be Good: Mystery Bomber of WW II*, which chronicles a crew's inspiring attempt to survive following the crash of a B-24 Liberator bomber in North Africa, and *The Legend of Colin Kelly: First American Hero of World War II*.

When we returned from the barnstorming tour, I rented a J-3 Taylor Cub and took it for a spin. It had a sixty-five-horsepower engine. When I tried a snap roll in it, the fabric that was rib-stitched to the top of the wing ripped apart. I caught hell for that, but that J-3 flew a lot smoother than the E-2.

Those days spent with Denny and the later ones in Europe and Africa with the rest of my military buddies were remarkable. There is an easy camaraderie among pilots and soldiers. We all knew that staying alive depended on protecting one another.

I am very proud to have been a member of this unique fraternity. Denny McClendon was just the first in a long line of courageous men who made my life richer through their friendship.

At Columbia, our unit was meshed into the Army Air Corps. Orders came down that enlisted men could apply for flight training if they passed a series of written and physical exams.

I passed the written test, but almost ended my flying career before it got started.

I couldn't read the eye chart correctly when my eyes were dilated. The 105th Observation Squadron flight surgeon, Capt. Bob Patterson, knew I was a capable pilot and was disappointed that I was having a problem with the test.

Finally he told me, "Bob, I'm going to leave the room for a few minutes to check on a couple of things. I'll be back in twenty minutes." When he left, I studied the charts and memorized the letters. When Captain Patterson returned, I whizzed through the test.

Bob Patterson even thought of a solution for future problems I might have. Before I departed for flight training, Captain Patterson said that if I ever had to undergo eye tests and someone wanted to dilate my eyes, I should tell them I was allergic to the eyedrops.

Bob's words of wisdom stayed with me as I readied myself for flight training. New adventures in the sky lay straight ahead, and I was anxious to learn all I could under the watchful eye of Uncle Sam.

2

Going to War

Twenty dollars' worth of good ol' Kentucky bourbon saved me from a life as a bomber or transport pilot.

In the 1940s, the Air Corps had a policy of sending the short pilots to fighter training and the taller ones to train in bombers and transports. At six foot two inches, I was definitely headed toward the latter until I used a little friendly influence to alter my fate.

It wasn't that I hated bombers and transports. Hell, I would fly an old Dodge truck if they put wings on the sides. During training, I had flown the Curtis AT-9, the Cessna AT-17 Bamboo Bomber, and the Lockheed Hudson. But I wanted to fly fighters, so I went into action.

I learned a "short" friend of mine preferred transports and bombers. I convinced him to agree to a switch and then gave twenty dollars' worth of bourbon to a sergeant in personnel to swap our orders.

This was a pivotal event in my career. It came after graduation from advanced flight training. Prior to that I had completed primary and basic training. My primary training took place sixty-five miles south of Memphis, Tennessee, in the small Arkansas town of Helena. I don't even think the base had a name.

I reported to Helena in December of 1941, shortly after the bombing of Pearl Harbor. There I was assigned to Capt. Bart Renno.

In 1975, I received a wonderful letter from Bart. It read in part:

> At the risk of mimicking the TV program *This Is Your Life*, Bob Hoover, let us reminisce to the year 1941.
> The Army Air Corps, as it was known at that time, had established

one of its many primary flying schools in the city of Helena, Arkansas, situated on the banks of the Mississippi River, south of Memphis, Tennessee. The airplane being utilized was the Stearman PT-17.

The standards of perfection, necessary for graduation from these primary flying schools, were enormous. In fact, only four out of every ten cadets survived these rigid standards to continue on to basic and advanced flying schools. Precision, alertness, ability to think, coordination, and safety were the prime requisites to be met if any cadet was to continue his Air Corps flying career.

It was my fortunate lot in life to have assigned to me one Sgt. Robert A. Hoover as one of my cadets.

We proceeded with the flying curriculum, and after two or three hours of dual instruction, performing takeoffs, landings, airwork, and traffic rules and procedures, it became very evident to me that I had an extremely talented student on my hands, and I decided, against Air Corps regulations, to advance you to the aerobatic phase of the curriculum required for graduation. Your grasping of these aerobatic maneuvers in a short span of time was phenomenal.

Since Air Corps regulations forbade any student from soloing the airplane before receiving a minimum of six hours flying time, I distinctly remember how we would leave the immediate airport area and perform our aerobatics in a location where we would be undetected.

As the time for your graduation drew nearer, I arranged for other instructors to ride with you to prove to them that you were in a class by yourself. They all agreed, without exception, that you were the answer to a flying instructor's dream. I even went so far as to request the commanding officer of the base to give you your forty-hour "check ride." Upon completion of this "ride" the commanding officer agreed that Sgt. Robert A. Hoover graded higher than any cadet he'd ever "checked."

The day of graduation had to come, and when the commanding officer called upon you to put on a thirty-minute flying demonstration for the benefit of the other cadets, I was probably the most proud man in the world. The eight-point slow-roll that you had perfected was a thing of beauty and the envy of everyone on that air base. Your performance in that thirty minutes was the epitome of Air Corps primary flying and, I am certain, will never be equaled or surpassed.

That PT-17 Stearman primary trainer I flew was a 225-horsepower biplane with two wings and two cockpits, fore and aft.

The maneuvers performed included a normal loop, four-, eight-, and sixteen-point hesitation rolls, a falling leaf (see glossary for description), and a landing out of a loop. Being asked to perform for all of those airmen was quite an honor, especially since I had just turned twenty years old.

During basic training at Greenville, Mississippi, I learned how to fly using instruments. That was difficult for me since I preferred to be guided by visual references or by the "feel" of the plane.

Relying on instruments was a new ball game, and I admit to being skeptical of whether I could convince myself to rely on readings set before me on the cockpit instrument panel.

The first stage involved ground school. We learned what the system was all about, how the instruments operated, and the indications we would see under different circumstances. All the pilots then spent time in what was called in those days a Link Trainer.

We would sit in a room that was set on an axis. It couldn't go up or down, just left or right. The same instruments we had in the cockpit were on a board before us. A controller/instructor sat in the back of the room to observe and put us through our simulated flight.

At that time, we did not have the navigational aids we have now, so a pilot was guided by what he heard. While it was necessary to control airspeed and altitude, the task at hand was to listen to Morse-code signals that were broadcast into each ear.

If a pilot heard the sound *dit dah*, he knew he was left of the intended path. *Dah dit*, on the other hand, meant the plane was too far to the right. The key was to get the sound equal, which meant the plane was on course toward what was called the "cone of silence." Silence meant the pilot was over the station.

The pilot checked the next heading from the charts, then proceeded toward that location. All the while, the controller/engineer was changing the volume of the *dit dah* and *dah dit* tones and evaluating the pilot's performance.

That system took some getting used to. I floundered at first, but after a while I picked up the sequences.

My passing grade in the Link Trainer meant it was time to take to the air. I trained in a BT-13 (Vultee Vibrator). An instructor was in the backseat as another pair of eyes.

Making certain that a pilot believed what his instruments were telling him was critical, especially if the disorienting condition of vertigo occurred. When that happens, pilots become so confused they may think they're turning left when they're actually heading in the opposite direction.

Overruling the brain is difficult to do, but a pilot must disregard what he thinks and obey what the instruments tell him. I've had vertigo, and it made me want to ignore the instruments. Fortunately I've always been able to fight off the impulse.

After basic training, I went to Columbus, Mississippi, for advanced twin-engine training. I then reported to the Twentieth Fighter Group stationed at Drew Field in Tampa, Florida, where I was the only pilot who had not trained in a single-engine AT-6 trainer. But I employed the same method I used in learning aerobatic maneuvers: I taught myself.

I also experienced firsthand at Drew the unequal treatment given noncommissioned enlisted pilots compared to the officers. Our commanding officer was strict and uncompromising, and he had never taken a shine to enlisted pilots. While our quarters were bare-bones, the officers stayed in much more pleasant surroundings. The enlisted men were forced to clean latrines and do KP duty, while the commissioned officers were not.

That hierarchy seemed very unfair. Many of us made our feelings known. Fortunately for me and the other sergeant pilots, a transfer in leadership occurred. Lt. Col. Joe Moore, who later became a three-star general and vice commander of Pacific Air Command under Gen. Hunter Harris, became the CO. The enlisted men were suddenly on equal footing with the officers and could concentrate on our fighter training tactics instead of peeling potatoes.

When I first joined the squadron, I was ordered to enter P-40 training. That plane had a good reputation since the AVG (American Volunteer Group) had successfully used it in fighting the Japanese in China.

In fact Eddie Rickenbacker, America's ace of aces in World War I, once compared the P-40 with the Japanese Zero. In his autobiography, *Rickenbacker*, he says:

> The P-40 has seen more combat than any of our other fighters. How does it compare with the Japanese Zero? The Zero is an excellent climber. It is very maneuverable. In these two respects, it surpasses the P-40, but only in these two. The P-40 has more firepower, heavier guns, and carries more ammunition than the Zero. . . . To all of these factors, add our superior training of the flight crews, and you will see why our P-40s destroy Zeroes better than two for one.

I learned how to fly a fighter plane in a slow-landing P-40. Its deficiencies still didn't detract from the fun I had flying that plane. I felt right at home in the fighter. It was a true love affair, but I did hanker to take up the more streamlined P-39 Airacobra. One day I was set to take my number 46 P-40 up, but on the way to the airplane, I saw a crew chief working on a P-39 with the same number.

"Do you know how to start the engine?" I asked.

He did. A few minutes later, I was airborne.

The P-39s, which were single-seat, low-wing fighters, had a reputation as "widow-makers." In fact, among the fighter pilots, there was an old song that went, "Oh, don't give me a P-39. Because the engine is mounted behind. She'll spin, crash, and burn. So don't give me a P-39."

The next verse went, "Oh, give me a P-38. The props that counterrotate. She'll not spin, crash, and burn. So give me a P-38."

The Airacobra's engine was mounted behind the pilot with a drive shaft to the propeller in a channel underneath the pilot. Most pilots felt that the midmounted engine made the P-39 susceptible to tumbling and flat spins when dogfighting. When that happened, we were told there was no recourse but to bail out.

Contrary to the views of my superiors and fellow fighter pilots, I fell in love with that plane. I really surprised my commanding officer when I took the badgered Airacobra up and put it through a series of loops, rolls, and spins.

At ten thousand feet, I pulled the nose up steeply, cut the power, and presto, the plane started to tumble. A flat spin followed, and I panicked for an instant trying to get my bearings. I tried conventional recovery controls, but none of them worked.

Instinctively I dropped the landing gear and lowered the flaps to upset the gyroscopic effect. To my amazement, the P-39 went into a conventional nose-down spin. I recovered the airplane with plenty of room to spare. Satisfied with the effort, I couldn't wait to land and share my experience with the other pilots.

Later, the commanding officer asked me to perform the same maneuver for all of the pilots to see. The entire squadron stood in the blazing sun at Pinellas County Airport near St. Petersburg, Florida, as I put the Airacobra through its paces once again.

Reaction to my maneuvers was positive. I felt good about contributing to our efforts to successfully fly the P-39.

I found through some experimenting with control applications that I could predictably get the airplane to tumble and achieve a recovery without getting into a flat spin. Many years later, a Czechoslovakian pilot gave the maneuver the name Lomcovak, which is the Czech word for headache.

I also duplicated the maneuvers in the P-39 when I took up the P-40. I found that plane could be tumbled and recovered as easily as the P-39.

Another pilot who flew the P-39 at that time was Tom Watts. A good-natured fellow from Globe, Arizona, Tom would become my closest buddy in the service.

Tom was a lot like me, very aggressive, always wanting to push himself a little harder, be a little better. I wanted to be the greatest fighter pilot who ever lived, and Tom planned to compete for the title.

During the war, Tom kept a journal. He sent pages back to his family in Arizona, and they gave me a copy when I returned home to the States.

In that journal, Tom talks about the first few times he took up a P-39:

When I started the engine, it was like starting some powerful diesel. It frightened the daylights out of me momentarily. But the big thing was after I had aligned myself on the runway for takeoff. I was due for a surprise and didn't know it. Nothing serious: I just felt like Buck Rogers when I opened the throttle and went tearing down the runway.

The first Mayday I ever experienced was in a P-39 over Tampa just as I was climbing out of the traffic pattern. The plane suddenly overheated, causing me instant concern.

In those days, pilots wore a cloth helmet that had earphones inside with wires that were sewn in and connected to the throat mike. The mike picked up points on either side of the Adam's apple. A pilot could be understood despite all the engine noise because the sound was transmitted from the voice-box area rather than from the pilot's mouth.

In the Tampa tower, Lt. Willie P. MacBride, the flight leader who was on duty, heard my frantic words: "Tampa tower . . . Mad Dog 3 . . . Emergency. . . . I've got an excessive temperature on the coolant gauge and smoke in the cockpit. Clear the traffic pattern . . . I'm comin' in."

Seconds later, MacBride and his tower operators spotted my plane. Huge flames were spewing from the engine.

"Mad Dog 3 . . . you're on fire . . . get the hell out of there," Mac-Bride roared.

Those words tightened my belly button. *Fire* is not a word a pilot wants to hear.

Still committed to saving the plane despite the presence of heavy smoke, I faced two choices: open the windows to try to get some air and take a chance on drawing the fire into the cockpit, or leave them closed and risk losing my vision and suffocating.

Believing I could clear out the smoke from the cockpit, I opened the side window by turning the hand crank. Bad choice. The rush of air sucked even more smoke into the cockpit. I continued the approach with severe visibility restriction and with increasing heat within the cockpit.

With no oxygen mask and sucking in more and more smoke with every passing second, I was coughing with every breath. Quickly, I shut the engine switches off. And then somehow managed a reasonable dead stick (no-engine) landing.

After the plane stopped, I saw the flames were headed straight up. Since the fuel tank could explode at any second, I jumped out and ran as fast as I could.

I saw the fire trucks on the horizon. They put out the fire. By the time they extinguished it, there wasn't much left of the airplane.

That Mayday experience was scary as hell, and I knew I was fortunate to have escaped unhurt. Tom kidded me about losing the plane, both in person and in his journal. He described the accident by saying: "A P-39 on fire had caused a forced landing, but there were no scratches, bruises, hits, runs, or errors."

Many people wonder whether a pilot panics in a situation like that. Panic is undeniable, but there are ways to control it. I got scared like anybody else, but I just tried to focus on ways to save myself and the plane. The butterflies in my stomach notwithstanding, I tried to stay calm. That way I could consider carefully every alternative open to me.

I had also rehearsed over and over again my emergency procedures for every type of situation that might occur. In an emergency then, I felt in control because I had already considered how to deal with that particular problem.

My ability to handle those types of situations is directly attributable to my military training, first at Maxwell preflight training and then at Helena. There they emphasized the importance of discipline and the ability to stay in control when faced with a wide range of situations.

For instance, we were trained how to respond appropriately when somebody said something really funny in a serious situation. That training took place when all the cadets were lined up at attention, and an upperclassman would say, "Mr. Jones, what are you famous for?" And Mr. Jones would be standing there in line with the rest of us. We couldn't crack a smile and had to look straight ahead.

Then Mr. Jones would say, "Sir, I am famous for cutting toilet seats in half for half-ass upperclassmen like you, sir!"

Of course, we all wanted to burst out laughing because our fellow airman had really insulted the upperclassman. That's funny any way you put it. But we knew that if we smiled, we were going to be carrying a parachute around the perimeter of the parade grounds for the next four or five hours. So we didn't smile. Believe me, that teaches discipline and self-control that is essential in times of crisis.

On other occasions, a squad leader might say, "Hoover, your head isn't erect enough. Pull those shoulders back. I want to see twenty-seven wrinkles in your chin. You look in a mirror and count twenty-seven wrinkles before I see you tomorrow." Not laughing at something as stupid as that isn't easy, but it's a must.

If cadets did screw up, they got demerits. For example, we had to eat "square." Seated at the table, all the men had to sit up straight and look straight ahead. We also had to pick up our fork, bring it up level, and then bring it back straight to our mouths. If somebody missed their mouth right across the table from me and I laughed, the next thing I heard was "Mr. Hoover, that's five demerits for you."

So many demerits meant so many laps around the parade grounds carrying a heavy parachute. Carrying that burden on a boiling-hot day convinced me to control my emotions next time out.

The next time my career as a pilot almost ended was near St. Petersburg, Florida. My squadron, in flights of four, was flying over the water near Mullet Key Bay when a near-disaster occurred.

We had been firing at a water slick created intentionally with patches of dye. Each of us fired individually at the target and then set up a rectangular traffic pattern similar to a landing pattern, only at high speeds. Then we dove toward the dye in the water, firing our guns at the water slicks.

All of a sudden, without warning, my P-40-K Kitty Hawk began to shake. My first thought was that the engine had failed and was tearing itself apart. Smoke and fire cascaded from the cowling around the engine. Heat intensified in the cockpit. I tried to assess the damage and think quickly about what to do.

I was close to the water and couldn't climb high enough for a safe bailout. My only alternative was to dead-stick the plane into the chilly waters. I had never attempted landing on water, so I was apprehensive. Fortunately, the water landing went smoothly. That is, until the Kitty Hawk and I began to sink to the bottom.

I tried to get out of the cockpit, but radio cords and shoulder straps pinned me to the seat. The water was now rushing into the plane. I was going to drown in my airplane. I knew there were only a few seconds left to escape. Just as I was about to go under, another frantic tug on the cords inflated my life vest. I was able to ease out of the cockpit and away from the plane as it sank to the bottom of the bay.

My heart was still pumping in overdrive as I floated in the water. If those cords hadn't broken loose, I would have been a goner.

Forty minutes later, a fishing boat retrieved me from the frigid water. I can still remember the warmth of the men's hands as they lifted me into the boat. They took me to a secluded beach where Joe Moore, the CO, rescued me in an L-4 reconnaissance plane.

Since the P-40 had a history of engine trouble, the superior officers assumed that was the cause of my crash. Someone, however, decided to salvage the plane from its fifty-foot depth.

When a floating crane snagged the Kitty Hawk from the water, we were all shocked to see that more than fifty bullet holes had pierced the plane. Further investigation disclosed that a fellow pilot who was close behind me in the gunnery pattern had accidentally machine-gunned my plane out of the sky!

While friendly fire upsets everyone, it was easy to understand how it could happen. The camouflage paint on the plane was the same color as the water. Everything blended together.

That softened my feelings about the pilot's miscue. I harbored no ill feelings toward him.

Orders of a transfer to the European theater came shortly after that incident. I was ready. I remember all of us being called together. We were told to pack and be prepared to leave the following morning. Tom Watts recorded the scene at the railroad station in his journal:

> The railroad station was a madhouse of heroes-to-be rushing back and forth; some with sick looks kissing their wives or sweethearts; and some with eager looks, rushing around madly endeavoring to strengthen their alcoholic supply and add ham, cheese, and hamburger sandwiches to it. By the time the train blew its last whistle, it was pretty well drunk out [the men had been drinking heavily].
>
> As the train began steaming slowly out of the station, there seemed to be a magnet pulling pilots out of all sorts of cracks and corners. How everyone finally made that train with no one left behind, I'll never know.

There were probably some who didn't want to leave for Europe, but not many.

It was a combination of patriotism, the love of flying, and the adventure. I was twenty years old and prepared to take on the whole German Air Force single-handedly if necessary.

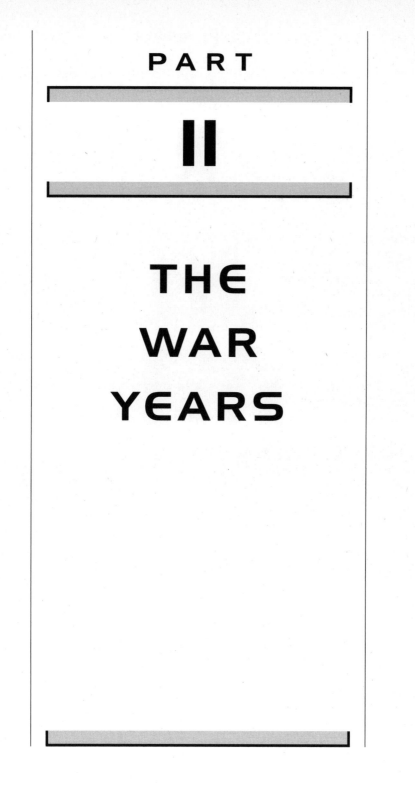

PART

II

THE
WAR
YEARS

3

Fighting the Germans

Before we left the United States, the Army issued us backpacks, standard infantry uniforms, and old World War I "doughboy" helmets and rifles. Marching down Fifth Avenue in New York City in full regalia caused quite a scene. Thousands lined the streets and supported us with their cheers.

We had not fired a shot, but we already felt like heroes. An hour later we boarded the *Queen Elizabeth*, an enormous cruise ship that had been converted for troop transport. Even though the military had made the ship functional, they had not been able to corrupt her beauty.

Submarines couldn't keep up with the *Queen Elizabeth*. Several times during the trip from New York to Scotland, we heard that German subs were on our tail, but they never caught us.

Even though I was just a sergeant (see Appendix) I was put in charge of sixty-seven pilots. This was an awesome responsibility for a twenty-year-old. Apparently my superiors felt that the experience I'd gained as a pilot qualified me to lead the men. Today, I fully understand what an honor that was.

On board the *Queen Elizabeth*, the other enlisted pilots and I ran into the same discrimination that we had witnessed earlier in fighter training. We were forced to ride in what had been the gymnasium with the infantry troops while the officers occupied the luxury suites.

Tom Watts wrote about the conditions in his journal:

Our quarters were in the gymnasium. Its size was 35' × 20' × 12', and there were 92 of us in it. Bunks were four layers and made like a box. There were four strips of lumber for the bottoms, a thin mattress, no pillow. Everything was discolored with filth.

Our life preservers were in our bunks, too, and they were shamefully grimy. Before we could even get in there, we had to remove all of our equipment and carry it because the bunks' aisles were only 25 inches apart. A soldier all decked out with his equipment could not pass through.

We also found that we were unable to stretch out to full length, since the bunks were 5 feet in length and only 3 feet in width.

Because of the trickle-down effect, all hell broke loose when men on the top tier of bunks experienced nausea and vomiting from seasickness. The stench was awful.

To keep the trip interesting, Tom Watts and I pulled a practical joke on the Army captain we reported to on the ship. He had been a fighter pilot in World War I.

That captain was always concerned about his waistline. Tom and I decided to needle him about it. We slipped into his quarters each night and trimmed a quarter inch from his Army webbed belt. Believe me, the captain started cutting back on his eating in an attempt to get his belt connected. By the time the ship reached Scotland he was on a starvation diet.

Our first look at the continent of Europe came when the *Queen Elizabeth* made its way up the Firth of Clyde, a narrow bay that leads to Glasgow. Tom Watts described the scene in his journal:

We docked in the little town of Greenock (pronounced Green-uck and said usually fast). All along the Firth, Spitfires were buzzing us and hedgehopping the whitecaps around us . . . what a prize we would have been with 20,000 men and 3,500 pilots aboard.

We spent one more night on the *Queen Elizabeth* and then boarded boats that Tom called "a cross between a ferry and a tug." It was deathly cold the morning of December 1, 1942, the first day I set foot on European soil.

The townspeople of Greenock were curious. I felt proud to be an American as I passed by them.

After a few hours, we boarded a train for England. Our unit was sent to a small town called Stone located near Shrewsbury, north of London.

Just a few miles from there were three munitions factories located out in the countryside. When I first heard about these factories, I couldn't believe our good luck. While there were just sixty-seven of us, there were over *ten thousand* women staying at the hostels and working at the munitions factories. Since we had ample free time while waiting for our assignment, we made ourselves available to "entertain" the ladies during our leisure hours.

The housing accommodations at Shrewsbury made access to the women a snap. Think of a wagon wheel; that was the configuration of the housing we had. They were called hostels, and each of the spokes housed a hundred or so people. The pilots had one spoke and all the rest housed women.

In the hub, they had a recreation hall and dining area, and we used to stand there when the buses returned the women from the plants. We had our pick. It was like having heaven on earth for a young single man.

And lively women they were. Tom Watts probably shocked his parents back home when he wrote about them in his journal:

> One would really think these girls had never seen a man before. Never have I seen a more eager bunch of females. They were like she-wolves in heat and employed similar tactics. The boys in our group went "hog-wild." Some even attempted to employ the attention of three or four girls in one evening.

Shortly after arriving in Stone, our outfit received orders to report to an airfield nearby called Atcham. We were quartered in Nissen huts, which were round half-cylinders, capable of accommodating eight to ten pilots. In the middle of each hut was a potbellied stove.

The English countryside, which was often blanketed in snow, was enchanting. But we had little sight-seeing time since we needed to focus on learning what was in store for us on the fighting front.

The aircraft identification training was intense. The instructors had small models of German and Italian airplanes hanging like mobiles. Split-second images of aircraft were flashed on a projector screen, and we had to identify them. This was repeated over and over until we could recognize the planes and ships in an eye-blink.

We were taught not only to identify the aircraft and ships, but to determine how many were in view.

Fliers at Shrewsbury were instructed on how to behave if they fell into enemy hands. If captured, we were under direct orders to give only name, rank, and serial number.

Training personnel explained how the underground worked in different countries and about some of the terrible torture that captured pilots had experienced. The worst one I heard about was inflicted on a

P-38 pilot shot down over Sardinia. He was strapped to a table with his feet hanging over the side, and when he would not talk, they beat his feet with two-by-fours. When he still refused to cooperate, they tied his genitals with a cord and yanked them off. He bled to death.

I would become a POW later in the war and learn firsthand that someone had broken the code of silence and informed on me. A German interrogation officer knew too much about my fighter squadron, and I knew someone had given him the information. I was very bitter and thought the behavior was criminal and that the guilty bastard was a traitor.

Initially I wanted to see that he got court-martialed. But, I came to understand that a lot of factors affect the way people respond in situations as difficult as that one.

Apparently, this fellow was married and had a baby that he had never seen. I guess he was convinced the Nazis were going to kill him if he didn't talk.

We never did much flying in England because of the rain and fog in December. I can't say I'm sorry.

England is about the size of Minnesota. The sky was thick with aircraft since pilots couldn't fly more than two hundred miles in any direction without leaving the country.

Problems with visibility made landing pure guesswork and luck. When a pilot was vectored in over an airfield, ground control would shoot a flare to let him know he was over the airfield. Pilots would then circle until they broke out of the overcast. That alone was scary enough, but there was a hill near the base, and if the pilots' circles were too wide, they crashed into the hillside.

While at Atcham, we enlisted pilots found a sympathetic officer named Colonel Grubb. As head of the reassignment group, he wondered why we had not received officer commissions.

We had assumed that we would be promoted before leaving New York since we had learned that pilots preceding us, who were staff sergeants, had been. As leader of our outfit, it was my responsibility to take this matter to the CO.

While no one knew the exact clause in the regulations that said so, I informed Colonel Grubb that enlisted men could refuse to fly combat without being court-martialed. Of course, nothing could have been further from the truth. We would have gone into combat as buck privates.

Colonel Grubb was first-class and he really did go to bat for all of us. On December 20, 1942, a brief ceremony was held. We were designated flight officers. That rank was equivalent to warrant officer in the

Army. It didn't mean we were commissioned, but we got pay and privileges similar to those of commissioned officers.

The Allied invasion of North Africa occurred in November of 1942. In January of 1943, our outfit was alerted that it would be transferred there. We boarded a train and traveled back to Greenock, Scotland.

At Greenock, our unit boarded a small but luxurious passenger ship called the *Strathnaver* and headed for North Africa. The accommodations this time were terrific, as evidenced by what Tom Watts wrote in his journal:

> When we were shown to our port rooms, we nearly dropped with surprise. Here were lovely beds with sheets and washbasins with running water. A valet was assigned to each one.
>
> The individual rooms were nearly as large as the entire gymnasium on the *Queen Elizabeth*. In these rooms there were twelve only instead of the ninety-two on the *Q.E.* Mmmm. Extreme comfort!
>
> The dining room was something out of a dream book. There were lovely large tables with fine cloths on them and enough silverware to make that famous lady of etiquette pull her hair. Each meal was served in seven courses with Portuguese waiters in formal dress serving. There were no meals missed on this voyage.

Good fortune smiled on us in other ways as well. The ship was transporting the Ninetieth General Hospital Unit, which included more than two hundred nurses! In addition to three great meals a day and evenings filled with feminine companionship, we could take time every afternoon to grab a nurse and attend teatime where crumpets and tea were served.

Our first stop in Africa was in the port city of Oran in French Morocco. We stayed there briefly before proceeding to St. Lucian, described by Tom Watts as a "mudhill for infantrymen." Next up was Tefaraoui, and then La Senia.

They had no beds in the barracks at La Senia, and we were forced to sleep on the cement floor. To keep from freezing, we wore our fleece-lined winter flying clothes over our regular uniforms and then curled up in a ball. Those nights in Africa felt more like nights in the dead of winter in Alaska.

After five days there, we were transported to Casablanca in DC-3s. We were then moved to Mediouna, about thirty miles outside the city.

Several of our flying buddies from Drew and Pinellas Fields in Florida joined us there. Denny McClendon, my barnstorming buddy during my stay at Columbia, South Carolina, was one of them.

Denny remembers our first meeting on African soil:

> A fellow Tennessee National Guard member named Leslie Wright and I were standing near an outdoor stand-up bench eating lunch in a little town called Nouvion, Algeria. It was the home of an old French Air Force base, and the barracks and eating station were all positioned up on a hill.
>
> All at once, from the direction of the airfield, we looked out and here came a P-40 headed right at us. The pilot startled everyone standing around by doing a precision eight-point roll right over the hill before flying away.
>
> At the same instant, Les and I turned to each other and said, "Uh-oh, Hoover's here!"

Sometime later, I ran into Denny at the La Senia Airport in Oran. We decided to do the town. The only problem was that every nightclub from Cairo to Casablanca had a sign on it, OFFICERS ONLY. Military police were there to enforce the rules.

Since I had been made a flight officer in England, I was okay. To qualify Denny, we merely "borrowed" a set of blue bars and promoted him on the spot.

Even though I wasn't happy about being stuck at a supply depot, I still felt combat was imminent. I tried to be patient, but I couldn't wait to fulfill my dream of dogfighting with the enemy.

When we arrived at Mediouna, all of the pilots were disappointed to learn we had been assigned to a replacement pilots' pool. One of the men decided we should rename the group the Sad Sacks to show our displeasure with not being ordered into combat. Tom Watts recorded the incident in his journal:

> Coates had the idea that the 67 of us should get an insignia for ourselves on the basis that we were somewhat of a rare collection. We [learned] we were not supposed to have been sent to England in the first place. We had gone to different places there, and they had no idea what to do with us.
>
> We were sent to five places in Africa, being received the same way we were in England. . . . Everyone agreed to Coates' proposal that we should be the 67 SAD SACKS, with the group title of SNAFU (Situation Normal All Fouled Up). Immediately, we donned our insignia, which, painted on leather, had the large numbers 67 with a face in the background of a sack weeping sadly; below was SAD SACKS, on top was SNAFU.

I knew the "official reason" I was not given an assignment to fly fighters when I first arrived in Africa was because my experience made me more qualified to test new aircraft.

I felt nothing could be further from the truth. The discipline involved with the routines I performed was indicative of my mind-set toward military regimen. Given the chance, I knew I could be a team player with any combat outfit in the Air Corps.

Combat pilots gave me a hard time about not being one of their brethren. Their attitude was illustrated by an incident that occurred at Telergma, Tunisia, the home base for the first fighter group. I had landed at that base for fuel and was relaxing at the officers'-club tent. It was nearly dark, and we didn't fly then because light illuminating the airfield would give the Germans a ready target.

Denny McClendon tells his version of the story:

> One drink led to another, and finally a smart-ass fighter pilot said, "Well, if you're such a hotshot pilot, Hoover, how come you're not flying combat?"
>
> Never one to back away, Bob responded, "Well, I'll tell you what. You know that suspension bridge right up the road over the canyon near Constantine? You jokers be in the middle of that bridge at eight hundred hours, and I'll fly the P-40 I'm driving down under that bridge and then loop around it."
>
> Those pilots cracked up with laughter at Hoover's boast. Flying a fighter under the bridge was considered to be next to impossible, and they were certain he'd never show up.
>
> Nevertheless, the next morning, six P-38 pilots were standing smack dab in the middle of the bridge when Bob roared up the canyon. When they saw him, half of them scattered, but the others stayed and watched the show as he flew under the bridge and looped back around, not once, but twice!

Denny was indeed a close friend. Years later, he sent me a copy of his book *The Lady Be Good*. His message on the inside cover was very special:

> To Bob Hoover. My oldest and best friend of the days when men were men and airplanes had real wings. When boundary layer, control pounds of thrust, state-of-the-art aerospace black boxes, and inertial guidance were for ground-pounding eggheads only. When a pilot flew by the feel in the seat of his pants with a small assist from what his eyes and nerves told that little black box inside his head. Where I work, Bob, you are known as the world's greatest pilot, and you deserve that title for my money.

It was signed *Denny McClendon, Pentagon, 1962.*

The commanding officer at Mediouna was Col. John Stevenson, a combat veteran. He later became a prisoner of war when his A-36 dive bomber was hit. During an escape attempt, he nearly lost a leg when a guard shot him.

Stevenson was an Army Air Corps man who loved to fly. A few days after we arrived, he assembled all the pilots and gave us the news that a French major would be delivering a brand-new Lockheed P-38 Lightning. This was a single-seater, twin-engine, twin-boom fighter, and I would be allowed to take it up. I couldn't wait to fly that twin-tail airplane.

When it came time for the major to give us a demonstration of the P-38's capability, all the troops gathered, and the pilot took the plane through a few uninspiring maneuvers. No one was too impressed since his maneuvers were performed at altitudes above three thousand feet.

When it was my turn, I was determined to outperform the French pilot. On takeoff, I barrel-rolled the "Fork-Tailed Devil," as it was referred to by the Germans. I flew the P-38 through a series of low-altitude aerobatics. They included one and then both propellers-feathered (dead) engine rolls at very low altitudes.

After fifteen minutes of flight, I landed the P-38 to the applause of everyone except Colonel Stevenson. The moment I was out of the plane, he was eyeball-to-eyeball with me. I can still remember his biting words: "Young man, you are grounded. Report to my office."

Once there, Colonel Stevenson slammed the door, and I readied myself for a good, old-fashioned tongue-lashing. A few nervous seconds went by as I stood at attention, awaiting his verbal barrage.

The colonel's stern face suddenly turned into a smiling one. He then extended his right hand toward me and uttered the comforting words "At ease."

I was dumbfounded. I extended my hand as he began to speak. "Flight Officer Hoover," he said, "I'm sure you've gotten me in serious trouble since other, inexperienced pilots will try to do what you just did, but let me shake your hand. I've flown the P-38 for more than three hundred hours, but I've never been able to do that!"

My heart was still racing, but I relaxed enough to respond, "It's a great machine, sir."

"Now, son, I'm going to have to make everyone believe I reprimanded you because I can't have my pilots busting their asses trying to duplicate your flights."

Seizing the moment, I decided to bring up the subject of a possible transfer to a combat unit. This one-on-one chance might not happen again, so I let the colonel have it with my best plea for a combat assignment for not only me, but Tom Watts as well.

I promised the colonel to leave his office acting as if he had disciplined me. He in turn promised me the first combat assignment out of there.

I believe that Colonel Stevenson carried out his part of the bargain too, but his superiors had other plans for me and Tom. We were sent back to the base at Oran to test new P-40s brought over in crates on cargo ships. Trying to hide my disappointment, I attempted to make the best of things and test-flew P-39s, P-40s, Spitfires, and the Hurricane, the British plane that fought in the Battle of Britain.

Tom and I really did put the P-40s through some ambitious tests. He recalled our flights:

> All these ships were brand-new P-40s, never flown, sent from the States in a crate and pieced together right here by GI mechanics. We were to test them, putting the slow time on the engine.
>
> We had the idea that we'd really test them by putting them through spins and dives and all the maneuvers, recording all reactions. The first day, however, Hoover was grounded for doing a few maneuvers over the field for the boys in the maintenance crew. . . . We merely went out of sight of the field and continued our routines.

Later on I was alongside Tom when we both encountered trouble in P-40s. It occurred over a valley about fifty miles out of Algiers. Tom described the incident in his journal:

> I tried to call Hoover, but my R/T [radio transmitter] was out too. I continued and in a few moments my electric prop went out. This old ship was so beaten and uncared for that the breaker points (prop) were evidently corroded, for even my manual increase and decrease RPM were inoperative. I knew I couldn't last much longer, and now Hoover's ship was leaving a stream of black smoke.
>
> I had just wiped the perspiration from my brow and was coaxing this heap over a peak barely making it, when—sputter—sput—and then she conked. First, I dropped my belly tank and like a fool lost a thousand feet watching it tumble to earth. (It didn't explode.) I took a second to pick my nest, and another second to decide whether to belly in or land with the wheels down.
>
> I started pumping my wheels down. At about halfway down the pressure on the hand pump entirely disappeared. Here I was with halfway landing gears. That wasn't funny in a P-40, for the way the gears operate, this is the surest way to be thrown on your back.
>
> I kept pumping and for some reason His hand was on my shoulder again, for the gear started coming back down. They finally locked into place and I had about eight feet altitude. Working furiously with my gear, I had drifted slightly from my intended pattern. I was over an erosion pit. I nearly kicked the rudder pedal through the floor and skidded her over to the right, and my wheels touched about a foot over the edge. I stopped after a short roll and the plane wasn't scratched—but God, I was nervous. I jumped out of the thing and praised the earth my feet were standing on.

I buzzed by and saw Tom salute to let me know he was all right. Now I had to figure out a way to get him off the ground. Tom wrote about that rescue attempt in his journal:

> He [Hoover] had an engine that was missing terribly. He pulled around and dragged the field, and then his gear moved down slowly and locked. Was this damn fool going to land? He did and a beauty. He brought his ship over alongside of me. My buddy wouldn't leave me.

I knew Tom would never have left me in a similar situation. I was determined that we'd either both make it back to base or neither one of us would.

The main problem of course was that the P-40 was a single seater. That and the fact that my ship wasn't exactly running on all fours made Tom and me do a bit of thinking. Here's what he remembered:

> We were in a hell of a desolate spot. After deep thinking and preparation, careful planning and such, I got on his shoulders and away we went. When we got about ten feet in the air, his engine began missing.
>
> Our would-be runway was surrounded by sharp, rocky knolls. If I had had a chute, my seat would have sewed button holes in it about that time [expression meaning his anal area is tight].
>
> However, we struggled into the air. My head and shoulders were in the slip stream, and I could hardly manage to keep my head on my body. Through the rearview mirror, I noticed my cheeks were being blown about three inches past my jaws—a hideous sight, and cruelly painful, indeed.
>
> I had no idea there was such elasticity in the skin. If I had lost my goggles, I would have lost my eyes.

With Tom hanging on for dear life, we lifted away from the valley and started to pass over a rugged part of the Atlas Range. I thought maybe we'd make it, and then the engine on my P-40 quit entirely. Tom recalls what happened next:

> Neither one of us had chutes. We couldn't have both gotten in the plane, especially with Bob six feet one and one-half inches tall. At approximately 800 feet from a subrange [smaller group of mountains], after gliding 6,200 feet, our engine began sputtering its answer to Bob's feverish and desperate work. Both of us thought this was "it."
>
> We approached our destination at 8,000 feet. But again our engine conked about ten miles out. When we radioed in, they thought we were being insubordinate to the authority of the tower. They cleared the field, though, for our emergency landing.
>
> Bob set her down nicely. We both got out and kissed the ground and answered questions of the crowd that seemed to come from everywhere. Bob had a kink in his back that kept him most uncomfortable

for days. I had a stiff neck, and my cheeks were so sore I could hardly wash my face.

We found later that the alert crew had found my ship and had it repaired. The local test pilot went down to fly it out and, after the first two attempts, tore the ship to pieces. People rushed up to find him strapped to a seat with a joystick in his hand [he was dead], and that was all that was left of the airplane.

Tom's write-up of this incident resulted in the award to me of the Soldier's Medal for Valor.

The next stop for Tom Watts and me was at Oujda, north of Rabat.

A few years back, I received a letter from aviator Bob Beynon, who recalled a rather humorous incident from those days in Africa:

> It's 1943 and my outfit . . . and the 438th Squadron have retreated back to Rabat, Morocco to regroup, etc. At this big base, P-51's are shipped in crates, bolted together, and guess who takes 'em up, Bob Hoover. . . . My outfit is living in pup tents and they are lined up along a company road which dead-ended at our three-hole latrine.
>
> One fine day I am in the latrine facing down the company street when suddenly I see Hoover in a P-51 on the deck coming right at me. Me and that latrine almost went over from the wash. I think I was constipated for a week!

Checking out planes from dawn to dusk kept me out of trouble for the most part, but not entirely. Looking for an instant cure for a severe case of body lice, I fell for a caper by a glib captain, who told me that soaking in gasoline was the answer to my woes.

It's hard to imagine that I was that naive, but I actually believed him. I rounded up a big tub and filled it with 100-octane gasoline. Naked as a jaybird, I eased down into that smelly fuel. After a while my body started to rebel, but I continued to sit there for quite a few minutes. Much to the enjoyment of those in on the joke, that fuel burned my skin so badly I couldn't sit comfortably for days!

One of my first close calls in the skies over Africa occurred when my Airacobra suffered an impeller explosion shortly after takeoff. To save the aircraft, I executed a sharp 180-degree turn. This was risky at low altitude. The engine was engulfed in flames, but I was able to land downwind and the fire crew saved the airplane.

Another incident, this time in an A-20 Havoc (twin-engine light bomber), almost caused the death of a flight-crew member. The bomber had a crew of three. The line chief, Raychard Paul, was in the nose, and a mechanic sat in the aft gunner's compartment.

When the landing gear would not extend, I knew we were going to be forced to make a belly landing. Realizing that since the only exit from the nose was from the bottom, I wanted Paul to bail out of the plane.

The communication system in the A-20 had failed, so I quickly scribbled a note to Paul telling him to open the hatch and jump. I passed it back through the instrument panel. He wrote back that he was not about to bail out.

Passing notes seems quite comical when I think back about it. Sign language would have worked better.

I didn't know any so I wrote back to Raychard saying that being trapped in the nose when we landed was one thing, but if the airplane caught fire, he wouldn't be able to get out. While all this correspondence was going on, I climbed to 11,000 feet. I wanted him to have plenty of time to get the parachute opened.

Although I respected Raychard for his loyalty, I was firm in my final note. He finally bailed out. I kept waiting to see his parachute open, but it didn't appear until I caught sight of it at a very low altitude.

Tom Watts said later that Sergeant Paul had obviously seen too many movies because he thought he was supposed to count to ten before pulling the rip cord. His error could have cost him his life if we had not been gaining altitude while writing and passing notes. As it was, the snap of the chute opening broke his right shoulder, and when he hit the ground, he dislocated the other one.

The mechanic in the back of the plane was unhurt when I bellied it, but for some reason, he'd opened his lower escape hatch. When the belly of the plane hit the grass, mud and gunk bombarded him. He was covered with wet, muddy sod when he got out. Neither of us cared. We were just glad to get out.

My most serious adventure over Africa happened in the Vultee Vengeance A-31, a single-engine, two-seater light attack bomber. During a routine test flight, my mechanic and I realized that each time we lowered the landing gear and reduced the throttle to idle, fire spewed out around the cowling next to the exhaust stacks.

Worried that this condition, known as torching, might occur when the plane touched down, I took a flyby, but the ground crew noticed no problem. So I climbed a few thousand feet and completed my tests. When it was time to land, I reduced the throttle to idle.

That's when we experienced a huge explosion. I was jolted in my seat. I saw both of the bomb-bay doors blow away. We were completely engulfed in flames. I could see the flames were already licking my legs and feet. I told my mechanic to jump. He hesitated.

Tom Watts wrote about the incident in his journal:

> The sergeant was afraid to leave, and those flames weren't doing Hoover's legs any good. Finally, when Hoover waved a wrench in a

gesture of bouncing it off his head, the sergeant decided he'd move. He started out the right side, but the flames were so bad he turned to the left.

A few seconds went by before he finally jumped. When I looked back to make sure he was safely out, the poor fellow was dangling over the side of the plane. His parachute harness had caught on the stowed .30-caliber machine-gun mount in the rear cockpit.

My feet and legs were still being singed as I rolled the plane and shook the sergeant loose. When I saw him float off, I focused on getting myself out of trouble.

By this time, I knew I was too low to parachute. I added full power and rolled the plane from its inverted position. That got rid of the fire. I climbed to ten thousand feet and shut off the fuel supply. I then dead-sticked the Vultee Vengeance back toward the field.

Tom Watts recalled my landing in his journal:

> [Hoover] was on his final approach when it [the plane] burst into flames. After setting her down, he jumped out and ran like hell. The fire department acted quickly. Hoover was recommended for the Distinguished Flying Cross. [not awarded]

Another incident occurred on one of my first flights delivering planes to different bases. I piloted an A-20 twin-engine light bomber over to Tunis from Algiers. A captain at the base needed a lift and I agreed to take him with me.

The bomber was not armed since we expected no trouble. Twenty-five miles from the Tunis base, however, I was told to delay my arrival since German fighters and bombers were attacking.

I reduced the power to conserve fuel, but the captain let me know he was a bit nervous about flying around without any defense whatsoever. His trepidation increased when ground control advised us to circle while they filled in many of the knee-deep craters in the runway caused by the bombing.

If there had been another delay, I think that captain would have wet his pants. He wanted off that plane—the quicker the better.

When I was finally cleared to land, the nose wheel caught in an area of soft dirt used to fill the craters. It collapsed and the plane skidded on its nose with the tail thrust in the air. With the plane still moving, the captain decided he'd had enough. He leaped from the plane and down on the pavement, breaking both ankles.

While I was testing aircraft, I was test-firing their weapons as well. As part of checking them out, I would fly in and hit a series of ground targets. I became proficient at this, then decided to see if I could hit the targets while upside down.

To make the routine as difficult as possible, I tried to see how round I could perform a loop. Most people go up and do an oval-shaped loop, but if a pilot does a loop like the competition aerobatic pilots, the loops are round, permitting consecutive loops starting and recovering at the same point for each loop. What I wanted to perfect was firing those guns into the same target four out of four consecutive loops.

After some experimenting, I found I could indeed accurately fire the guns at the targets at the bottom of four consecutive loops. None of the pilots made much of it, and since many of my superiors were not aviators, they did not show a lot of interest in my exploits. The firing technique was more for my personal satisfaction than anything. If the situation arose during combat, I might have a skill that could save my life.

The bottom line was that while I had carved out a reputation as a good test pilot who could fly many different aircraft, those skills continued to pigeonhole me. I knew my commanding officer was reluctant to let me go and join a combat unit since he didn't have an able replacement.

Every chance I got, I carried my request for combat down to the CO's office. Every request was turned down.

4

The Distinguished Flying Cross

Serving my country as a test pilot gave me intense satisfaction, but I wanted to engage the enemy. Time and time again I coveted the experience of my fellow aviators as they climbed into Spitfires and streaked across the sky on combat missions.

In early 1943, I thought I had finally broken free of my commanding officer's desire to keep me on board as a test pilot. Tom Watts was already over with the Fifty-second Fighter Group, and I had the opportunity to plead my case to a major whose name I thought was Melvin McNickle.

During my brief stay in England, I had met a Major McNickle. Much to my delight, I thought I spied him one day in the operations office at Oran.

I walked over to the major, slapped him on the back, and said, "How ya doin'. It's Bob Hoover!"

I was surprised when he didn't respond as I had expected because I thought we had become pretty good friends. Instead, it was a few seconds before he broke into a grin.

"Marvin McNickle," he said. "Melvin's twin brother. What's your name again?"

We talked for a while, but it wasn't long before I shared with him my disappointment about not being in combat.

Major McNickle was on his way to take over the Fifty-second in Palermo, Sicily. He had earned a British Distinguished Flying Cross for flying Spitfires for them in late 1942 at Dieppe in France.

"Sir," I said, "a few of my buddies and I have flown Spitfires. It's a great plane and we're ready to fly combat, but we're having a devil of a time getting anyone to listen to us."

"What seems to be the problem?" the major asked.

"We've all put in for transfer, but they say they need us here. All we do is test planes crated in, and that's all right, but we want to fly combat."

"Well, young man, I appreciate anyone who wants combat. I'll tell you what. You get a transfer and I'll back you up on the other end."

Talking to Major McNickle got my hopes up, but that transfer didn't occur for some time.

First, I was ordered to report to the Twelfth Air Corps headquarters in Algiers. I was sure this would be my opportunity for combat.

That turned out not to be true. The Twelfth Air Corps was organizing a ferry command. Their commander, Colonel Eppwright, had requested me to be his operations officer because I had experience in so many aircraft.

This was a great disappointment. Instead of flying combat, I checked out pilots in airplanes they had never flown before. Then I led them in a North American B-25 Mitchell bomber to where *I* wanted to be—airstrips on the fighting front. I also brought pilots back to Algiers to pick up planes that would replace those lost in combat.

Meanwhile, Colonel Eppwright batted down any attempts for a transfer to the fighting front. I became very discouraged. Fighting was what I wanted to do, and no one would give me a chance. They kept telling me that because of my experience in so many aircraft, they needed me right where I was.

Months after my encounter with Major McNickle, I had occasion to fly a B-25 bomber and lead six P-40 fighters to Licata. This occurred immediately after the invasion of Sicily. My mission was to escort the fighters over and then transport the pilots back to our home base at Algiers.

As I waited outside the operations tent, I watched with envy as fighter pilots returned from their missions. They were flying support for the ground troops commanded by Generals Patton and Montgomery. Mistaking me for one of the combat pilots, a two-star general named Joe Cannon began to question me about my mission.

Having a two-star general strike up a conversation was an opportunity not to be lost. I didn't pass up the chance to once again plead my case for combat.

"I want to fly combat, sir," I told the general, "but I'm being held back."

"What seems to be the problem, son?" he asked.

"General Cannon, my CO, will not let me join the Fifty-second and fly combat."

As the conversation continued, I tried to give the general an idea of my flying skills and why I was ready for combat. I wasn't usually one to wave my own flag, but this time I didn't hold back.

I even went so far as to tell General Cannon about my ability to hit ground targets coming out of four consecutive loops, both rightside up and upside down. I also told him that Maj. Marvin McNickle had invited me to join him if I could gain a transfer.

He listened carefully, and at the end of our conversation, General Cannon said, "Son, I'll see what I can do. I promise you that."

After writing down my name and unit, the general returned to his P-51 and off he went. I felt confident that if Marvin McNickle told Cannon he wanted me, and Cannon kept his word, I would soon be flying combat.

The waiting was the toughest part. I was very hopeful at first, but then weeks went by with no answer. I continued to check out newly arriving pilots and to lead formations of new aircraft that were headed for the front lines.

My frustration grew, especially during an air-raid alert we experienced one evening right after dark. The attack came from the Luftwaffe bomber command. I could hear the engines of the bomber formation even though the sirens were wailing and the antiaircraft firing was almost continuous.

The huge spotlights made the bombers visible. I didn't see a single plane get hit even though the sky was a blanket of ack-ack (streams of bullets) and lit up like a fireworks display.

That raid made me yearn to take to the sky, but if not for the favor of a corporal who worked in the office of Colonel Eppwright, I might never have received my orders to fly combat. Almost three weeks to the day after my talk with Gen. Joe Cannon, the corporal met me after one of my test flights.

"Hoover, I've seen your transfer orders," he told me. "They've been here for two weeks."

"They've what?" I replied, my indignation apparent.

"The colonel has been sitting on them. He'd skin me alive if he knew I told you, but I thought that you ought to know."

"Where's the transfer to?"

"The Fifty-second."

Armed with this information, and at the risk of being disciplined, I confronted Colonel Eppwright. "Colonel, I had a call from somebody wanting to know why I haven't reported to duty at the Fifty-second Fighter Group!"

"I'm not letting you go. No one else has the experience you do. You'll just get killed in combat, but here at the base you can help our war effort . . . and you might make a great test pilot after the war."

Despite his obstinacy, I held my ground. "Sir, those orders are made out and I'm supposed to be with the Fifty-second. I don't believe you have any choice."

"Well, we'll see about that, soldier," he bellowed as he abruptly dismissed me.

Looking back, I am flattered that the colonel wanted to keep me. He even suggested that I should stay there so that after the war I could go to Wright Field (in Ohio) and fly experimental aircraft.

Leaving Colonel Eppwright's office, I still had no idea whether he'd let me go. He seemed hell-bent on keeping me with him for the duration of the war.

The next day, I was scheduled for a B-25 training flight to check out two pilots. Seconds before I dropped into the cockpit, that same corporal raced up with copies of my transfer orders.

I didn't want to hang around and give Eppwright a chance to reconsider, so I headed straight for Boco de Falco Air Base at Palermo, Sicily, which had just fallen to the Allies. Once I was airborne, I gave out a victorious war whoop that must have been heard all across Africa.

I joined the Fifty-second Fighter Group in September of 1943. Lt. Col. Marvin McNickle was indeed the commanding officer. I was assigned to the Fourth Fighter Squadron and would remain at Palermo until I was reassigned to Calvi, Corsica, when that island was captured.

Being a part of McNickle's outfit was a remarkable experience for me. I had been trained to be a fighter pilot, and now I was going to get my chance in combat. While many of the pilots were just counting every mission, wanting to go home as soon as possible, I never felt that way. I wanted to stay at Palermo or wherever I could until the war was over.

Within days of my arrival, Lieutenant Colonel McNickle told me he wanted the pilots to see firsthand the Spitfire's capabilities. I was asked to display my aerobatic skills for the fighter group so they would have confidence in the aircraft. He warned them that he would reprimand anyone who tried to duplicate my routine.

The performance went off without a flaw. The response from the men was very positive. I was nearing my twenty-second birthday, and it was quite a charge to have everyone so excited about the maneuvers I'd performed.

My initial duties in the Fourth Squadron involved escorting Allied ship convoys who brought much-needed supplies. These escort excursions never resulted in any dogfights with the enemy. I soon became restless again even though I carried the designation *combat pilot*.

I was, however, able to link up with Tom Watts, who had been transferred to the Fifty-second sometime earlier. He was also upset that he hadn't seen more combat time as evidenced by an entry in his journal dated October 9, 1943:

> Hoover and I got a couple of test ships and some dogfighting against one another. We usually team up to get someone else, shining together [getting the opposition in between them]. I guess things must really be rough when we have to resort to fighting each other. It was a vicious affair. The circumstances of no one knows put us in a hole about five miles wide with peaks walling it in [accidentally found themselves in a valley surrounded by mountains].
>
> To top all this our fighting was from 50 feet not to exceed 1,200 feet. Most of the time our ships were vibrating violently, as they were on stalling edge throughout the flight. We were in a semistate of blackout to help the situation. That was really fun. Hoover has never been defeated in a dogfight, but this one was a tie.

I was asked to put on an air show when the boys from the Thirty-fourth Air Depot Group had a P-38 that needed a test flight.

Tom Watts and I talked over what maneuvers I might perform. We decided that I should include one where I feathered the prop on both engines (engines dead) and then did a loop off the deck.

Tom recalled the show in his journal:

> Bob's takeoff was very clean and a bit fancy. He climbed to an approximate altitude of 10,000 feet. I was happy to see him feel it out with tight maneuvers, for he hadn't flown an exhibition on the deck for some time.
>
> The time he has had here has been so stretched between flights and flights so few [Bob flew very rarely] that it makes a difference on this particular type of flying. But I was to find that it wouldn't make too much difference with his gifted abilities.
>
> He streaked over our heads so low that we could see him grinning in the cockpit. He did some climbing rolls to about 600 feet, turning on its back and flying her through to give us a haircut on the way back. He then did some inverted rolls off the deck, several loops at exceedingly low altitude, and repeated all these at the same altitude with a prop feathered on one of the engines.
>
> Due to a very weak battery, Hoover wisely disconsidered the double-prop-feathered loop off the deck. Everyone appreciated the great art he displayed and no one was displeased except Hoover himself when he found that one of our favorite sergeants had bet ten dollars that he would perform the originally intended double-prop-feathered loop off the deck maneuver.

That P-38 was a great plane. Just after that air show I went to our flight operations officer, Captain Scott, and told him that it would be interesting to see how it matched up with the Spitfire. I told him I would pilot the P-38 and Tom Watts would battle me in a Spitfire. Tom wrote about the dogfight in his journal:

> We went to our planes but found we were hard-pressed for time because of an oncoming storm. The sky was overcast now, but there was still a 7,000-foot base.
>
> We took to the air to fight over the vicinity of the field, finding the weather rapidly dissipating to give us more room. For a solid hour we fought hard, tiring ourselves to complete exhaustion. We did find, how-ever, that the Spit 9 is by a damn sight better than the Lightning. The turning ability is about equal; the climbing ability of the Spit 9 is twice that of the Lightning.

Later that week, we lost Captain Scott. He was returning from a mission and his engine failed. He didn't have enough altitude to make it to the airfield.

Two of our pilots were riding in a jeep near the field. When Scotty's plane crashed, they rushed to help him. The fuel tank ruptured and burst into flames. His boot had gone through the stirrup above the rud-der pedal and they couldn't get him out of the cockpit. The heat was so intense they had to back off and stand there while they heard his cries for help. I can only imagine the horror and then the nightmares the two men must have had after that tragedy.

My friend Denny McClendon was assigned to Palermo for a short time.

When I checked Denny out in a P-40 War Hawk, he fell in love. He decided on the spot that he wanted to be a fighter pilot. When he went to Marvin McNickle with his request, he was told, according to Denny, "Get your ass home and go to gunnery school because right now you don't know your ass from a hole in the ground about fighters, and all I'll do is lose you and a good airplane."

After that, I didn't see Denny for a while. He was stationed down in Sicily near a monastery. That was shortly after General Patton had cleared out the area, and all of the monks had fled in panic since the Germans had told them that the conquering Americans would castrate them all if they were captured.

After some time, a bit of excitement finally did come my way at Palermo. My experience with aerobatics and knowledge of many types of aircraft paid off. I would have a chance to win the coveted Distin-guished Flying Cross.

Colonel Blair, my commanding officer in Casablanca, called Lieu-tenant Colonel McNickle to see if I would be interested in retrieving a B-26 Martin Marauder that had been shot up. It had bellied in on a very short stretch of beach in the Straits of Messina. The damaged plane had been repaired and was needed by the forces back at the base, but no one felt they could get it airborne since there was so little room to lift off.

I was told that if I could not find a way to save the aircraft, it would be abandoned, since there was no equipment in the area with which to disassemble the bomber. I had never flown the Marauder, but was intrigued by the challenge of saving the aircraft. I was also challenged by the prospect of being awarded the DFC.

My buddy Tom Watts wrote about this event on November 20, 1943:

> You may see Bob Hoover in a newsreel someday. A B-26 had a forced landing after a mission on the beachhead about fifty miles west of Messina. It's in such a small, narrow, highly obstructed place that the bomber pilots refused to fly it at all. They asked Hoover if he would do it, and of course, he would.
>
> So the picture men are going to make an issue of the fact that bomber pilots refuse to fly their own planes and a Spitfire pilot soars it to safety.

My only reservation about flying the B-26 was its reputation. Pilots used to say, "One a day in Tampa Bay," to describe the Marauder when I was stateside, since so many of them crashed into the bay. That plane would go on to have a great track record in combat, but it had a poor reputation in training.

My mechanic for the escapade was to be my old friend Sgt. Raychard Paul. We flew an L-4 reconnaissance airplane, a small two-seater capable of landing in a short distance, over to take a look at the bomber.

The B-26 was setting up on its landing gear on a crescent-shaped stretch of sand just a little more than a thousand feet long. At one end of the beach, there was a twelve-foot drop-off to the water. The challenge would be to lift the bird off the uphill-grade portion of the beach before it catapulted over the drop-off and crashed into the Straits.

Sergeant Paul and I circled the Marauder several times, trying to gain a bead on how I could get it out of there and back to Palermo. I also studied several manuals describing the plane's capabilities.

From first look, I knew there was no way I could lift the B-26 off before the drop-off with the plane at normal weight. There was simply not enough space. To lighten the load, Sergeant Paul and I decided which different parts of the B-26 could be eliminated. Then, we requested ten good men to assist us.

Two days later, Sergeant Paul and his handpicked crew began dismantling the plane. When they were finished, the copilot's seat, most of the instruments, and everything else that wasn't absolutely essential to flying the plane was no longer on board. Less than a hundred gallons of fuel was put in the tanks. That was just enough for the trip to Palermo.

Even with the lighter plane, I knew that I needed as much runway as possible. We had the crew lay down three hundred feet of steel matting across the soft, sandy beach. An additional three-hundred-foot extension of chicken wire was laid down beyond that and mixed in with the sand to provide additional firmness.

With several curious observers on the scene, I decided to make a first try. That attempt to free the Marauder was aborted when the electric propellers overspeeded. I couldn't even get to where the chicken wire was located.

What a fiasco. I could almost hear the skeptical onlookers snickering about my inability even to come close to getting the plane airborne. That only stiffened my resolve.

Besides new batteries for the propellers, I decided that I needed three hundred more feet of steel matting. Our ground crew stirred into action.

Getting everything right for the recovery effort took more than a month. Finally, I was ready to make the attempt. Several hundred troops as well as a reporter for the *Stars and Stripes* newspaper took their stations to watch the action.

The pressure was on, but I was confident. I'd show my detractors I could lift the bird from the beach.

As I readied for takeoff, Sergeant Paul, who was in his early forties, stated, "I'm going with you." I told him that wouldn't work since we didn't even have a seat or a seat belt for him. "Doesn't matter," he said, "I'm in for the ride. You can't close the hatch without me, and I refuse to do it unless you let me go."

Since I was burning precious fuel while arguing with him, I finally gave in.

I ran up the R-2800 engines, dropped my quarter flaps, and off we went. The propellers operated efficiently this time, and the acceleration was better than I had anticipated because of the wind on the nose.

The propellers disturbed the sand, sifting it past the windshield as the B-26 accelerated quickly down the makeshift runway. Just in case the plane didn't make it, a fishing boat was positioned offshore so that we could be rescued from the water.

There was only about four feet of clearance on each side of the matting, so I had not only to get up to speed, but steer the beached bird straight ahead. A slight drift to the right or left on the takeoff would have been disastrous.

Ever cautious, I watched the airspeed indicator closely as it climbed to twenty knots, then thirty, then to fifty.

At that point, I only had about four hundred feet of matting left. The end of the beach was quickly approaching, and the nose still wasn't up.

Perspiration dampened my forehead, but forty more knots of speed permitted me to gently lift the nose of the B-26 upward, and ten more lifted the plane completely off the sand. The Marauder pitched its way skyward, stretched out over the drop-off, and took off as if it slipped from an aircraft carrier deck.

Sergeant Paul and I proudly flew the B-26 back toward Palermo. When I got back near the base, I realized I was fat on fuel. Feeling frisky with the DFC in my pocket, I spotted a P-40 and decided to do a bit of dogfighting with him. He was overconfident at first, but the ol' Marauder surprised him. I may have been flying a bomber, but that baby weighed so much less than normal that it was probably an even match.

Even though fuel was low after the dogfight, I still had enough to give my Allied buddies a few aerobatic maneuvers over the base. When Sarge and I landed and emerged from the Marauder, the pilots gave us a rousing ovation.

Tom Watts recorded the event for posterity in his journal:

> Today, [Bob] attempted again and was highly successful. He brought her in for a beautiful landing. Many a pessimistic one [at the base] gave an envious look as he climbed out of the B-26 with a big grin on his face.

Since I was the only pilot on the base qualified to fly bombers, I took four or five pilots back to Algiers in a B-25, then led a return flight of new Spitfires to replace planes lost in combat.

On New Year's Eve of 1943, I had three aviators with me who had completed their fifty missions and were on their way home. In some theaters, the number was more and in some less, but where we were based the magic number was fifty.

Before we took off, I was sitting in the bar with the three pilots headed for home. As they got in the ink, they kept telling me how slim my survival chances were. They then described the fate of their buddies, some of whom were dead, others captured. As I listened to their grim accounts, I realized perhaps for the first time that there was a chance that I wouldn't make it back to the States in one piece.

Despite their doom-and-gloom attitude, belief in my ability to fly capably any Allied aircraft gave me comfort. I was confident no German pilot could shoot me out of the sky.

5

The Spitfire Goes Down

I'd rather dogfight than eat steak and mashed potatoes on Sunday. My best memories are of duels with other pilots ten thousand feet above the earth.

Strategy is the key to dogfighting. Both aircraft begin by flying in formation, then each pilot makes a ninety-degree turn and heads off in the opposite direction. A minute later, after one pilot calls out, "Time," each airplane turns toward the opponent.

Except for the always-pass-on-the-right rule, pilots can employ whatever strategy they choose. I always thought it was best to add power while heading toward the other aircraft and then, the moment the planes pass, head straight up.

I also kept an eye on my opponent to see what decision he made. All the while, I attempted to convert airspeed to altitude, and when I finally rolled the plane, the other aircraft was down below me where I could go after him.

The greatest dogfighter I ever saw was Chuck Yeager. In his book *Yeager*, he says, "I loved to dogfight. It was a clean contest of skill, stamina, and courage, all in one."

Chuck and I battled each other in all kinds of aircraft, after the war at Wright Field in Ohio. We usually fought to a draw because we knew each other so well that one could never get the best of the other. Many times, we had to break it off before we both crashed and burned. Afterward, we'd have a few cold ones and relive the excitement.

Other than fighting to several "draws" with Chuck, and one with

Tom Watts, I never lost a dogfight. I have had a lot of skirmishes, but one occurred at Palermo that I will never forget.

An American pilot who had shot down several airplanes in the area called to challenge me to a dogfight. The match was arranged and side bets were made. I laid a few dollars out myself.

There were about twenty P-40s and several Spitfires at the depot. My opponent and I had our pick of the group. I walked down the flight line with the pilot, who was a captain, and asked him to choose his weapon.

He picked the P-40 and proceeded to get into it as I chose mine. While I was getting settled in, one of the ground crew came up and said, "The airplane we put him in has a bad mixture of coolant and water. There's no way he'll whip you."

While I appreciated the allegiance, I didn't want to play the game that way. I got out of my airplane and told the other pilot to take the one I had been in. I found another that was fit and up we went.

I expected quite a dogfight, but to my surprise, the ending was quick and easy. I don't know if the captain was nervous or what, but I was on his ass less than thirty seconds after we went at it.

We must have gone at each other four or five times, but each time I fell in behind his tail and nailed him. When we landed, he was totally humiliated. While my comrades were patting me on the back, that poor guy shuffled off by himself somewhere. I felt bad for him, but he's the one who came after me.

Tom Watts recorded the dogfight in his journal on October 18, 1943: "While we were waiting for the next series of events, one of our boys jumped Bob in a Spitfire V and was literally made a fool of."

Needless to say, word of my victory got around. Each time the story was told, it grew in stature. Before it was over, I'd mastered the Red Baron himself.

Off the northern tip of Corsica, there was a small island occupied by the Germans. Most of those islands had been purged of the enemy, but not that one.

The Germans were still running barges across the channels. To stop the flow of men and supplies, we were ordered to strafe them.

When the barges came into view, we swooped down with guns blazing. The hundred or so men on board tried to counterattack with rifles, but they were not effective. Before long, we could see no movement. The Germans were either dead or had jumped overboard.

That ghastly mission bothered me more than I could have imagined. The pile of bodies haunted me, and the recurrent image of the carnage plagued me at night, making sleep difficult for weeks. That incident still troubles me today when I think about it.

Despite my reservations about that type of assignment, Tom Watts and I were always trying to find ways to get more time in the air. We weren't going to become aces sitting on our butts, so we took advantage of any opportunity that came our way to gain flight time.

The day after Thanksgiving in 1943, we had our chance. I didn't drink at the time and neither did Tom, but several of the pilots went on a holiday binge. They were drinking a strange concoction: grain alcohol mixed with grape juice.

We knew that most of the celebrants would really be suffering the next morning. Tom and I went into action. We approached some of the more enthusiastic drinkers and said, "You know, you're not going to be feeling too well in the morning. How about letting us take your mission?"

It worked. The next day Tom and I flew four different missions! Unfortunately, we didn't encounter one combat opportunity. Enemy planes just didn't come that far away from the front lines.

One day, however, it looked as if I might become an ace during a single enemy encounter.

That's the goal of every fighter pilot. It's the pinnacle. I wanted to be an ace more than anything else in the world.

A pilot needed five confirmed kills to become an ace. That meant that I had to shoot down at least five enemy aircraft.

A fighter pilot can't focus on the human loss involved in these encounters. Shooting down planes is the main goal; the fate of the enemy pilot is a secondary concern.

Eddie Rickenbacker, the ace of aces in World War I, put it this way in his autobiography, *Rickenbacker:*

> I had no regrets over killing a fellow human being. I do not believe that at the proper moment I even considered the matter. Like nearly all air fighters, I was in automation behind the gun barrels of my plane. I never even thought of killing an individual but of shooting down an enemy plane.

My chance to become an ace came in September 1943. Tom Watts and I had a duty assignment for alert scrambles. That required sitting in the cockpit of a Spitfire adjacent to the runway for two hours at a time waiting for enemy aircraft. We kept the engine running intermittently, ready at the call.

When radar picked up a bandit (enemy), a green flare would shoot up in front of the airplane. That meant it was time to take to the air as quickly as possible.

That green flare triggered excitement that came from flying into an unknown situation. There was no way to determine if there was one plane or a thousand planes to face in a potential life-or-death struggle.

On this occasion, I saw the green flare. As soon as Tom and I scrambled into the air, we were advised that over a hundred enemy aircraft were heading toward Palermo.

The excitement built as Tom and I entered the airspace and checked our headings. The drama intensified when ground control confirmed, "Bogies at 360, one hundred plus." That meant more than a hundred enemy planes were coming from the north.

With a clenched jaw and ready eye, I focused on the sky in front of me, looking for specks on the horizon that would signal enemy aircraft. All at once, I thought I saw one speck. Then another. Suddenly, I could see more of them. Before long, nearly a hundred planes were in clear focus. The sheer number was staggering. They darkened the sky.

Quickly I glanced out toward Tom's plane. He gave me a thumbs-up. We were both ready for the flight of our lives.

Once I closed in on the Italian armada, I could see that while there were a few fighters, most of the planes were bombers. I figured my best strategy would be to make the attack on the left flank since the fighters were on the right.

Tom and I angled up and over the top of the planes to get into position for the kill. I wanted to come up from behind and dive before they knew what happened.

Ready for the kill, I clicked on the gun switch. Tom was in position, and we were seconds away from spitting bullets at as many enemy aircraft as possible before ducking for cover.

Just as I closed in on the first target, ground control blurted out, "The Italians have surrendered. You are to escort those planes to base. Do you read?"

My heart dropped to the basement as I acknowledged the message. I removed my hand from the gun switch and relaxed my hold on the controls. If that message had been relayed only moments later, I would have been an instant ace.

Instead, I was forced to move out and ahead of the lead airplane in the tight formation. As I flew by, the same men that I would have killed waved cheerfully as they fell in behind Tom and me.

We led the armada back to base. I got dangerously low on fuel while flying around watching the parade of planes pass by.

When I finally landed, Tom and I commiserated with one another. "We were awful close," I told him, "awful close."

Before the Italians had surrendered, my love for old airplanes led me to fly a vintage World War I Italian Fiat while stationed at Palermo.

The victorious pilots who had captured the Boco de Falco airfield discovered the Fiat hidden behind one of the damaged hangars. Restoring it became a project for the base mechanics, and before long the plane was used to fly mail to other bases.

That Fiat was a single-seat, high-wing monoplane. When orders came for the Fifty-second to relocate to Corsica, I was flattered that Lieutenant Colonel McNickle asked me if I wanted to fly the Fiat to the new base.

Since the fuel capacity of the plane was limited, I had the mechanics install extra fuel tanks between the engine and the cockpit. The scheduled flight called for me to fly to Sardinia, refuel at what we thought was a recently captured base along the way, and make my way across the Strait of Bonifacio to Corsica.

The trip would cover nearly three hundred and fifty miles on the first leg to Sardinia. A group of Spitfires were scheduled to fly a wide fingertip formation over my flight path to let me know I was on course.

The Fiat had no radio, so I couldn't keep in voice contact with either ground control or the other planes set to pass over me after I took off. The airplane was unarmed, and the magnetic float compass wasn't quite up to par. That was a problem because if I veered too far off course, I could easily end up defenseless behind enemy lines in southern France or Italy.

I didn't know that the flight of the Spitfires had been called off because Sardinia and Corsica had not been secured by the Allies. With no Spitfires to guide me, I meandered over the water toward the coast of Sardinia.

It was a beautiful flight. It was hard to imagine that the world was at war. When I spied a coastline, I didn't know if the landfall was Sardinia, France, or Italy.

I made a safe landing on a field in Sardinia that was filled with Macchi fighters. The Macchi C.202 was Italy's best fighter. It could fly at almost 375 miles an hour, making it a solid opponent for Allied pilots.

I had planned to land, fuel up, and fly to Corsica. Instead, as I taxied down the runway, I saw a weary bunch of Italian aviators headed my way.

My first instinct was to decide how to defend myself. But, something about the way the men were approaching me made me relax.

They turned out to be stragglers who had been marooned on the base after attacks by the Allies. The portly commander and his men stopped in formation and gave me a smart salute. But I could tell they were puzzled in spite of the formality. What in the world was I doing in a World War I Fiat?

I approached the commander, who spoke very little English. I was shocked when I realized what was going on. These men were trying to surrender to me!

I tried to explain to the Italian commanding officer that I couldn't accept their offer, but he insisted. He then invited me to join him for lunch. I ended up sitting with my former enemy under a tent awning on the lawn while we ate lunch and discussed the war.

There was even entertainment. After lunch we sat on the well-manicured grass and watched an Italian pilot perform aerobatics in his Macchi 205. I kept my comments about his performance, which was mediocre, to myself. I only wished I was flying the 205.

I finally convinced the commander that I had to continue on to Corsica because I was concerned about reaching my destination before dark. He had the ground crew fill the Fiat with fuel. It wasn't until I'd flown away from the airfield that I realized what a bizarre afternoon I'd had.

My adventures in the Italian Fiat were not over, however. A strong headwind began to impede my progress. The normal four-hour trip to Corsica would take much longer than anticipated.

I had been cruising for a couple of hours when a flight of American P-38s appeared on the horizon. Before I knew it, the P-38s were all over me with the intent to kill. To them, I was just another Italian enemy plane.

My lack of speed in the Fiat turned out to be a blessing. The P-38s whizzed by me so fast they couldn't get a good clear shot. I was waving frantically, hoping to focus their attention toward the Allied markings on the side. I wasn't having much luck. I did some quick turns to evade them, but I knew that sooner or later they would hit me.

I was anticipating the first blast when one of the pilots spotted the marking. He gave me the thumbs-up, apparently radioed his fellow fighter pilots, and without missing a beat, sped away from me.

What a day! The Italians tried to surrender and the Americans tried to shoot me down.

Upon arrival at Calvi, Corsica, I was shocked that no Spitfires were on the airfield. The only airplane was a battle-damaged B-17 Flying Fortress bomber, later dubbed the "plane that won the war," that had made an emergency landing.

I learned that the French had invaded the day before and accepted the surrender of the Italian ground troops. The situation was still chaotic. I ended up sleeping in a tent with some French soldiers and eating with them until my squadron arrived.

The next day I noticed that the Italian troops were out of supplies. They were eating the garbage from the French soldiers' kitchen area. Little did I know that before long I would be hungry enough to welcome such a scavenging opportunity.

* * *

The night before my fifty-ninth mission, a group of pilots and I sat around our quarters. Among them was James "Monty" Montgomery, who had been shot down a few months earlier. He had spent three days in a life raft before being rescued.

Monty was my closest friend in those days. The two of us were roommates.

Monty was easygoing, a natural with an airplane, and equally determined as I to get into combat.

Monty and a pilot named "Andy" Anderson normally flew the dawn patrol. Ever ready for any chance at combat, I tried to convince them to let another airman and me take their place. I still wanted to dogfight with the Germans, and I thought enemy fighters might be lurking about on that early patrol.

"Why should I let you go up there?" Andy asked.

"'Cause they might shoot your butt down. My buddy and I have had a lot of simulated dogfights. We can handle 'em."

The disgusted look on Anderson's face let me know I had struck a nerve.

"Oh, is that so?" Andy asked.

"Can I have all your personals when you hit the deck?" I said, trying to goad him further.

Unfortunately, nothing I could say changed Andy's mind. The next morning Monty and Anderson took off and headed out over the Mediterranean Sea. With no warning, the engines on both planes quit.

Monty managed to make a miraculous turnaround and landed safely. Unfortunately, Andy's plane, the one I could very well have been flying, crashed into the sea.

His body was found the next morning. Later that day, investigators found salt water mixed with the fuel in Monty's plane. Apparently someone had sabotaged both planes during the night. We never knew whether it was the enemy or someone from the base with a score to settle.

By this time, even though I hadn't personally encountered many combat situations, casualty rates among our squadron were high. There had been thirty-four pilots when I arrived; now there were thirteen.

On January 24, 1944, my twenty-second birthday, Tom was shot down near the coast of Calvi, Corsica. He had successfully bailed out of his Spitfire, but the force of the high winds dragged him into a reef of rocks offshore.

I flew over the location where Tom went down and could see his body and parachute in the crystal clear water. He had been such a part of my life that I could almost feel the impact of the reef on his body as I flew away. It only deepened my grief.

I remember the day Tom and I sailed together for England past the Statue of Liberty. I think it was my fondest memory of our time together. I learned later that it had been memorable for him as well. He'd recorded it in his journal:

> On the little narrow deck [of the *Queen Elizabeth*], I leaned on the rail and took a gander at New York harbor for the first time and definitely not the last, I HOPED. All along the way were busy cranes loading and unloading the different ships.
>
> Finally, through all these sights was singled out one sight I had been hoping for—the Statue of Liberty. When people raved about her beauty, I thought they were just patriotic. When I saw it, though, it was quite different. There was a new kind of thrill in it for me; one that was deep, and I began thinking of my folks at home.

Tom would never see the harbor, the Statue of Liberty, his home, or his folks again. But, Tom died doing what he loved most—being a fighter pilot. He wrote a preface to his journal that revealed those feelings. He titled it "Spitfire Mk9."

> There is a man who sits looking over a calm sea who dreams of the love he enjoys in his fighter aircraft in which he trusts his life day by day. His love is similar to the love man enjoys in a lovely maiden, and his heart aches, too, as he dreams of his unmatched worship.
>
> He knows, when he is in the cockpit flying high above the rest of his fellow men, he has no challenge for he is master of himself, and his strength of life that guides him through the heavens. He loves his thought and clings to it before his dream ends the thought to change to another beauty.
>
> He glimpses the world below—this world with its wars and death that prevail—and knows that in time to come his job will be done and he will be taken from this love that enchants his life.
>
> His judgment ponders the challenge to leave this beauty, but he knows he someday must. He shall never forget, and throughout his life his heart will be heavy and moody in every relative thought. Signed: Tommy.

A part of me left the day I packed up Tom's belongings and sent them back to the States. Shortly after I returned to the States, I fulfilled a promise I made to my friend and visited his home and family in Globe, Arizona.

That trip to see his folks was one of the toughest things I've ever done. Tom's family came to meet my train. His mother was deluded from her devastating loss. She climbed up into the train car and searched everywhere for her son. Her family calmed her down somewhat, but she steadfastly refused to believe that Tom wasn't coming home.

His family treated me with great courtesy, and I told them every-thing I could remember about Tom. When I left, I knew the depth of their grief. They had lost a son who would never have a wife or a child or ever share laughter around the dinner table with them again. Tom's death created a deep and lasting sadness for those of us who knew him.

By this time, I had been promoted to flight leader. Flying Spitfires from the new base at Calvi, my four-plane-formation mission was or-dered to patrol the waters off the Italian and French coasts.

On this particular day, February 9, 1944, I was flying Black 3, a supermarine Spitfire Mk. Vc s/n MA 883. It bore the squadron code WD*R. The mission began about one-thirty in the afternoon.

We were charged with search and destroy, attacking enemy ships and shooting up trains. Our Mark V Spitfires carried belly tanks for extra fuel. If an attack came, we were prepared to drop the extra load so we could compete with the German fighters.

The area of patrol for the harassment missions stretched from Cannes to Genoa. Dirtying up the sleek Spitfires with bombs and drop tanks wasn't something I favored, but my fellow pilots and I success-fully destroyed a German freighter in the harbor near Savona, Italy. We then flew to home base to refuel.

We returned to patrol and found a German convoy coasting through the waters near Nice (just across the Italian border in France). Even though we used World War I ring and bead gunsights, there were two or three direct hits, and then our Spitfires sped away in all different directions.

I was ready to rendezvous with my fellow pilots, including Monty Montgomery, and head to home base.

One problem we had with vertical dive-bombing was that it was necessary to turn the plane to keep the gunsight on the target. Making a corkscrew dive left us all spread out when we recovered. As I looked around to see how we might get back into formation, my eyes caught sight of four German Focke-Wulf 190s.

This was Germany's most versatile aircraft. It was an air-to-air and ground-attack machine, and a reliable reconnaissance aircraft. Be-sides the P-51 and the Spitfire, I felt the FW-190 was the best airplane in the sky during the war.

One unidentified pilot told of his first look at the FW-190: "Never had I seen so beautiful an airplane. A rich, dappled blue, from a dark, threatening thunderstorm to a light, sky blue. The cowling is a brilliant, gleaming yellow. Beautiful, and Death on the wing."

Once I had identified the enemy, I quickly called out their position at twelve o'clock high. I saw that one of the FW-190s was right on

Monty's tail. I frantically called out for him to break (turn abruptly) left to avoid gunfire.

The adrenaline was pumping hard. This was real combat, not a dog-fight with comrades, the real thing. To have a chance, I knew I had to get rid of the external fuel tank. I quickly pulled the tank release handle. It came off in my hand. "Damn," I screamed, realizing that the superior turning ability of the Spitfire was now my only defense.

I headed straight for the German fighter and spit out a burst of .50-caliber gunfire. My hand was frozen stiff to the trigger. My mind raced as I attempted to hit the weaving FW-190.

Then I saw the billows of smoke as they streamed through the sky. I had hit the FW-190's engine. It was my first kill of the war.

But there was no time to celebrate, Monty had been hit. The shock of seeing him struggle to save his doomed plane knocked the breath right out of me. I watched it burst into flames and spiral toward the earth below. I prayed he'd make it, but I doubted he would.

Now, two FW-190s were after me. Quickly, I dove left to avoid them. I took comfort in knowing that I had two other buddies nearby to help me, but suddenly, they veered off and left me stranded.

I used every curse word I could think of to let them know how I felt about their abandoning me. The base crew heard my ugly expletives on the radio. I learned later that the two deserters were chastised severely when they returned safely.

Now all alone, I turned my attention to the 190s.

The German fighters struck like copperheads, but the external fuel tank that wouldn't jettison made my Spitfire so slow that they overshot and missed. Two more turned in toward me, but I was able to turn inside them.

I fired and hit one of the FW-190s. Just when I thought I was going to escape, I heard the shells hitting the engine cowling from underneath.

The FW-190 pilot had hit me with a high-angle deflection shot that I had discounted as impossible. A split second later, severe pain shot through my lower extremities.

I glanced in the rearview mirror to see another FW-190 closing in on my tail. The pilot swooped in underneath me and then pulled up right in front of my nose. He must have thought I had no firepower, but I let him have it with a burst of gunfire. I never knew whether I hit him or not because seconds later my engine exploded. The entire nose of my Spitfire was a ball of flames. I was also blinded by a mask of oil that covered the windshield.

Fear gripped my senses as I tried to react to the explosion. I attempted to bring the nose of the Spitfire up, but there was no power. I tried to think of other options. There were none. I knew I couldn't save the plane, so I radioed for a British Dumbo (a walrus amphibian rescue plane).

Now I hoped the canopy jettison on the plane would work properly. I opened the cockpit, released my shoulder and seat straps, rolled the plane inverted, and I was away from the fire.

Almost fifty years later, I would receive a letter from a publishing company in Germany. They employed an artist who was an aviator, and he wanted to paint a picture of my getting shot down. They also told me they had located the pilot, Siegfried "Bamm" Lemke, who had shot me down. In part the letter read:

> He [the pilot] is seventy-three years old and in a wheelchair after both his legs were amputated in 1985 as the result of a disease. Other than that he seems to be in good health, and his mind and memory are crystal clear.
>
> Anyway, you may be very interested to learn that it was actually one and the same pilot who shot you, Bishop, and Montgomery down that February 9, and even a fourth Spit [of which I am not certain whether U.S. or British] that same day. The German pilot was actually renowned for having succeeded in shooting down several planes in one mission on various occasions. He ended the war as commanding officer of one of Germany's most traditional *Jagdgeschwader* [the German equivalent of a fighter wing] with more than seventy victories to his credit, for which he won the Knight's Cross.

A profile of the pilot who had hit me was not on my mind as I separated from the Spitfire. The unthinkable had happened. I'd been shot out of the sky. Despite the shock, I tried to get my bearings and pull the parachute rip cord.

As I was falling toward the Mediterranean Sea, I saw the flames trailing behind the Spitfire like a comet as it plunged into the sea and disappeared into the silence. It was a sickening sight.

I continued to try to open my parachute, but I was inverted and faced with a streamer (a parachute that would not open properly).

I was only three or four hundred feet above the water now and falling fast. My arms were flailing as I wrestled with the parachute. Nothing worked. All I could do was brace myself for a violent crash in the water.

Then suddenly the parachute blossomed; I'd found the correct riser just in time. I heard the familiar pop, and the canopy filled with air. I had just enough time to inflate my Mae West life vest before I hit the water.

The impact stunned me. I was not prepared for the staggering pain I felt when the cold salt water hit my wounded legs and buttocks. My life raft would not inflate. It was riddled with shrapnel. All I could do was float in the icy water, untangle the parachute lines, and wait to be rescued.

I was some twenty miles off the coast of Nice, France. I waited to hear the familiar purring sound of a Rolls-Royce engine. These were the engines used in British fishing boats that patrolled the area. I also kept watch overhead for the Dumbo. I prayed one or the other would find me.

My hopes of rescue heightened when I watched four Spitfires approach. I waved and splashed with the fervor of a boy showing off in a swimming hole. Unfortunately, a group of FW-190s swooped down on them. One went down; the others got away. I was sure I had been spotted, and that they would find a way to rescue me.

Time went by slowly. My mind was filled with a million thoughts. Had Monty made it out alive? No, not possible. Who would find me first? The Germans or friendly faces?

I tried to think back to survival training. What had I learned? "Keep calm," I told myself, "someone will come along."

Two hours went by. Then three. The water was freezing. My feet were numb.

I had been shot down at 3 P.M. A little after seven, I heard a faint sound in the distance.

There's a certain rat-a-tat a diesel engine makes, and I knew a ship was approaching. When I first saw the vessel, it must have been no more than 150 yards away. The distinguishable sound of water slapping against the hull followed. I just floated there in the icy water, praying that the ship was a friendly one.

Finally, the vessel came close enough for me to realize it was a German corvette. Somehow German intelligence must have spotted my plane going down and given the ship my location.

My heart sank. I was a sitting duck. Defenseless.

When the sailors on board threw me a towline, I made a small protest by refusing to grab it. The banter of indistinguishable German filled the air, and the vessel made a U-turn.

The corvette made its second pass. It came so close to me that the sailors, members of the German merchant marine, could reach out and pull me from the water. Cold, wet, and wounded, I was now Robert A. Hoover, prisoner of war.

6

Prisoner of War

I was strip-searched on the corvette. Then given dry clothes. When I was offered coffee, I refused it. Name, rank, and serial number was all I provided, but I was not mistreated for my insubordination.

I learned that the corvette had been searching the icy waters looking for two Luftwaffe pilots. When they saw me, the ship made a bee-line for my position.

The captain of the corvette was a seasoned military man who was surprisingly cordial. He had served in World War I and seemed to have some compassion for my plight. I tried to be matter-of-fact with him. Show no weakness.

On the way toward shore, I wondered what the reaction would be at the base to my being shot down. One man who wasn't surprised was Col. Marvin McNickle:

> All of the men at the Fifty-second were stunned to learn that Bob had been shot down. I wasn't because I knew Bob would either get shot down immediately or become an ace. That was because he always wanted to be right in the middle of the action. Pilots like me were a bit more conservative, but Bob loved being a fighter pilot. He would have taken on the whole German Air Force if they'd let him.

The ship docked at Nice, France, a little after sunset. I could see a damaged German freighter in the harbor. Was that damage the result of my squadron's efforts? Were the covered bodies laid out in formation along the dock area the result as well?

Onshore, French and Italian civilians pressed against the fence that cordoned off the dock. They flashed the V-for-victory sign for me as I passed them. They offered me bread and cheese. I was hungry, but I couldn't take their offering. I thanked them with my eyes as the German guards goaded me on.

Further along the way I heard someone yell out, *"Viva l'americano."* That encouraged me to believe that somehow, with the assistance of the French underground, I would escape to freedom. That was my only goal. To escape and fight again.

The German guards escorted me to a waiting car, and I was taken to a local jail. The steel door of the tiny cell made a thunderous clank behind me. I believe I was more frightened than I had ever been in my life. I was surrounded by the enemy, alone in a dark prison cell. Powerless and despondent, I slumped to the floor as the rats came from every crack in the concrete walls. They were more free than I.

Even though I had been searched on the German corvette, no medical attention had been given to the shrapnel wounds on the back of my legs and buttocks. Too stubborn to ask for assistance, I sat in the jail cell and awaited my fate.

In a short time, I heard the loud clang of the steel cell door. I was ordered out and transported to the Continental Hotel in Cannes. This was the headquarters for German officers. The commander there told me that he was worried about his two sons who were in combat on the Western Front. Then he asked me about my wounds. I started to answer, but then just gave him, "Robert A. Hoover, Flight Officer, 20443029."

He continued his interrogation for some time, but became frustrated at attempts to gain information from me. He called the guards. I was strapped to a marble column in the lobby of the hotel.

Angry wives, mothers, and children of German soldiers were encouraged to walk by me. I was a spectacle. I'm sure they had lost family members through Allied bombing raids in Germany, and they wanted me to suffer for it. They cursed in German. They spit at my feet and slapped me in the face. Their cruelty was degrading. I was absolutely helpless.

This degradation continued for two days. Then I was transported down the southern coast of France toward Marseilles. My accommodations there were a slight improvement over those at Nice.

The cell had a straw mattress and an old metal chair. It was six by eight feet. There were two narrow windows with three bars across each one. When I moved the chair over by the window to look outside, I saw the six-foot-high barbed-wire fence and two German sentries with growling, mean-spirited police dogs by their side.

To my surprise, when I grabbed one of the bars, it moved slightly. They were set in the concrete that surrounded the window frame.

I got off the chair and removed one of the metal support bars from the back. Banging away at the cement frame would bring the guards' attention, so I used my flight jacket to muffle the clanking sound and the rubber heel of my shoe as a hammer.

After I removed the first bar, I used it as a makeshift tool to chip away at the cement. I hid the residue in the straw mattress.

I was startled when I heard a guard approaching. I sat on the bunk as if I were waiting for my food. After he put a plate of boiled potatoes on the floor in front of me, he left unsuspecting.

After eating, I chipped away again. Soon the bars were loose enough to remove. I then sat and waited for darkness. My nerves were on edge as the time passed slowly. When nightfall came, I squeezed through the opening and crawled out onto the ledge. The ten-foot drop to the ground surprised me. Could I jump that far without causing a disturbance?

There was no turning back. The guards would be around to check my cell momentarily.

I put my hands on the outside ledge of the window. Then I slid down the roof and dangled down as far as I could before jumping. I landed with a loud thud. Instantly, the sleeping dogs came to life. My heart was racing as I ran across the yard toward the barbed-wire fence.

Just as I was ready to mount the fence, bright lights illuminated me, and the first dog clamped his jaws into my leg. Two more German shepherds attacked as I clung to the fence. I'm sure they would have ripped me apart if the guards hadn't pulled them off.

The guards dragged me across the frozen ground. I covered my head to avoid the butts of their guns.

My punishment for trying to escape was a dark basement cell. The night was filled with nightmares, fear for my life, and fresh pain from the dog bites. I had never experienced such isolation.

My fear of being shot kept me awake. That night seemed as if it lasted forever.

The next morning, guards ordered me out of the cell. I was taken to a train station a short distance away. My captors turned me over to two German soldiers, who treated me with complete disdain.

My wounds had still not been treated. They hadn't been serious, but without treatment I was certain they were infected.

The Germans were not even remotely concerned about my condition. I was unceremoniously herded into the train and thrown into a compartment with two new and even more unpleasant guards. When the train left the station, I knew we were headed north. The sun was to our right.

I was handcuffed, and the two German guards, who resembled a deadly sinister Laurel and Hardy team, stayed with me every second. They alternated sleep so one could always keep a close eye on me.

I slept very little since I wanted to see where we were going. I was knowledgeable of the terrain and knew we would be traveling near the Swiss border.

We were headed toward Switzerland, and all I could think of was escaping so I could ask for asylum. As we slowed for each railroad station, I began to concoct an escape plan.

Just prior to the next stop, I signaled to the English-speaking guard that I had to use the bathroom. One of the guards escorted me toward the toilet and removed the handcuffs.

The bathroom was very small, requiring the guard to wait outside the door. When I was safely inside, I saw the escape route—a small window above the sink.

With the train slowed to around fifteen miles an hour, I went into action. A swift kick broke the glass. I cleared the windowsill of slivers and squeezed through the tiny opening.

We were a few miles from Mulhouse, France, near the Swiss border. My second attempt at freedom was doomed by the elements. There had been a huge snowstorm, and when I dropped from the train, I disappeared into a huge snowbank. I struggled to my feet, but it was almost impossible to move forward.

In search of safe ground, I made my way along the tracks. After about five paces, I heard gunshots. I froze and put my hands in the air. Why the guards didn't shoot to kill, I'll never know.

Guards surrounded me from every direction. I was forced down on my knees with my hands behind my head while one of the German soldiers pressed his gun barrel against my neck.

I was thrown back on the train and shackled to a seat. Zero for two in escape attempts, I reconciled myself to a trip to Germany as the frozen countryside swept by.

When we arrived at Mulhouse, I was tossed into a jail cell. The German practice was to punish the guard who had let me attempt the escape. He was thrown into the cell next to me. He hammered on the wall and screamed every German obscenity he could conjure up at me.

Since the jailers were sympathetic to the guard, it didn't make my stay there any easier. They never caused me harm, but their tendency to yell and scream made me confused as to what was going on.

The German Luftwaffe "bad cop" interrogation headquarters were located several hundred miles north of Mulhouse at Oberursel near

Frankfurt. Reminiscent of many of the dreary German manufacturing centers, the city was home to a prison filled with captured Allied fliers.

I was put in solitary, given bread and water, and then my first taste of German cabbage soup. It had been a week since my capture.

On the third day in solitary, a German lieutenant named Schafter entered my cell. Wearing an International Red Cross insignia, he said he was there to comfort me. That was bullshit. He asked me about the type of airplane I was flying. "We need the information so the Red Cross can notify your parents that you are alive," he told me.

We had been warned about such tactics. I knew he had no connection with the Red Cross. He got name, rank, and serial number from me and that was all. He asked about my squadron, saying he wanted to help me, but again I gave him the standard answer. When he finally figured I wasn't going to open up, he no longer disguised his frustration and anger, slapped his clipboard on his knee, and left the cell.

I only had one visitor a day and that was an ill-tempered guard who brought cabbage soup and two slices of bread. What I would have given for service rations during this time.

Isolation is cruel and punishing. The small space in the cell made it impossible to move around. There is no way to measure time, and the future is incomprehensible. There is only the past.

I began challenging myself for details about my early years. What was my first-grade teacher like? What did we do in class? Who was my first date? Did I meet her parents?

I also thought about Berry Field and Louie Gasser and my early days of flying. I tried to remember details about the hot summer days I had spent with the family clan at the Camp.

The Germans had still not offered to treat my injuries. Besides the wounds on my legs and buttocks, my genitals were beginning to swell from some type of infection. The Germans continued to interrogate me daily, but I was determined never to let them get the best of me.

It was impossible to know how long I'd been a prisoner. At first, I tried to keep count of the days, but after a while I gave up.

I awoke one morning to a voice I recognized. It was the same German lieutenant who had tried to pose as a sympathetic Red Cross worker. I was disoriented and the sounds were muffled, but I could hear him talking to an American sergeant in the next cell. I knew the airman was a gunner in a B-17 Fortress.

I knew because he told the German lieutenant. He then gave his inquisitor the name of his commanding officer and wing commander. I couldn't take it anymore. The information he was giving out could cost fellow airmen their lives.

I started yelling, "Shut up," but the sergeant kept talking. He talked about the plane's bombing mission and their targets. I screamed for him to stop, but he just kept giving out information.

My protests finally brought an enraged German guard racing to my cell. He stuck a gun to my head and told me that if I didn't shut up, he'd kill me.

I tried to make contact with the sergeant the next morning by tapping on the cell wall. I heard no return tap, and efforts to rouse him through conversation were unsuccessful.

I felt alone and frightened. I wanted to hear the voice of another prisoner, someone to talk to. I called out, "Are there any Americans in here?" a few times, but nobody answered. I was in the middle of yelling it again through the door when it blasted open. I was thrown back on the floor.

Yanked up by the scruff of the neck, I was pushed into the corridor and marched out of the cellblock. Along the way out, a scraggly toothpick of a man with shoulder-length hair and full beard reached his hand out through the bars of his cell.

The jaundiced man had hollow cheeks and bulging, bloodshot eyes. I detected a British accent in his weak voice. "Don't tell 'em anything," he said. "Whatever you do, don't tell 'em anything."

I was taken to a dingy interrogation room where I was pushed into a chair. The stiff prison guards stood at attention on either side of me.

I was seated before a gruff-looking German officer with wire-rimmed spectacles who ignored me for several minutes. He was thumbing through a file folder. He said nothing, and his silence made me more nervous by the minute. He studied the papers, shuffled them, then finally looked over at me.

From behind, a soldier entered the room. Before I saw the food, I smelled the aroma. For the last few days, I had eaten nothing but cabbage soup. I felt weaker with each passing hour. The cut beef, boiled potatoes, and fresh vegetables were a cruel temptation.

To the German's annoyance, the food-for-information ploy didn't work. Name, rank, and serial number was all they got.

I also resisted his attempt to have me confirm his knowledge about the airplane I was in when I was shot down.

"We know you were flying a Spitfire," he told me. "That Rolls-Royce engine really gave you a lot of power."

I wouldn't budge from my pledge of silence. The captain became so agitated that he bolted from his chair. He signaled for the guards to remove me from the room. I was half-dragged back to my cell.

The next day, they tried again. My inquisitor this time was a man with little patience. Just minutes into the interrogation, he startled me by saying, "Cooperate or be shot." To this day, I don't know how I managed to speak. I was wounded and near starvation, and his words terrified me. The tone of his voice and the evil in his eye made me realize this man would kill me. I meant nothing to him.

After a few seconds, somehow I slowly gave out my name, rank, and serial number. My voice steadied as I barked out, "20443029."

The captain became more infuriated. He barked loud bursts of German orders. I was jerked from my seat by the two guards and marched behind the captain's desk and out the back door.

The glare of the sun on the bright snow blinded me for a few seconds. The guards threw me to the ground. I felt the wetness on my face. A guard yanked me up and pushed me forward. As I groped along half-stumbling, I saw a pockmarked cement wall. It was riddled with bullet holes.

I was forced to stand against the wall. One of the guards kept shouting at me in German. Their handguns were leveled right at my forehead. I anticipated death at any second.

The captain stomped into the courtyard. I could hear him slapping his swagger stick on his knee as he walked toward me. He stood forcefully in front of me. When he finally spoke, his raging eyes were within a few inches of my nose. He was so close I could feel the offensive breath of the man who could very well order my death within the next second.

I stared straight ahead, showing no emotion. I knew the captain was trying to determine if he could break me.

His words were simple, "You have one minute to answer my questions or you will be shot."

I tried to remember the guidance I'd received at primary training. The ability to withstand a verbal barrage was now paramount. I could be executed at any second.

"Will you answer the questions?" the captain bellowed. In a voice I barely recognized as my own, I said, "Robert A. Hoover, Flight Officer, 20443029."

The captain barked an order in German. The soldiers put away their handguns and picked up their rifles.

With a wry smile on his face, the captain began the countdown. At "Ready," the soldiers' rifles were brought to shoulder height. I remained stone-faced, determined to show no fear. I pressed my body back against the wall in a futile attempt to put more distance between me and my assassins.

Despite my attempts to stop them, a trace of tears welled in my eyes. I didn't want to die this way. Alone and humiliated, without a chance to defend myself.

A few seconds later I heard the second command, "Aim." The guns were cocked. I winced at the sound.

My brain froze as I waited to hear "Fire." The captain was staring straight at me, an ominous smile on his face, waiting to see if I would crack.

Seconds passed as if they were hours. Finally, the captain turned from view and retreated into the building. At that, the soldiers lowered their weapons, returned me to the cellblock, and threw me inside. I sat there trembling, more frightened than I could ever describe.

The whole episode had been a ruse for the weak at heart. I spoke with other POWs who had endured the same horrifying experience.

The escapade with the captain made me more determined to escape. It didn't take me long to devise another plan.

At the interrogation center, there was a row of cells along one wall and another along the opposite wall. In between was a narrow hall that led to a large corridor. An office located at the midway point of the hall had windows around two sides of it.

For many days, I planned my escape. I was finally ready. I had a long-sleeved turtleneck shirt that had been given to me by the captain of the corvette when I was picked up at sea. I still had it on under my military clothes when I was put in prison. I pulled the turtleneck over the top of my other clothing so I wouldn't look like a prisoner. The guards didn't notice. They had their minds on other things.

I then requested that the Germans let me go to the toilet. It was located off to the left of the row of cells by the office. In the opposite direction was an exit that went directly to the grounds outside the building.

I entered the bathroom and closed the door. But I left the latch so it wasn't quite closed. When my guard walked away to chat with a comrade, I slipped out of the bathroom and closed the door behind me.

I got down on my hands and knees and crawled back around toward an exit door. I reached up and eased the door open and headed outside. To avoid detection, I acted like an afflicted person and hobbled toward the main gate.

I limped along for quite a ways and nobody paid any attention to me. I finally arrived at the gate and was ready to walk out when a guard started talking to me in German. Realizing something was wrong when I didn't respond, he grabbed me by the shoulder. I kept on walking, mumbling incoherently all the while. Finally, he yanked me back and began screaming at me.

At that moment, the guard from my prison block came running up to us. He drew his Luger and ordered me back to the cellblock. There he proceeded to kick me over and over as I lay defenseless on the floor, unable to strike back.

That beating resulted in painful head and facial injuries, severe enough to have caused residual scars that remain today.

More than a week went by before the guards came for me again. This time, the interrogator was a tall, striking captain right out of central casting. Dressed smartly in his Nazi finest, he also sported a monocle. The aviator's wings on his chest were impressive, and he spoke with me pilot to pilot in almost perfect English.

"As an aviator much like yourself, I understand all about airplanes," he began. "I know that you were a member of the Fifty-second Fighter Group under the command of Col. Marvin McNickle. The plane you flew was a Mark V Spitfire."

As the captain spoke, the hair on the back of my neck bristled. Someone was a loose-lipped traitor. My face flushed with anger as the captain continued.

"The code name for the mission you flew, Airman Hoover, was Snake Grace. There is no need for you to tell me anything because I already have it firsthand from a fellow flier."

"Robert A. Hoover, Flight Officer, 20443029," I bellowed, correcting his reference to me as an airman.

I wondered who it could be. Who was the traitor who collaborated with the enemy? If it was the last thing I ever did, I told myself, I would see the coward court-martialed.

"Now, *Airman* Hoover, you are well-known and have flown many different kinds of aircraft," the captain said. "You can provide us with much information."

Just as I was ready to repeat my name, rank, and serial number, the captain asked about my injuries.

"I understand you have been wounded and are suffering from an infection. Drop your trousers and let me see."

The last thing I wanted to do was obey his order. Reluctantly, I decided to do so, realizing he could have me stripped by force.

I dropped my trousers and underwear. My testicles were enlarged, and the rest of my groin was red and inflamed. The wounds to my buttocks and legs were weeping with infection.

Seeing the disgusting nature of my lower body, it wasn't long before the captain spoke.

"You obviously have contracted syphilis," he observed incorrectly. "You need immediate medical attention."

I was then returned to my prison cell without further interrogation. The next day, guards came for me. I was taken to the train station for a trip toward the Baltic Sea and Barth, the location of the notorious Stalag Luft I prison camp.

7

Escape from Stalag I

My fellow prisoners and I were stuffed into a narrow-gauge boxcar that was standing overnight in the marshaling yards near Frankfurt. A British navigator who had been looking through the cracks in the boxcar suddenly called out, "There's the pathfinder . . . oh, no . . . we're the target!"

We all dropped to the oily boxcar floor. We knew what to expect. The British navigator had seen a spiraling flare dropped by the lead Allied bomber. The Allies used it as a pathfinder and dropped their loads as near to its position as possible.

Within seconds, we could feel the shock of thousands of tons of bombs exploding all around us. Our German guards raced off to bomb shelters, leaving us like caged animals, targets for our own unsuspecting Allies.

My hope was that somehow our boxcar would be damaged just enough so that we might escape, but that never occurred. The horror of war did leave its mark on all of us when the fourth car down from us, packed with prisoners, was hit. It exploded, killing everyone inside, the result of friendly fire.

Fortunately, my comrades and I were unhurt during the raid. When morning came, we saw the incredible destruction that had been inflicted on Frankfurt. The success of the Allied bombing reinforced my determination to escape and rejoin my squadron at first chance.

* * *

The gaunt faces of hundreds of undernourished prisoners greeted us as we entered Stalag I. They were pressed against the barbed-wire fence watching the bizarre parade of new arrivals.

As we walked toward the main building, one of the prisoners behind the fence said, "Damn, they've got Hoover." In some paradoxical way, I felt like a celebrity, but at the same time embarrassed and diminished by having been shot down and captured.

The prison camp was called Kriegsgefangenerlager No. 1 der Luft-waffe, better known as Stalag I. It opened in 1940 and was used to house captured Royal Air Force pilots.

The camp was closed for a time because of so many escape attempts, but security was tightened and it reopened in 1942. By 1943, when the air assault by the Allies against Hitler was at a fever pitch, Stalag I was in full operation. More than a thousand American airmen were incarcerated there.

The camp was laid out in a reverse L-shape and located on the low-lying Baltic peninsula near Barth. The area was covered with dense woods and scrubland. The isolated location and high water table made escape difficult.

Several different compounds were strategically placed around the prison grounds. The barracks were built on wooden studs, leaving a two-foot clearance between the floorboards and the ground. German shepherds could squeeze into that small space to search for tunnels or prisoners who attempted escape.

The individual compounds were surrounded by double ten-foot barbed-wire fences. Coils of additional barbed wire kept prisoners from crawling out the bottom. Another similar fence enclosed the entire camp. There was also a "warning wire" beyond which any prisoner would be shot on sight. As a final precaution, guard towers had mounted searchlights that illuminated the entire area.

Those double rolls of barbed wire and sharpshooting watchtower guards discouraged escape attempts at Stalag Luft I. In fact, the double-barreled efforts had stopped every escape attempt. My fellow prisoners and I were never deterred, however, and we never ceased our obsessive pursuit of freedom.

Approximately 120 men were in each POW or "Kriegie" barracks with twenty men assigned to a room. After so much time in solitary, I welcomed the company of the other men.

Each barracks contained a central corridor with small rooms on either side. The rooms were stuffed with four-tiered beds with mattresses filled with wood shavings.

Regardless of the regulations in the Geneva convention, it had now been more than a month and my wounds had still not been treated. Finally, a fellow prisoner, RAF Lieutenant Colonel George Hankey, who had been captured at Dunkirk, came to the rescue. His efforts certainly saved both my legs, if not my life.

For a few months the food was far better than at my interrogation stops. Toward the end of the war, though, it became scarce. Potato peelings and Red Cross vitamins got me through, but I did lose nearly fifty pounds. A great majority of the other prisoners suffered from severe malnutrition.

During the days at Stalag I, we witnessed unimaginable heroism from our comrades. Perhaps the most compelling was an inspirational speech given by our commanding officer, Col. Russ Spicer.

On that occasion, in front of several calloused German officers, the colonel described the Nazis' war atrocities, referred to his disgust with the German soldiers, and told us by no means to be friendly with "Jerry."

One prisoner's account of the speech was forwarded to me after the war:

> Morning roll call was over. The German officer, Major Steinhauer, had given the colonel permission to dismiss the group. Before dismissal he ordered the men to assemble in front of Block 7.
>
> "Lads, as you can see, this isn't going to be any fireside chat.
>
> "Someone has taken the steel bar off the South Latrine door. The Germans want this bar back. They have tried to find it and I've also tried to find it. We have had no success. The Germans have threatened to cut off our coal ration if this bar isn't found by twelve noon. I don't know if this is a threat or not, but we must return the bar to the Germans. Anyone having information report to my room after this talk. There will be no disciplinary action taken against anyone.
>
> "Yesterday, an officer [Major Brunson] was put in the cooler for two weeks. He had two counts against him. The first was failure to obey a German officer. That is beside the point. The second was failure to salute a German officer of *lower* rank.
>
> "The Articles of the Geneva convention say to salute all officers of *equal* or *higher* rank. The Germans in this camp have put out an order that we must salute *all* German officers whether *lower* or *higher* rank. My order to you is: Salute all German officers of equal or higher rank.
>
> "I have noticed that many of you men are becoming too 'buddy-buddy' with the Germans. Remember, we are still at war with the Germans. They are still our enemies and are doing everything they can to win this war. Don't let him fool you, around this camp, because Jerry is a dirty, lying sneak and can't be trusted.
>
> "As an example of the type of enemy you have to deal with, the British were forced to retreat in the Arnhem area. They had to leave the wounded in the hospital. The Germans came, took the hospital, and machine-gunned all those British in their beds.

"In Holland, behind the German lines, a woman with a baby in her arms was walking along the road evacuating the battle zone. Some British prisoners were passing her. She gave the V-for-victory sign. A German soldier saw her and without hesitation swung his gun around and shot her on the spot.

"They are a bunch of murderous, no-good liars, and if we have to stay here for ten years to see all Germans killed, then it'll be worth it."

(Loud cheers from all the men)

The colonel then turned to the German major and noncoms standing to one side, saying, "For your information, these are my own personal opinions and I'm not attempting to incite riot or rebellion. They are my own opinions and not necessarily the opinions of my men."

(More loud cheering)

Then facing the men again, he continued, "That is all, men, and remember what I have told you."

That same prisoner also recalled that "within a few hours, the colonel was in solitary confinement, and Lieutenant Colonel Wilson, next in command, had been threatened with solitary if the iron bar did not show up." He went on to write:

Colonel Spicer was put in solitary and did not get out until midnight of April 30th [1945], when the Americans took the camp.

He was court-martialed by the Germans and sentenced to death—to take effect in three months. This was at the end of December 1944, and April 1, 1945, was set as the day. However, things were so hot in those times that the sentence fortunately was not carried out.

My own recollection is that Russ was in solitary for nine months. What bravery he exhibited! He didn't know from day to day when or if his execution would be carried out.

The words he'd spoken became the creed for all of us. When times got tough, we had only to look at Colonel Spicer for inspiration.

Back home in the States, word of my being missing in action reached the *Nashville Tennessean* newspaper. Their account on March 17, 1944, read in part:

NO WORD RECEIVED FROM MISSING FLIER

Flight Officer Robert A. Hoover, son of Mr. and Mrs. L. F. Hoover, Sr., reported missing in action on February 9 [1944], has not been heard from since that date, his parents said this morning.

The March 22 edition of the newspaper announced my capture by the Germans:

ROBERT A. HOOVER PRISONER OF NAZIS

Flight Officer Robert A. Hoover, 22, son of Mr. And Mrs. L. F. Hoover . . . is a prisoner of war in Germany, according to a telegram received from the War Department yesterday by his parents.

Missing in action since February 9, it had been one month yesterday since Mrs. Hoover had received the notification that her son was missing.

The telegram said a letter from the International Red Cross would follow with details as to his capture.

Overseas 17 months, serving most of that time in North Africa, Officer Hoover, holder of the Distinguished Flying Cross and the Air Medal, was made a flight leader just before his capture. . . .

An article in the February Palermo, Italy, *Post* bulletin had also commented on my capture.

HOOVER FINALLY GOT IT BUT HE'LL COME BACK

12th Fighter Command Headquarters—They used to say that the Jerry who got Hoover would have to get up very, very early in the morning and practice for a long, long time. Somebody must have done just that, though, because Hoover and his Spitfire parted company the other day about ten miles off the coast of France after a fierce dogfight with some FW-190s.

Hoover is Flight Officer Robert A. Hoover, 22, Nashville, Tenn. The tense is present, because his buddies on the flight, 1st Lt. Bradley Smith, Yonkers, N.Y., and 2nd Lt. H. E. Montgomery, New York, N.Y., saw him bail out over water.

Hoover is a legendary figure to ack crews, radio operators and the hill people in Corsica. He used to do eight-point slow rolls all over the place and fly upside down just to keep from being bored. In his flying career he had been at the controls of 40 different types of airplanes and had never lost a mock dogfight with any American or British pilot.

Hoover first learned to fly when he was working Saturdays at an A and P store back in the States. He earned a dollar fifty on a Saturday and took the money to his local airdrome and spent it on 15 minutes' flying time on Sunday. In eight or nine months he had enough time for a private pilot's license.

The tall, black-haired pilot went through regular AAC (Army Air Corps) pilot training and joined a Spitfire outfit in Sicily. That must have been kind fate, because he could never have been happy flying anything but a fast, light plane that he could wring out. But his buddies say that if he had landed in a B-17 outfit, he'd have been slow-rolling and looping them just like he did the fighters.

Hoover met a major in Sicily last summer and the two got to comparing notes on the number of airplanes they'd flown. Hoover chalked up his 40 and the major, with a hell-you-ain't-seen-nothing-yet attitude, said he had been at the controls of 300. After that Hoover wasn't so very cocky.

He never was very cocky though, even after he had slow-rolled a B-26 or brought a B-25 in for a perfect landing with both engines dead.

His aerobatic ability was what made his squadron buddies believe he would never be shot down. This ability doesn't make the best fighter pilot in the world, because a fighter has got to be able to shoot straight. But it is one of the most important, if not the most important thing in fighter flying.

Hoover had piled up 1,400 hours of flying time when his flying career ended—at least temporarily, it ended. They figure he's a prisoner of war now but that he'll come back one of these days and fly the pants off another Spitfire like he used to.

Despite German boasts to the contrary, my fellow prisoners and I knew the Allies would prevail in the war. We knew firsthand that the streets of Berlin were being hit hard by Allied bombers. We had seen the incredible damage to homes and buildings through the cracks of the boxcar while traveling to Stalag I.

We had also seen thousands of Allied planes fly over the prison camp in box formation. Prior to that, only a few planes had appeared in the air at a time. The buildup in England of the Allied armada while I was in Africa and Italy triggered more and more deadly flights over Germany's targets.

A sky thick with a thousand bombers lifted our spirits. Swarms of Allied fighters destroyed German defenders. Everyone in the camp knew Germany wouldn't survive the barrage. They were just too drastically outnumbered.

Eyewitness accounts of Allied supremacy countered German boasts that London was in flames. In spite of our captors' grim predictions, newly arriving prisoners disputed their claims. We knew they couldn't hold out much longer.

Guards boasted that no one had ever escaped from Stalag I, but that didn't stop us. There was never a day when we weren't planning some sort of escape attempt. We never ceased trying to weasel our way out of there. On one occasion, I was the leader of a group who decided to tunnel out. To hide some of the dirt, we stored it in our pants legs and dropped it while we were out for daily exercise. The rest we stored in the attic of the barracks.

We were making so much progress that we were sure we'd be able to escape. Unfortunately we hadn't counted on seismographic equipment that the Germans used to detect underground noises. I would learn later that even though they were aware of tunneling schemes, they permitted prisoners to proceed with their work. Just before completion, the guards would storm the barracks. This would make the escape failure even more devastating.

The Germans were denied their foray in this situation because our escape idea literally fell in our faces. One night we heard a creaking noise overhead in the tunnel. The ceiling gave way, and we were buried in dirt. German guards and their dogs quickly responded to the commotion.

Without coats or jackets, we were ordered outside into the freezing cold. The angry commandant threatened to leave us there to die if the leaders of the escape attempt didn't come forward.

That threat left me in a difficult position. Since I was the ringleader, I wanted to accept responsibility. But our experience had taught us that the Germans would not stop until they had the names of every man involved. Even though the German officer in charge kept demanding that the guilty ones speak up, we all remained silent. Tense moments of silence passed by. Finally the Germans backed down. They sent us to another barracks where we slept on the cold floor. We could handle the discomfort and inconvenience, but the knowledge that our plan to escape had failed was devastating to morale.

Despite the failure, I soon came up with another plan. To make it succeed, I needed the help of a fellow prisoner named Jim Foster. He was in charge of our building and responsible for all of the 120 men held there. His title was a weird one. The Germans called him a "block-head."

Jim was also in charge of the coal detail. Officers couldn't be forced to work hard labor according to the Geneva convention, but many volunteered for the coal detail just to get outside the barbed wire.

At Stalag I, they had horse-drawn wagons to transport the coal. Each compound was allotted so many bricks of coal per day for the potbellied stove that was used for both cooking and heating in each room.

The coal shed was actually a long, wooden building with a huge door cut in the middle. Enclosed within a single fence, the shed was located outside the double-row fence that had coiled wire in the middle and on top. To get the coal, the detail would follow the horse-drawn wagon outside the double-fenced area into the coal yard with the single fence.

My idea was to be buried in the coal inside the shed. I would protect my head with a cloth before the prisoners covered me with coal. After dark, I would unearth myself, climb over the single fence, and make my way toward the countryside.

Since I knew the coal dust would cause me to sneeze, I practiced for hours until I could sneeze without making a sound.

On the day of the escape, I hunkered on the concrete floor and my fellow prisoners covered my body with coal. They then carefully stacked blocks of coal around my head and neck.

Everything went according to plan. I never moved a muscle and hid until dark, hoping there would be an air raid to divert attention away from the coal area. None came.

Time was critical because I had to escape before the guards made their head count the next morning. The coal dust did make me sneeze, but none of the guards patrolling the area ever heard a sound.

Sometime in the middle of the night, I began to quietly wiggle myself out of the coal. With extreme caution, I opened the main door, crawled over to the fence, and climbed over it.

When I hit the ground, my mind was filled with excitement since I was moments away from freedom. Easing away from the fence, I saw the wooded area less than fifty yards away. That's when I nearly collapsed after running right into a startled German guard. We stood there staring at one another. Finally he yelled, "Halt," and I raised my arms in surrender.

Two weeks in the cooler was my punishment. Fortunately my next-door neighbor was Russ Spicer. He and I spent the long nights talking through the walls. Even though the Germans kicked us around for talking, those conversations were worth it. Russ was my hero and his inspirational words made me never think of giving up my desire to escape.

Believing the end of the war to be near, Allied Supreme Commander Gen. Dwight Eisenhower issued orders to Allied prisoners not to try to escape.

There were now ten thousand prisoners at Stalag I. This was a significant increase from the twelve hundred or so who were there when I arrived sixteen months earlier.

Despite General Eisenhower's directive, most of us still kept trying to devise ways to escape. We believed we had a good chance in April of that year (1945), since a great many German guards had deserted. They had heard the Russians shelling their cities. It was now obvious even to them that they were going to lose the war.

We also continued to plot our escape since we were concerned about what the civilian population in the area might do to us if we weren't under military protection. Massive bombing raids had resulted in heavy civilian casualties. Civilians hated all pilots and crew members of Allied aircraft, referring to us as *Terrorflieger*.

Besides the potential for civilian revenge, boasts by fanatic SS troops about a planned slaughter of POWs caused us unrest. No one could predict what treatment POWs might receive from them. In addition, Russian troops were now invading from every direction, and they were as unpredictable as the Germans.

We were desperate to get out of Stalag I. An American named Jerry

Ennis, from the Fifty-second Fighter Group, a Canadian airman named George, and I decided to attempt another escape. While other prisoners staged a fight to divert the guards' attention, the three of us broke out of the compound. We half-crawled, half-ran across the yard, climbed the inside barbed-wire fence, pushed a board across and over the outside fence, and crawled the rest of the way.

We ran from that prison until our lungs ached and we had to fight for every shallow breath. We struggled through the densely wooded area and collapsed on the shoreline of the frozen waters of the Baltic Sea. Our courage faltered as we realized we would have to swim from the peninsula to the mainland without freezing to death.

But we had to keep going. We went back into the woods and picked up long, narrow logs. We used grapevines to tie the logs together and fashioned a crude raft. It had enough buoyancy for one person.

George and I slipped nude into the water, shocked by the icy cold water. We pushed the raft while Jerry Ennis held our dry clothes. When we reached the other shore, we quickly covered our wet bodies with dry clothes. Then we ran again, all the while looking over our shoulders to see if guards had given chase.

We encountered no one as we continued across the countryside. We had heard that a Russian invasion was imminent. No one wanted to be caught by them due to their reputation for extreme brutality.

We came to a deserted German farmhouse and spent our first night of freedom under the warmth of the hay in the barn. The next morning we entered a very small village. We stayed on the outskirts while attempting to scrounge up something to eat. We ate unwashed and uncooked potatoes and turnips we found in a field. It was a feast.

Later that day, we stole bicycles that were leaning against a wall outside a public meeting place near the village. Nobody tried to stop us. We just walked over, took the bicycles, and headed out of town.

Our Canadian friend decided to try it alone. We bid him good-bye and headed on. We never saw him again. I still don't know if he made it.

Jerry and I were unsure of our location, but we continued west. We were hoping to find Allied lines, but we wanted to avoid the Russians even though they were considered to be our allies.

Despite the fact that we stayed off the main roads, we finally encountered Russian troops near another small village. Jerry, who spoke French, tried to communicate with one of the soldiers. He attempted to convince them that we were not prisoners of war but simply Allied soldiers evading the Germans.

This was the first of many confrontations where we had to convince the Russians we weren't prisoners. They considered any prisoner to be an enemy collaborator. Escaped prisoners were either whisked off to the salt mines or shot on the spot.

In this instance, Jerry prevailed, and without hesitation the Russians offered us shelter and food. Since we hadn't had a good square meal in months, I was excited. That was until a plate was put before me that contained a large chunk of raw beef. It was about three inches thick and the blood had coagulated on the plate. Hungry as I was, I couldn't force myself to eat the meat. I did take the bread they offered.

We spent the night with the Russians. The next morning, we pedaled away. Another group of Russian soldiers stopped us at a nearby village. Those Russians didn't question us much. Then they invited us to follow them toward a church. Since the soldiers were pretty drunk and extremely friendly, we couldn't tell what they had in mind.

We entered the darkened church. There before us were hundreds of German women and children huddled together. Finally Jerry figured out what was up. "The Russian soldiers want us to choose a woman, any woman, and rape her," he whispered to me. This savage offer of hospitality was one we didn't want anything to do with. "What do we do?" I asked Jerry.

Jerry walked toward a group of women, acting as if we were making our selection. He found a woman who spoke French. "I'll tell her we're going to fake it," he told me.

Luckily, the tiny woman understood our intentions. Two women joined Jerry and me and went over into a dark corner where no one could see. We laid on the women and moaned and groaned enough to make our sexual attack seem real.

All the while, the Russian soldiers were hooting and hollering. They shined a light over toward us just to make certain we were raping the women.

Our performance convinced the Russians. They invited us to spend the night in a small abandoned house. We had no choice, but we left those disgusting soldiers as early as possible the next morning.

When we arrived in a nearby German village the next day, a woman in her fifties approached me. She had a bloody cloth wrapped around her hand. "Are you an American?" When I told her I was, she said, "Do you realize what your Russian allies have done? They're barbarians, animals."

The woman then unwrapped her hand and I saw that one finger was cut off. "They wanted my gold band. It wouldn't come off, so they cut off my finger."

I was still staring at her hand in horror when she turned and said, "You must come with me. I want you to remember this forever." She took us into an abandoned department store. All of the people who had worked in the store were dead, their throats methodically slit. Every one of them the same.

We followed her to a ravine that was two blocks out of town. She said, "You cannot believe me without seeing this." I looked down and there were hundreds of bodies, all slaughtered and thrown like kitchen scraps into the open grave.

Seeing the pile of bodies made me almost throw up. The senseless brutality made me ashamed that I was somehow allied with the Russians.

Before we left the village, Jerry and I went into a house looking for food. Several Russian soldiers were squatting near the base of the toilet. It was the type where the water bowl is at the top of the wall and a chain is pulled to flush it.

One of the soldiers would pull the chain and then they all watched the water. They'd never seen a toilet before. Under any other circumstances, the scene would have been comical, but somehow the humor was absent in the presence of the display of cruelty we had already witnessed.

The farmyards in Germany were enclosed with brick or stone walls that often rose eight feet high. They were like small fortresses. Inside the wall was the farmhouse, the barn, and a few toolsheds.

When we arrived at one of these compounds, there must have been eighty people staying there. They were mostly French except for a handful of Germans. They were all trying to get away from the Russians.

These people were conscripted labor. When France fell, the Germans took whole families of people into Germany and put them into forced labor. The group we encountered had been forced to work on farms after they had cleaned up the rubbish left from the bombings in the cities.

One woman gave us a small pistol, which would come in handy later on. The people were generous, providing us with food and shelter.

As we slept in a hayloft alongside the refugees that night, suddenly Russian tanks arrived. We could hear screams and gunshots as the Russians rampaged through other parts of the compound.

Moments later, they stormed the barn, screaming and yelling. Nobody moved or made a sound.

The soldiers had lights and lanterns to illuminate the barn. They just started jabbing through the hay with pitchforks. They finally hit several people, who involuntarily screamed from the pain. Without hesitation, the soldiers opened fire, killing the refugees.

Jerry Ennis and I stood against a back wall with our hands up as the soldiers roamed around. Suddenly one of them slit a pregnant woman's throat. She was full term and ready to give birth. We could see from the lantern that the woman was dead. Nevertheless, soldiers started lining up with the cheerful tolerance of young men waiting for baseball tickets. Then they raped her, one after the other.

We could do nothing since we would have been killed on the spot for our intrusion. All Jerry and I could do was watch the most atrocious act of barbarism I would ever see in my lifetime.

Several of the soldiers who had finished their part in this dreadful scene pulled us away. Jerry's voice cracked when he asked whether anybody spoke French or English. When no one responded, I pointed to their clothing. For some unknown reason one soldier wore an American jacket and another had shoes and pants from the USA. We tried to show them that we were wearing the same clothing so they would understand that we were Americans. We finally got through to them, and they let us go.

Jerry and I walked away from what had been a peaceful family farm before the war. We had both seen the unbelievable. It was literally an unspeakable horror.

I used to fantasize at Stalag I about not only gaining my freedom but somehow stealing a German airplane to accomplish it. That dream came closer to reality when Jerry and I came upon an abandoned Luftwaffe base. A very few ground crew were around, but twenty-five or thirty Focke-Wulf 190s were hidden in revetments all over the airfield just inside the border of Germany.

I had some knowledge of the plane because of a fellow Stalag I prisoner, Gus Lundquist. Hour after hour I had listened as Gus told me what he'd learned about it.

His experience with the 190 came from flying captured German aircraft when he was sent to England after being a test pilot at Wright Field. He was only there for a short time before he got shot down and captured. Our captors at Stalag I never found out Gus was familiar with their airplanes or he would have been subjected to severe torture.

The revetments (U-shaped mounds of dirt) at the airfield shielded the planes from enemy aircraft strafing attacks. Unless an enemy pilot could somehow shoot straight down, the plane was protected.

Jerry and I found an FW-190 that looked to be in fairly good shape. It had a few holes in the wing and tail, but otherwise it wasn't damaged. Best of all, the plane had full fuel tanks.

Using that .25 automatic we had been given by the Frenchwoman, Jerry "convinced" a ground crewman to assist our effort. "If my friend here doesn't get airborne, I'm going to kill you," he told him.

Ignoring Jerry's threat, the defiant crewman reached into the cockpit and yanked up the landing-gear handle, which retracted the tailwheel. That took a few hours' work to fix, but soon the plane was ready for flight.

Jerry held the gun on the agitated crewman while I taxied out. He'd already decided not to join me in flight. Later we'd meet up in the States and talk about our escape to freedom.

I was exhausted from our long trek across Germany, but I taxied out and took off. Although I kept a close eye out for Jerry, I felt some sense of freedom. I was flying away from prison, isolation, torture, near-starvation, humiliation, and cabbage soup.

The FW-190 performed capably and I headed north along the tree line. I knew that if an Allied plane saw the swastika on the 190, they'd blast me out of the sky. It was overcast, but I followed the coastline to the Zuider Zee (inlet) in Holland since I knew it had been liberated.

I couldn't land at any ex-German airfields since they would probably be mined. I chose instead an open field, but when I landed, the rollout was a bit too long and I saw an open ditch not three hundred yards ahead. I quickly ground-looped the plane, wiping out the landing gear, but that maneuver stopped me short of the ditch.

My nerves relaxed a bit knowing that I was in safe country. Darkness was approaching, so I climbed out of the FW-190 and tried to figure out which way to go. I decided to walk toward a small village I had spotted off in the distance. Just as I started to walk in that direction, a group of Dutch farmers armed with pitchforks came running toward me.

I waved my arms and frantically spoke to them in English, trying to convince them that I should not be pitchforked. Since I'd landed in a German plane, they thought I was an enemy deserter. Confusion reigned for several moments since I had no identification other than my dog tags. Despite reservations, they escorted me into a small town where they turned me over to the British.

I don't think those farmers ever believed I was an American, but I convinced the British officials. They showed me the direction I needed to go to find the Americans, and I started walking toward their headquarters. My energies and emotions were spent, but I was a free man for the first time in almost a year and a half.

Some months later, the November 25, 1945, edition of the *Nashville Tennessean* published a belated account of my escape to freedom.

SGT. ROBERT HOOVER FLEW GERMAN PLANE TO FREEDOM

When an Army pilot is recommended for the Distinguished Flying Cross before reaching combat, he is "doing pretty good," but when he does get into combat, is shot down and captured and then escapes in the enemy's airplane, he is "flying high."

Twenty-three-year-old Robert Hoover was shot down and taken prisoner by the Germans.

After having spent such a prolonged period [16 months] in the company of such unpleasant individuals as the Germans, Hoover decided it was time to go home. He [escaped], found an airfield, preflighted a damaged enemy Focke-Wulf 190, started the engine, casually checked his instruments, headed it into the wind and sassily wiggled his wings at the astonished Huns as he zoomed across the edge of the field. . . .

Ordinarily, Hoover, being a "hot" pilot after having flown every type of combat aircraft as a test pilot and surviving 17 "crackups" due to structural defects, might have been tempted to circle the field for a "hangar-top buzz," but having a "borrowed" airplane, he didn't want to take the chance of wrecking it so he headed for Holland and crash-landed in a plowed field. . . .

When that article was published, I was in Nashville with my parents. After I escaped, I took some time to roam around France and England, where I saw my brother Leroy. Then I caught a ship for New York.

I had spent nearly two and a half years overseas. It was an experience I'll never forget. I had seen the extremes of bravery and brutality, of kindness and cruelty, of loyalty and cowardliness. Above all, I knew more than ever what it meant for one to lose that precious gift of freedom.

TEST-FLYING FOR UNCLE SAM

8

Dogfighting over Ohio

Even though I was flying a P-38 prop fighter, I headed straight toward the Bell jet that was circling Wright Field in Dayton, Ohio, spoiling for a dogfight. The pilot in the P-59 may have been startled to see me challenge him, but he never backed away.

In the early fall of 1945, the jet fighter and my P-38 battled toe-to-toe. Neither one of us could gain the advantage. As soon as I made a vertical climb to the stall to try to get an advantage on the P-59, it was right there staring me in the face.

Later, the pilot in the P-59 would describe the action that day in his autobiography:

> I whipped the jet around and pulled straight up into a vertical climb . . . and I stalled going straight up. I was spinning down and that damn P-38 was spinning up, both airplanes out of control. . . .
>
> When we went by each other, not ten feet apart, my eyes were like saucers and so were the other pilot's. Finally, he said, "Hey, man, we'd better knock it off before we bust our asses."

If my memory serves me right, I wasn't the one who called things off! Nevertheless, once we landed, I laid eyes for the first time on the man who would come to call me Pard, Charles "Chuck" Yeager.

"Man, I didn't know the 38 could swap ends like that," he bellowed while extending his hand.

"Those eyes of yours were bigger than a stripper's knockers," I shot back.

That was more than fifty years ago. Somehow I knew right then and there that Chuck and I would always be friends.

He and I arrived at Wright Field about the same time. My commanding officer in Corsica, Col. Marvin McNickle, had told me that when the war was over, he'd attempt to get me assigned to the base in Dayton, Ohio.

That was not an easy task, according to McNickle, who was assigned to the Joint Chiefs of Staff at the time:

> Bob was not qualified to be a test pilot. He might have been a fine "seat of the pants" flier, but he didn't have the educational background, or the engineering knowledge, necessary to become a test pilot. I saw firsthand though what a fine aviator Bob was overseas. He had the "touch" and everyone who ever rode with him came back to tell me that he could really make a plane sing. I therefore wrote a letter to Gen. Fred Dent, commander at Wright-Patterson, asking him to give Bob a chance.

Wright Field was a beehive of activity for experimental planes. It was the principal fighter, bomber, cargo, and helicopter testing facility for the Army Air Corps. My experience with testing aircraft overseas would come in handy.

Flying as a test pilot was just as dangerous as flying combat, but in a different way. Fighter pilots are trained to believe that they are the best pilots flying the best planes. They must believe they can outwit and outperform the enemy in life-and-death encounters.

Test pilots also face life-threatening situations. Flying experimental aircraft is by definition trial and error. Yet, test pilots cannot afford to make errors. They aren't dodging bullets, but the possibility that the plane will fail is a constant threat.

At Wright Field, my first assignment was to perform compressibility tests on the Republic P-47 "Jug" fighter as well as captured Japanese and German aircraft.

I was also very interested in flying the German Henkel 162. Made of plywood and other nonstrategic materials, it featured springs on the gears and engines that could easily be detached.

The one I flew had a wolf's head on it. It was so difficult to pilot that I had to use both hands on the stick since there was no boost and the aerodynamic forces stiffened up the controls.

I flew the He 162 plane at Muroc Air Force Base in California. It was my first trip there, and I remember the visit well. Colonel Gilkey, the commanding officer, asked to have his picture taken with the test pilots before we flew. He wanted the picture taken then in case we were killed. I recall laughing at the time, but looking back, I guess it wasn't so funny.

In addition to our test-flight duties, Chuck Yeager and I began to put on air shows in all types of aircraft in the late months of 1945.

Buoyed by the success of our fighter aircraft in World War II, air shows were extremely popular. Chuck and I were only in our early twenties, but we attained some celebrity status with air-show flying.

While many of the senior officers at Wright Field weren't interested in barnstorming around the country, Chuck and I were. We traveled to such places as New York, Alabama, Wisconsin, and Oklahoma, where we performed our loops and spins for thousands of people.

Patriotism was still running high then, and we were able to sell war bonds on many of those trips. I wasn't much of a public speaker, but I'd remind the audience that our country's military needed donations since our boys were still flying old aircraft left over from World War II.

Wright Field had the only jets in our Army Air Corps fleet. The P-59 was the very first one manufactured. It was built by the Bell Aircraft Company of Niagara Falls, New York, the same company that would later produce the X-1, which Chuck Yeager would pilot to break the sound barrier.

A single-seater, the P-59 had mechanical flight controls. It never saw combat, but I was impressed with its performance the first time I flew it.

What I noticed with the P-59 jet was that I had to watch the rate at which I opened up the throttle. With propeller-driven aircraft, there was instant power. When the pilot opened the throttle, the propeller revved up and the plane accelerated at a steady pace. By the same token, when the pilot backed off the throttle, deceleration occurred smoothly.

It was a different matter when it came to flying jets. They were driven by a powerful discharge of exhaust rather than by pistons. And the pilot had to open the throttle very slowly. Otherwise the engine would overtemp (become too hot) and be ruined.

Flying that first jet, and later the P-80A, was like nothing I had experienced before. I fell in love with the P-59 on my maiden voyage. That fascination with jet aircraft continues to this day.

While the P-59 was the first one built, the P-80A Shooting Star was the most impressive of the early jets.

Lockheed developed that plane in the midforties. It was equipped with cantilever wings and a turbojet engine enclosed with the rear fuselage. Engine problems haunted it for some time, and several test pilots lost their lives.

Tony LeVier, the chief test pilot for Lockheed, was the first pilot to fly the prototype. It was the successor aircraft to the P-80, which was affectionately known as Lulubelle.

The P-80A, or Gray Ghost as it was called, was quite a handful when he first flew it according to Tony:

> I thought flying it was going to be a piece of cake since piloting the P-80 had been a breeze. It turned out to be just the opposite. On the way to the airplane the morning of its first flight, I ran into Kelly Johnson, its designer. "How much do you want for flying this plane?" he asked me. "Just the normal amount," I responded. "Well," Kelly responded, "I think it's only worth half as much since you've already flown the P-80."
>
> We left the fee up in the air, and I proceeded to take off in the P-80A. It was the tenth of June, 1944, and that flight turned out to be one of the most dangerous I ever had. The plane was completely unstable and I was lucky I was finally able to land it safely. When Kelly heard all of my squawks, he and the other engineers made a lot of changes and finally that plane flew smooth as silk. By the way, when my paycheck for that flight came around, it was for $5,000, the full amount!

By 1947, the P-80A was known as the F-80. It set a speed record of nearly 630 miles per hour. Three years later, it would take its place in history when it successfully challenged a Russian MiG-15 in Korea in the first all-jet air-combat engagement.

That F-80 was a beauty. I can still remember the faces of people at air shows who stared in wonder. "How can it fly with no propeller?" they asked themselves.

Chuck Yeager would tease them by getting a volunteer to stand behind the tailpipe with a crumpled newspaper. Then Chuck would position himself so he had access to the ignition switch. Just as the volunteer lit the newspaper and held it up by the engine, the plane roared to life. It looked as if the startled volunteer had fired up the engine with the burning newspaper.

In mid-1946, I received orders to fly the P-80 Shooting Star to my hometown of Nashville. Upon arrival, I flew low over the downtown area and my old neighborhood. There were no maneuver restrictions in those days, but I later learned that buzzing those areas just as people were heading home from work upset a few residents.

I really enjoyed barnstorming, but those trips across the country were not without incident.

One of my escapades involved a flight I was asked to take to Beverly, Massachusetts, which is near Boston, in a P-80. The assignment came from Col. Albert Boyd. He had received a call from Gen. Toohy Spaatz, later chief of staff of the Army Air Corps, requesting that a jet be flown to Beverly.

I was concerned about fuel consumption because of the long distance, so I decided to have tip tanks added to the plane. This took some doing. By the time they were installed, it was sunset. I took off and step-climbed to a high altitude since we had learned that the P-80's range could be extended by flying as high as possible.

In those days we didn't have navigation systems to let us know exactly where we were. There was no pressurization, so the windshield would frost over with ice, blinding the pilot. When it was time to land, the pilot would put his thumb on the windshield and melt a small peephole.

On this particular flight, everything went well. I finally saw what I thought were the lights of Boston. I could also see that the city was engulfed in heavy fog. I radioed in that I needed to land at an alternative military site in the area. When a new vector was given, I headed in that direction.

All at once, the engine exploded and the sky lit up before me. I cut the engine because the fire warning lights were on and declared an emergency.

It was a wild ride. Lack of oxygen made it hard to focus. To see better, I jettisoned the canopy. Freezing-cold air smacked me in the face. Since there were no ejection seats, my alternatives were to ditch the plane and parachute over the side or somehow try to stretch the glide and land at a military base. I had made the decision to bail out when I saw what was called a Sandra Lightbeam (vertical light beam) off in the distance.

It came from the Westover Airfield at Chicopee, Massachusetts. My instincts told me I could make it there if I could just get the P-80 to start. I hit the switch, and miraculously it did.

However, both the fore and aft fire-warning lights illuminated. I got enough speed built up to make it before shutting off the engine. Since there were no runway lights, I couldn't see the surface of the airfield. I just picked a spot and landed.

Blind luck saved me because I didn't land on the runway. I ended up on a surface that was tucked between two huge revetments. A duty officer just happened to be driving by. He raced toward me with the lights of his jeep glaring in my face.

I was nearly frozen. I stayed in the hospital four days recovering from hypothermia and frostbite. To this day my fingers are extremely sensitive to cold due to that episode over Massachusetts. Nevertheless, I was back in the air in less than a week.

The P-80's skin was burned off all the way from the engine back to the tail. Lt. Col. Bill Counsel recommended me for the Distinguished

Flying Cross. Although I didn't get it this time, I appreciated the recognition.

That incident was written up in the *Dayton Journal* on September 28, 1946:

JET PILOT CHEATS DEATH AT 42,000 FEET

A Wright Field pilot last night fought a lonely, dramatic battle with death in his P-80 "Shooting Star" jet plane miles above New England. [Fortunately, he] landed his erratic aircraft safely.

First Lt. Robert A. Hoover, 24, of the YMCA, flying to a Civil Air Patrol show at Beverly, Mass., radioed that his oxygen supply and jet turbines failed at 42,000 feet.

His radio distress call was heard by flight control centers throughout Massachusetts. Then followed as breathless and astounding an experience as ever was linked with jet plane flying.

"My jet turbines are cut out," Hoover cried.

Maj. W. B. Harris of Columbia, S.C., operations officer of the AAF exhibition team, heard the call at the Beverly tower. Hoover's radio reports grew unintelligible. Airmen knew the Dayton pilot was suffering from anoxia (lack of oxygen).

Harris asked several questions of the pilot via radio, but the answers were jumbled. All fields in the state were alerted for an emergency landing. The pilot was advised to bail out as soon as the plane descended to 21,000 feet.

"My dashboard lights are blinking. I can't focus my eyes," Hoover mumbled.

The pilot told listeners on the ground that he was experiencing a choking sensation—that his hands were cold. A silence of five or six minutes followed.

Again Harris advised the pilot to abandon ship. There was no answer for several minutes. Then Hoover's voice could be heard faintly:

"I'm at 7,500 feet, ready to bail out."

Two minutes later, the pilot called again—his engine had started and he could see an airfield in the distance. There was a 15-minute silence while airmen awaited some word of the pilot's fate.

At 8:15 P.M. (EDT) Westover Field, Chicopee, Mass., radioed that Hoover had landed unharmed.

My favorite air show routine during this time was a P-38 act. It was a risky maneuver where I flew vertical hammerhead stalls. That involved chopping one engine as the plane stalled.

I then put the P-38 in a flat spin with one engine wide-open and the other off. When I got ready to stop, I'd open the engine that I had throttled back and pull back on the other one. The plane would spin like a top, but I could stop it wherever I wanted to.

I recall performing the routine at Stapleton Field in Denver in 1947.

I was at four thousand feet, going at high speed, when I went into the vertical. It was overcast, but I knew when I came out of the clouds, I would have enough room to recover.

I opened up the other engine on the P-38 and throttled back on the one I had wide-open. I made a couple of turns and swapped the engine, but it didn't take. I didn't have enough power to stop the rotation. I chopped the other engine and finally recovered. That was close enough for me. I never did a flat spin in that airplane again.

I also flew a P-38 to Offutt Field in Omaha where the Blue Angels were performing. They were the Navy's official demonstration team, led by my good friend Butch Vores.

My commanding officer at Wright Field forbid me to fly my energy management maneuver (both engines shut down), but General Harbold, who ran the program there, ordered me to.

The general secured a telegram for me from the Air Force chief of staff, Gen. Toohy Spaatz. That telegram, which relayed the chief of staff's request order that I perform my trademark maneuver, is still one of my most prized possessions.

At the briefing before my performance, the officer in charge said they were going to feature me in a P-38. I could hear snickering from members of the Navy ground crew. One said, "Well, our guys will out-fly Hoover; he's Air Corps."

As it turned out, one particular member of Butch's team planned to outdo me in a Bearcat. He went first. His single-engine F-8-F fighter, which came out right after the war, took off and pulled up to do a roll on takeoff. He dished out of the roll too low and too slow and went right into the runway. He killed himself in front of his fellow Blue Angel team members, several thousand spectators, and his family.

With all my war experience, I had seen death in its most brutal form, but seeing that young fellow crash and burn gave me a hollow feeling in my stomach that wouldn't go away.

There was a great deal of death and tragedy during those days. To lighten the load, Chuck Yeager and I loved to play practical jokes. In his autobiography, *Yeager*, Chuck recalls a beauty:

> He [Hoover] went over to a little airport in Dayton and signed up for flying lessons. He took the course taught by a really sharp-looking blonde, and when the time came for him to solo, a bunch of us went out to watch. He took off, climbed above the field, then dove straight down, did a roll and barely missed the hangars, looped and spun, and turned everything loose. His instructor hid her face in her hands and almost passed out, but when she saw us standing in our uniforms and laughing like hell, she knew she'd been had.

* * *

Chuck's memory is a good one. I can still see that lady laughing even today.

During that time, pilots were supposed to live in the Spartan base barracks at Wright Field. A few of us chose instead to move into the local YMCA in downtown Dayton.

Another pilot named Jim Little and I gave a sad-sack story to the base commander so he would approve of our living off base. We told him that the barracks reminded us of the World War II prison-camp buildings we so detested.

We were really just trying to save money. If we stayed in the barracks, there was no living allowance. If we stayed off base, we could save a few bucks from our housing allowance.

Since Chuck Yeager's wife, Glennis, and their new baby were back in West Virginia, he was a bachelor during the week. Sometimes I would fly him down to see her in one of the test airplanes on Friday, then pick him up on Sunday evening.

I also chanced a blind date while at Wright Field. The result would be my forty-eight-year marriage to my wife, Colleen, who remembers:

"On the blind date, I think Bob wanted to be with my roommate, but he got stuck with me. I didn't even know what a flight officer was, or what a test pilot did. He was a real gentleman though, and I kept seeing him. Later he took me for a ride in a Stearman that he bought with a fellow pilot named Jim Fitzgerald. I'll never forget the first flight—he made all these loops and spins in the plane. I was dizzy for a week, but I didn't get sick."

While Colleen's first flight with me was exciting, it was uneventful. The second one, however, could easily have ended our relationship before it began. Colleen recalls:

"My second flight was a bit more dangerous. He was bragging about how great a buy the plane was, but then the Stearman picked up carburetor ice, and we crashed between two trees. Luckily, I wasn't hurt and neither was Bob, but then an angry farmer came charging toward us, yelling and screaming, 'I hope you broke your necks.'"

I wouldn't say it was exactly love at first sight with Colleen, but I knew she was special. She was pretty, intelligent, and had a great sense of humor.

"I think the only thing that held Bob back was my maiden name of Humrickhouse," Colleen recalls. "Sometimes he'd just introduce me as Colleen Jones and avoid the hassle."

Shortly after we got the Stearman repaired, I asked Colleen to go with me to see my folks in Nashville. "It took him all winter to fix the Stearman," Colleen remembers. "And then he asked me to go to Nashville. I only went because I was afraid he'd take up with some Southern belle."

Regardless, Colleen climbed into the Stearman, and off we went. "Nothing too exciting happened on that flight," Colleen recalls, "except, of course, we nearly ran out of gas on the way back."

Even though Chuck Yeager and I were junior officers, the experiences we had testing the P-59, P-80, and P-84 apparently impressed the Wright Field head of the flight-test division, Col. Albert Boyd. A no-nonsense, tough-as-nails career soldier, Boyd was never one to mince words. When he designated us to be involved with supersecret test projects, it didn't occur to us to question him.

Colonel Boyd was feared by everyone, but we all had great respect for him. A protruding jaw and lean facial features gave him a stern presence. Colonel McNickle, who ended up a three-star general and spent thirty-six years in the military before he retired, called him a "straitlaced guy who never stood for any foolishness."

I learned right away that if you stood Boyd's test, he'd go through the wall for you. He was loud and to the point, but as time went by, I came to understand and respect his abruptness.

Colonel Boyd, who was chiefly responsible for establishing the flight-test center at Muroc in California, was also a capable pilot. He retired after thirty years of service and twenty-five thousand hours of flight time. At one point he held the speed record of 625 mph in a Shooting Star.

When Colonel Boyd first arrived at Wright Field, I wasn't test-flying at all. The previous commander had grounded me for an incident involving my friend Gus Lundquist.

Ol' Gus had been a test pilot at Wright Field before the war. He had flown many of the captured German and Japanese planes. While a fellow prisoner at Stalag I, he had familiarized me with the FW-190 that I ended up flying to freedom.

The unfortunate incident at Wright Field with Gus occurred on a particularly nice day in the summer of 1945. I was flying a P-38 and Gus a P-59 over the skies near the field. Against orders, we got into a furious dogfight.

Those types of personal battles weren't unusual. Pilots were dogfighting all the time. Some superior officers looked the other way. Some were "by the book." They had no sense of humor.

Lt. Col. Bill Counsel, who was the commanding officer, was one of those. As bad luck would have it, he witnessed the fray between Gus and me. When we landed, he called us into his office and read us the riot act. To our surprise, he informed us that we were being reassigned to fly B-17 bombers in Florida.

That assignment was the bottom rung for a test pilot. Gus said, "Yes, sir," and quit the program. He went back to school to obtain his master's degree and Ph.D.

Unlike Gus, I was determined not to be washed out of the flight-test division. Not only was I upset by Counsel's orders, but my fellow test pilots were outraged as well. They encouraged me to go to Lieutenant Colonel Counsel's base quarters and beg for mercy. A group of them offered to go with me.

Don Gentile, Johnny Godfrey, Steve Pisanos (who had flown with the famed Eagle squadron), Jim Fitzgerald, and Jim Little, all of whom had great combat records, joined me in driving to Lieutenant Colonel Counsel's home. Once there, I reluctantly walked up the steps and knocked on the door. My support team stayed behind.

Lieutenant Colonel Counsel's wife answered the door. She wasn't quite sure what I was doing there, but she invited me in.

The lieutenant colonel was asleep with his feet propped on an ottoman. The morning news splayed out on his lap. I knew his peaceful expression would soon be gone.

I hated to disturb him since he was mad at me already. But his wife bumped his foot, and he came to life.

"What the hell are *you* doing here?" he demanded.

I had left my buddies in the cars. Now I wished they were beside me as I proceeded to plead my case:

"Sir, after all these years as a fighter pilot, I don't want to fly bombers. I've always dreamed about being a test pilot, and that's all I want to do."

The lieutenant colonel stared me down. "You should have thought of that before you and Lundquist decided to play games in the sky."

"Sir, I'm sorry. That was a mistake. It won't happen again."

Apparently realizing I needed some additional support, Lieutenant Colonel Counsel's wife spoke up.

"Nobody ever gave you a break," she said as she glared at her husband.

Seeing a ray of hope, I pleaded once again. "I'll take anything you've got. I don't care how low-level it is. Let me prove myself to you."

Lieutenant Colonel Counsel was silent for a moment. He looked at me and then over at his wife, who was now a solid member of my support team.

"All right," he said. "You're grounded. You can be a damn clerk."

I accepted that and thanked him. I then nodded my appreciation to his wife before making a hasty retreat out the door. They never knew about my platoon of supporters waiting outside.

Later on, Bill Counsel would be instrumental in my becoming a member of the X-1 team. He gave me a second chance, and I'll always appreciate him for that.

If not for Lieutenant Colonel Counsel's sympathy, who knows where I would have ended up. My flying days in the service could have been over since I would probably have left the military.

Getting from a typewriter in the clerk's office back in the air wasn't an easy task. When Colonel Boyd came along to replace Lieutenant Colonel Counsel, I got my first break. Russ Schleeh, who was chief of fighter flight test at the time, suggested that I check out the colonel when he arrived at Wright Field. I got to know Boyd that way, and finally he asked Russ why I was a clerk typist.

Russ explained what had happened, but that I was a very capable pilot. "Right now," Schleeh told him, "he's just typing up operational orders. He should be flying."

Colonel Boyd took it upon himself to spring me from the desk chains. Soon I was back in the air doing what I enjoyed most.

In 1946, I had been assigned to a program involving the Me (Messerschmitt) 163 Komet. This was a rocket plane the Germans flew during the war. It was faster than anything we had in our country, and we wanted to learn as much as we could about their technology.

Gus Lundquist had performed the glide flights before he'd left the program. He had been towed like a glider to altitude by a B-17. I was to make the rocket-powered flights, but because of the volatility of the rocket fuel, the project was canceled.

Many years later, I would have occasion to meet Willy Messerschmitt in Hot Springs, Arkansas, where I was performing aerobatic routines in the P-51 Mustang for an aerospace symposium. He had started his aircraft company in 1923. Their Me 209 set a world speed record in 1939. The company was also responsible for building the world's first operational jet aircraft, the Me 262. I was very impressed by him, and his knowledge of the aircraft industry.

Later on, I flew the Messerschmitt 109. The plane looked like a P-51 or a Spitfire, but it was difficult to control.

That flight occurred during a visit to an outfit called the Confederate Air Force down in Harlingen, Texas. All the pilots were called colonels and wore gray uniforms. It was like a good ol' boy's club.

I was in Harlingen to participate in the annual Confederate air show. There was an enormous collection of airplanes there, and they had reenactments of World War II battles.

The Me 109 had a reputation of being tricky on landing. Operated off grass, pilots thought it was all right, but taking off on a runway was risky since the landing gear was canted toward the wingtip at an angle. If a crosswind came up or the pilot stubbed his toe on the gear sticking out, the plane would flip. In fact, of the thirty-five thousand 109s built, many thousands were destroyed on takeoffs and landings.

After I flew the 109, I entered the officers' club where I saw my old buddy "Gabby" Gabreski, who had been in prison camp with me during the war.

Gabby was one of our leading aces in War II with twenty-eight kills. I approached him. He said, "Well, Bob, what did you think of the Messerschmitt?"

After careful thought I told Gabby and his friends, "Well, after flying that miserable son of a bitch, instead of thirty-eight kills, Gabby, you should have had one hundred and thirty-eight!"

Gabby, who has always been a great inspiration to all fighter pilots, laughed at my remarks. Besides those thirty-eight kills in War II, he added six and a half more to his list when he flew the F-86 in Korea.

One of my first flight-test projects after the assignment to Wright Field had been to continue the dive recovery test in the Republic P-47 Thunderbolt. This airplane when dived vertical had a tendency to tuck under when recover was attempted at high speeds.

Two test pilots had lost their lives while trying to determine a consistent recovery technique. Even though the war was over, engineering hoped that we could learn additional knowledge about recovery from compressibility (a condition of the air flow over parts of the plane going from subsonic to supersonic).

They had designed a flat plate that was manually controllable in the cockpit and could be manipulated to vary angles of deflection. It was located on the horizontal stabilizer just ahead of the elevator controls.

Each of the test flights called for higher speeds checking out the effectiveness of the recovery device. After many flights, it was determined that I should go for maximum speed from the highest altitude.

My friend Jim Fitzgerald was in the chase plane for this final flight. His responsibility was to assess the test aircraft after the dive or identify my location in the event the airplane didn't survive the recovery.

Each flight on this test program was like a combat mission. It was an eerie flight into the unknown due to the uncertainty of the outcome for each dive and for survival if a bailout became necessary at speeds in excess of five hundred miles per hour. Of course, ejection seats did not exist at this time.

The final dive resulted in a speed of .83 Mach. During the recovery, Fitz advised me to pull more force on the controls since he didn't believe I had enough altitude to make it. I was using all of my physical strength to pull on the stick. The airplane was experiencing compressibility shaking prior to an over-g acceleration that flexed the wings so severely as to snap the landing-gear doors open. Because of the excessive speed, they separated instantly, which created an even greater buffet than the compressibility effect.

After slowing down, Fitz flew into a formation position and advised me that the gear doors were gone and that the wings were wrinkled from the excessive g force on the pullout from the dive. He was concerned about possible landing-gear damage from the landing-gear doors' separation. Fortunately, the landing gear extended and a normal landing concluded the test program.

Besides developing and testing new aircraft at Wright Field, the military tested all types of new military innovations there.

Fuel tests in the P-80 included for the first time the use of gasoline in a jet engine. Prior to that, the Army Air Corps had always used either JP (jet fuel) or kerosene to fuel the jets.

Kerosene or JP fuel was not available at bases across the country. The fuel had to be trucked in huge quantities to any base where a jet was to land on a cross-country trip. Logistics made this difficult. It was imperative that a new, more accessible fuel be tested in the jets. Gasoline seemed to be the answer since it was already available everywhere.

The question was whether its lead deposits and flash point would create a fire hazard in the jets. To find the answer, a three-step process was created.

Initially, an engine powered by gasoline was set up on a test stand. When that worked, the gas-powered engine was installed in the aircraft that was to be tested with the aft (rear) section of the fuselage left off.

To complete that phase of the test program, my job was to sit in an open cockpit with the canopy removed from the P-80. For one hour at a time, and fifteen hours in all, I sat in the cockpit as we ran the engine using gasoline.

Gasoline has a lower flash point than kerosene and is therefore more combustible. For obvious reasons, flight engineers stationed five fire trucks on either side and in front of the P-80. Spray nozzles were aimed right at me in anticipation of a deadly fire.

Fifteen hours in that cockpit was very unnerving. Kind of high-tech Russian roulette. I'd listen for any variation in sound or the slightest vibration, wondering whether it meant I'd be blown to bits.

Having a nervous audience didn't help either. That made me even more anxious, although I wasn't about to let anyone know it. The engineers paced around with their eyes focused on my helmet. Fire personnel stood ready to hose me down if they saw the slightest trace of fire.

The anticipation of spontaneous disaster was quickly replaced by boredom after the first few hours. I had to keep myself alert, ready to react in a split second. Fortunately, the test went off without incident. My days of being a human guinea pig were over.

Shortly after that successful test, Colonel Boyd then asked me to take the third step in the test process. I would perform aerobatic maneuvers in the gas-powered P-80 for General McNarny, the commander of Allied Forces in Europe, who was making a visit to Wright Field.

Everything went well during the first part of that flight. Suddenly, at ten thousand feet, the gasoline apparently coked up the burner cans (fouls up the burner section). The engine flamed out.

I set up an overhead 360-degree landing pattern. The only way to get the landing gear down was to pump a little side-stick that telescoped up for mechanical advantage. That provided a manual auxiliary pump for the hydraulics that permitted the wheels to extend.

I frantically pumped that side-stick thirty or forty times. The red light kept flashing. Nothing happened. The landing gear was still not locked down.

I knew I could not make the runway with the altitude and airspeed available. Ahead of me I saw a road with cars parked on both sides. There were only two choices. I could dump the nose and probably kill myself or try to stretch the glide and fit the wing of the plane in between rows of cars.

I chose the second alternative and banked the airplane at forty-five degrees. This permitted me to squeeze the left wing of the airplane between two cars.

The terrain on the other side of the road downsloped about thirty feet. After passing over the cars, I was out of airspeed and stalled. The impact with the ground was severe, forcing the landing-gear struts through the wings and breaking the fuselage back of the cockpit.

The normal and emergency canopy release mechanisms were jammed from the impact. My immediate concern was fire. I released the safety harness and tried to get my shoulders and back against the canopy to force it off. No luck.

I heard the sirens of the rescue teams approaching. I attempted to remain calm, but being trapped in the cockpit made me fidget with anxiety.

Then a fireman appeared out of nowhere. I gave him the thumbs-up to let him know I was all right.

Within a few minutes, an entire rescue crew arrived. They chopped the canopy to get me out of the cockpit. A cut lip and nose and a sore back were my only injuries. I'd dodged another bullet.

That afternoon I was ready to get back in the air. I was scheduled to finish up the tests of a one-of-a-kind P-51 that had ramjets on the wingtips.

Ramjets are a high-speed, high-altitude propulsion power plant. I had been testing the P-51 equipped with them for several weeks and had one more test flight to go before completing the project. I climbed into the cockpit, ready to start the engine.

About that time, Colonel Boyd drove up in his staff car. He had other ideas. "Lieutenant Hoover, what in the world are you doing in that airplane?"

"Ready to take it up, sir. Last flight in the program."

"Oh, no, you're not. This morning's episode was quite enough. You climb down from there and take a few days off."

"But, sir," I pleaded.

Test pilots can be egotistical as well as stubborn. I was a little of both that day. Boyd was equal to the challenge, and we argued for the next ten minutes.

There was no question that I was out of order. I tried to explain what had happened in the P-80 and used raw language to back it up. Boyd could have written me up for insubordination and court-martialed me. Instead, he got personal.

"Hoover, I've been counting up the number of dead-stick [engine failure] landings you've had. It's way more than anyone else."

He took a moment to let me think about what he'd said before he continued.

"Well, nobody else seems to be having these types of problems."

Finally, I'd had enough. I wanted to tell him that I had had more engine failures than anyone because I always requested assignment to high-risk flights. But he had gotten personal so I decided to do the same. My next comment could have landed me in the brig.

"Well, Colonel, if you'd come down here and fly more often, you could assume some of the risks too."

I thought Colonel Boyd was going to climb out of his staff car and come after me. He started to, but then had second thoughts.

"That's it," he said. "Get out of that cockpit. You're grounded until further notice."

That grounding lasted nearly two weeks. Once again, my friend Marvin McNickle came to the rescue. He gave me a temporary assignment to his laboratory. I flew test aircraft until Colonel Boyd relented and put me back in the flight-test program.

While Colonel Boyd was a controlled and imposing man, some of the other test pilots enjoyed introducing a little chaos into his life. When he bought a new Buick, Dick Johnson, head of fighter flight test, put some stones in the back right hubcap.

The men hid behind some bushes to watch the colonel's reaction. He was obviously proud of that new car as he drove away with a straight back and a smile on his face. When he heard the *clampty-clamp*, he slammed on his brakes and brought the automobile to an abrupt stop. Up went the hood and his frustration when he couldn't find the source of the problem.

Off he went, only to stop again when the rattling resumed. To hear that the "old man," as we kindly referred to him, had fallen for the prank was something all of us treasured for years to come.

As I mentioned, Dick Johnson was my commanding officer in flight test at Wright Field. He had been a fighter pilot with the Fifty-seventh Fighter Group in World War II. But by the time he arrived in the Italian theater, I was in prison camp.

Prior to the grounding I received from Colonel Boyd, Dick wanted to be checked out in an F-82, a long-range fighter that featured dual cockpits (two fuselages joined to one wing—referred to as the Twin Mustang) so pilots could switch off during long flights. I said, "Great, let's go," and off we went.

I was securely seated in one cockpit with Dick in the other. We flew over a section of town where there was a golf course. Dick Johnson remembers, "Bob and I flew many times together, but on this particular flight I told people later that when we flew over a golf course, we got so close the propeller knocked a golf ball off a tee."

On another occasion, I flew the plane awhile, then said, "Dick, you've got it," at about thirty thousand feet.

I let loose of the controls and sat back to relax. The F-82 flew without a hitch, sailing comfortably across the sky. At one point, I did have some concern because the plane was flying treetop high over downtown Dayton. We were perilously close to many of the office buildings.

Of course, I thought Dick was just trying to show off. To make him see how relaxed I was, I leaned back and put both of my hands behind my head. I looked over at him in his cockpit with a great big who-cares smile.

It was then that I noticed that Dick's face was as white as a sheet as he grappled with the controls. Quickly he steadied the F-82 and then yelled over to me, "For Christ's sake, Hoover, I thought *you* were flying the plane."

9

Bear Huntin' with Chuck Yeager

After World War II, the race for airspeed in an aircraft reached another dimension entirely. A German rocket plane, the Me 163, had gone nearly six hundred miles per hour, and then a British jet, the Gloster Meteor, surpassed that speed.

While the Germans and the British had experienced high subsonic speeds, no one had flown faster than Mach 1, the speed of sound. This was the magic number known as the sound barrier. Several aviators had been killed trying. Geoffrey De Havilland Jr., a British pilot, died in an aircraft called the Sparrow. Later a motion picture called *Breaking the Sound Barrier* suggested that De Havilland broke the barrier. But the design of that plane prohibited it from ever going that fast.

America's hope was the X-1. It was the baby of the Bell Aircraft Company, but progress on the project had been slow and meticulous. New tests had proven successful in 1947, however, and the plane was apparently ready. It was time to take dead aim at flying faster than the speed of sound.

Civilian test pilot Chalmers "Slick" Goodlin demanded $150,000 for the first flight to exceed Mach 1. It was considered a dangerous test flight, but the Bell Company and the military thought this was an excessive demand. They decided to find a military pilot qualified to fly the aircraft.

Until the news broke at Wright Field that they were looking for a volunteer to break the sound barrier, none of the test pilots there knew much about it. Despite our lack of knowledge, a number of us signed up. After several interviews, I felt confident I had a legitimate shot. I had flown many different types of aircraft and had a reputation as a competent test pilot who wasn't afraid of danger.

Lt. Col. Bill Counsel narrowed the candidates down, and I was his choice. This was before Colonel Boyd took over the flight test division.

Shortly after he replaced Lieutenant Colonel Counsel, an incident in the summer of 1947 killed my chance to fly the X-1.

A fellow pilot asked me for a favor. He had friends and family in Springfield, Ohio. He wasn't flying jets then but he wanted them to think he was. To impress them, he asked me if I would perform a flyby in a P-80 over the Springfield Airport. He would of course take credit for the flight.

If I had just made a flyby, everything would have been fine. But I decided to give those folks two inverted flybys.

What I hadn't counted on was that a Civil Aeronautics Administration (CAA), which later was known as the Federal Aviation Administration (FAA), official would witness my performance. He promptly filed a "safety violation" report. Although no one could read the numbers on the tail, an investigation revealed that, of all things, I was flying the only jet in the entire country on that particular day.

Colonel Boyd called me to his office. I stood stiffly at attention when he asked me if I had buzzed the Springfield airport. My response was, "Yes, sir."

The colonel looked at me and said, "I know two things about you. You are honest but you can also be irresponsible. I am going to assign someone else as the primary pilot for the X-1, and you will be his backup as well as fly the chase plane."

I can still remember the incredible disappointment I felt when I left the colonel's office. There are few opportunities in life to be the first to do anything, and I had missed out. I would not be responsible for one of the greatest breakthroughs in aviation history.

When Colonel Boyd announced that he had selected my friend Chuck Yeager as the primary X-1 pilot, I was delighted. Because of my respect for his outstanding flying ability and War II combat record, I knew that the colonel could not have made a better choice.

From the day Chuck was selected, we became an inseparable team. That included being involved in a number of bizarre experiments that the National Advisory Committee on Aeronautics (NACA), which later became the National Aeronautics and Space Administration (NASA), medical team felt warranted. They tested the limits of human endurance in the high-altitude pressure chamber and under high g loads on the centrifuge.

Chuck and I were locked in altitude test chambers and strapped on to various centrifuges (simulates gravity with centrifugal force). We wore bulky, tight-fitting capstan pressure suits that looked like something a primitive deep-sea diver would wear.

Recently, Chuck sent me a copy of the old records from Wright Field. His accompanying note said, "Pard—While I was back at W-P AFB last week I found these old records where we used to puke outside the centrifuge. Take care, Chuck."

That equipment exposed us to high g's to determine our level of tolerance before blackout and unconsciousness. Even today, I can remember the nausea I experienced from twisting around on the centrifuges. Those were brutal experiments.

They would lock us in a sealed chamber and then simulate flight at eighty thousand feet. On one occasion, the chamber technician neglected to open the valve on my oxygen supply. My face turned morning-glory purple. Chuck Yeager loves to tell that story, and it seems funny now, but at the time I was petrified. I can't express the helpless feeling of having your lungs locked in the middle of a breath unable to inhale or exhale.

I almost choked to death. If Chuck had not looked through the porthole window at that particular instant, I would been asphyxiated.

The David Clark Company of Worcester, Massachusetts, manufactured bras and girdles. While it may seem hard to believe, that was the company that was chosen to make our high-pressure suits for the X-1 program. *Cumbersome* is the only word I can use to describe them; Chuck and I could not even stand straight up.

The executives at the Clark Company were great when we visited there. They took us through the manufacturing section; bras were made in one area, girdles, panties, and other ladies' undergarments in another. An attractive tour guide led us around rows of attractive women busily tapping away on their Singer sewing machines. They even sent us home with boxes of frilly panties and bras.

Having those articles in our plane could have been embarrassing. I'm sure Chuck remembers our return trip from Massachusetts to Wright Field. We had our full load of underwear when we encountered severe weather and lightning over Ohio.

Seeing the sky brighten up like fireworks on the Fourth of July presented quite an unforgettable image. Then suddenly we heard the crack of a huge bolt of lightning. It hit directly on the nose of the plane and the Plexiglas disintegrated. I smelled a pungent odor of ozone. Chuck was alongside in the copilot's seat, and the force of the electrical blast temporarily blinded us both.

When I looked over at Chuck, the startled look on his face told me he was as shook up as I was. We both were virtually speechless, but finally he said, "I'm surprised you're still with me, Pard!" I felt the same way.

Since the only damage to the plane was to the Plexiglas, we were able to make it to Wright Field safely. If we had crashed, I don't know how the Air Force (until July 1947 known as the Army Air Corps) would have explained the women's undies to investigators.

Chuck Yeager and I knew that Slick Goodlin had taken the X-1 experimental aircraft to .8 Mach. He had made over twenty flights in the aircraft, but felt the danger involved in pushing the envelope past Mach 1 deserved the price tag he demanded.

Just the term *sound barrier* meant that there were those who felt that there was a "barrier" that would destroy any aircraft. No one knew for sure whether there was an "ultimate speed" beyond which the plane would disintegrate.

Chuck and I were confident that the X-1 wouldn't break up since it was designed for eighteen positive and eighteen negative g's. The only limitation would be man's capacity for surviving the loads.

To gain an up-close look at the X-1, Chuck and I and Jack Ridley, the engineer assigned to the program, flew a C-45 to the Bell plant in Buffalo, New York. Their engineers took us to the company's laboratories where we saw, among other things, huge vats filled with liquid oxygen. The vapor steamed over the sides, and I felt as if we'd walked onto the set of a science fiction movie.

Either to shock us or for some other diabolical reason, one of the scientists dropped a poor, defenseless frog tied to a string into one of those vats. At minus 290 degrees, the liquid oxygen froze the wide-eyed hopper, who split into several pieces when he was dropped unceremoniously to the floor.

Once the demonstrations were over, Ridley, Yeager, and I were escorted out for a closer look at the bright orange X-1. It was log-chained to the concrete floor in a hangar that had the back wall removed. Larry Bell, the president of the corporation who developed the plane, gave us the grand tour. His description of the aircraft's features echoed the sounds of a mother talking about her child.

We had been briefed on the volatility of the fuels being used to propel the X-1. I never looked at the X-1 as a difficult airplane to fly, but we all knew that keeping the dome pressures balanced was the key to survival.

The way the system worked, fuel needed to be powered into the combustion chamber. Nitrogen was the pressure head used to power everything. If the pressures were not just right, the plane could blow up.

Those first rockets had no automatic controls to turn them off as the later space shuttles would. Several of the X series of aircraft were destroyed due to explosions.

To Larry Bell's way of thinking, the X-1 was indestructible. I agreed. The plane, which was rocket-propelled with six thousand pounds of thrust, was built to fly well above the speed of sound, but the only escape was through a side door exit. Escape through that door looked like a death wish to me. If the pilot was lucky enough to get out, he was certain to be scissored to death by the razor-edged wings.

The bright orange X-1 did not take off like a conventional aircraft; it had to be dropped from the belly of a B-29 at twenty-five thousand feet. After learning all of this, I wasn't sure that Goodlin's request for $150,000 was all that unreasonable.

While at the Bell plant, Larry asked us whether we wanted to take a seat in the X-1 cockpit. Chuck fired up one of the rocket engine chambers, and the roar can only be described as deafening. Ridley and I covered our ears against the loudest sound we had ever heard. The X-1 strained at its chains like a raging, shackled beast.

When it was my turn to sit in the cockpit, I experienced firsthand how it lunged to be free. The X-1 was the most streamlined airplane I'd ever seen.

Colonel Boyd asked for our impressions when we returned to Wright Field. We probably sounded like kids who had been to an amusement park. An adventure of a lifetime was about to occur. I knew I had in all likelihood missed the chance to experience the thrill firsthand, but nevertheless I would have a front-row seat to history in the making.

For all practical purposes, Muroc in 1947 resembled an old Western ghost town. It consisted of modest War II barracks, a Spartan headquarters building, and two hangars. There was a general store near the base. The closest city, Lancaster, was several miles away.

At the makeshift base, it was not uncommon to have fifty-mile-an-hour winds distort the unprotected Joshua trees. Nothing I could recognize lived in the searing 120-degree heat. At night, pilots froze when the temperatures plummeted. During the daytime, the red-hot sun cooked unprotected skin in a few minutes.

The only saving grace around the area was a bar/restaurant called Pancho's. Later to be called the Happy Bottom Riding Club, Pancho's was owned and operated by a caustic woman named Pancho Barnes, undoubtedly the ugliest, most foulmouthed woman I've ever known.

Pancho looked as if her face had been frozen in a nine-G pullout. Chuck Yeager and I went to her quarters once, and she came to the door wearing only panties. The sight was enough to turn your stomach.

Pancho Barnes had been a race pilot for Lockheed before she became an innkeeper, cattle rancher, bartender, and den mother to all the pilots. If Pancho liked you, there wasn't a better friend in the world. If you got on her wrong side, heaven help you.

It's hard to accurately describe Pancho's foul mouth, but I can't remember a sentence she uttered that didn't have several F or GD words in it. She could outcuss any mule skinner, and Chuck Yeager says in *Yeager* that Pancho once complimented a general's wife at a party by saying, "For a bitch, you're a pretty nice dame!"

Despite her foul mouth and contemptuous nature, one thing was for certain: Pancho Barnes had been a gutsy aviator. She won a number of Tom Thumb races (short-distance, high-speed races) in the 1930s. Howard Hughes once built a special racer for her.

Pancho was fiercely loyal and didn't like big shots. Slick Goodlin used to hang out at her place. When she heard he wanted more than a hundred grand to fly the X-1, she gave him holy hell. "Yeager's makin' two bucks an hour," she roared, "and you're sittin' on the sidelines while history's being made."

One night Pancho asked why I was only a lieutenant. I told her promotions were frozen. Damned if she didn't pick up the phone and wake up the chief of staff of the Army Air Corps, a four-star general named Spaatz in Washington. She called him "Toohey." Since it was three in the morning, I winced when she said my name. I figured my flying career was over right then and there.

I never did get that promotion, but it wasn't due to lack of effort on Pancho's part. She did everything she could to help me, but the promotion wasn't in the cards.

Pancho Barnes always stood up for us when our ability to fly the X-1 was questioned by civilian pilots.

In *Yeager*, Chuck recalls Pancho's well-chosen words to a test pilot named Gene May, who questioned us as to why we thought we could fly the X-1. "Gene, these two [Hoover and Yeager] can fly right up your ass and tickle your right eyeball, and you would never know why you were farting shock waves."

Pancho's main contribution to aviation at the time was that she provided a place where pilots could get together and discuss flight-test data. They used Pancho's to gather information and try to learn from someone else's experience.

Fatality rates were extremely high in those days. Black-and-white photos of pilots who had bought the farm were hanging on the wall behind the bar at Pancho's. This was a constant reminder of the danger pilots faced.

Col. John Stapp, a pioneer in high-speed acceleration, called Pan-

cho's "a fraternity house for test pilots where they could celebrate surviving for one more day."

Even though Pancho had her share of problems with the government in later years, she was a feisty cuss who lived every second of her
life. Chuck Yeager says she once told him, "Damn it, I have more fun
in a week than most of the weenies in the world have in a lifetime."

While the X-1 was undergoing maintenance, Jack Ridley, Russ
Schleeh, Chuck Yeager, and I squeezed into my 1947 ragtop Roadmas-
ter to go bear hunting. We headed toward a logging area up on the
Kern River that Chuck had seen while testing a P-80.

Since we had begun drinking at "beer call" in the late afternoon,
the four of us were ready for anything. Armed with a .38 revolver, a
.22 rifle, and old 8-mm Mauser (automatic pistol), we roared toward
bear-huntin' country.

We ended up camping near a garbage dump, where we assumed
the bears would come in search of food. We aimed the headlights of the
car toward the dump and waited for a grizzly to make its appearance.

No bears appeared, so we decided to call it a night. Russ, the only
man to have been chief of both the bomber and fighter flight-test sections at Wright Field, and I won the right to the sleeping bags. Chuck
and Jack curled up on the cold leather upholstery in the car.

Not long after we'd fallen asleep, all hell broke loose when a pine
branch blew off a tree and gently brushed my nose. I thought it was a
bear licking my face. I tugged at the sleeping bag and leaped up to try
to get away. I fell backward head over heels down an embankment
toward the garbage.

Someone mistook my silhouette for a bear and tried to shoot me.
My cry of "You son of a bitch, you're gonna kill me" finally stopped his
firing. I guess he assumed a real bear wouldn't use profanity.

Yeager and Ridley never did let me live that down. That was my last
bear hunt.

The Air Force took great pride in the X-1 program and was more determined than ever to be the first to break the sound barrier.

Whoever decided that the tests on the $6-million X-1 should be done
at Muroc had one thing in mind: isolation. But perhaps more important were the miles and miles of dry lake bed for landing.

The isolation took care of another problem. Security. None was
needed and the expensive, top-secret aircraft was kept unguarded in
an unlocked hangar.

Besides Chuck, Jack Ridley, and me, there were only ten other men assigned to the project. The base commander ignored us as if we had some sort of disease, and our unit rarely socialized with the other people at the base.

The selection of Chuck Yeager and me to work on the X-1 was still the center of much debate. In *Yeager,* Bell X-1 project engineer and test pilot Dick Frost recalls:

> The rumor I heard about the two pilots [Yeager and Hoover] was that they were the most junior guys in the flight test section at Wright and therefore were the most expendable in a catastrophe. That was the kind of sour-grapes rumor I didn't believe. What I did believe was that they were supposedly two of the hottest fighter jocks in the Air Corps who always flew balls out.

I appreciate Dick Frost's accolades, but I think the rumor may have been right about our selection to the X-1 team. We were both young pilots, only twenty-four. Even though the powers-that-be had decided we were the most qualified pilots in the Air Force. I had a hunch that if the $6-million airplane and the millions more spent to test it went sour, our inexperience would bear the blame.

10

Hole in the Sky

I had my share of success in flight test, but there were those days when the planes humbled me. One occurred while Jack Ridley, Chuck Yeager, and I were at Muroc working on the X-1 program.

Headquarters at Wright Field asked us to evaluate the N-9-M Flying Wing (an aircraft that has only wing surfaces, eliminating the drag generated by a fuselage). We flipped coins to see who would be the first to fly it. I won the flip.

When we had watched the civilian test pilots take off in the N-9-M, they always seemed to bobble or porpoise. I felt the problem had to do with the trim-setting (pilot sets control surfaces for takeoff, landing, or level flight).

I had learned from experience in other aircraft that if those trim settings were properly set, there was less potential for what was known as pilot-induced oscillation. That phenomenon sometimes occurred when a pilot encountered rough air while holding the controls too tightly.

This caused the plane to porpoise. I figured that if a proper trim setting was in place and left alone, I could perform the smoothest takeoff in the N-9-M anyone had ever seen.

During takeoff, I concentrated solely on not touching the controls with my hands. With my feet planted heavily on the rudder pedals, the plane reached its trim speed, but I was still on the runway. Airspeed was increasing, but I stayed right there. All of a sudden, I looked out and saw the elevons open on both the left and right wings. I was surprised no one had told me they weren't interconnected. With both elevons open, they were acting as dive brakes.

Instinctively, I took my feet off the rudder pedals. As soon as I did that, the plane was way above its trim speed so it pitched up abruptly right to the vertical.

I immediately pushed forward on the controls with an overcontrol that had the N-9-M headed steeply back to the runway. Then I pulled back again on the controls, which caused perhaps the most gigantic porpoise ever witnessed in the history of aviation.

Not only was the experience embarrassing, but frightening as well, since I could easily have slammed into the runway. Instead of making me and the Air Force look good, I could almost hear the snickers from the civilians about know-it-all Hoover and his flying circus.

In order to redeem myself in front of the entire base, I tried to think of something I could do to make up for my boondoggle. I remembered that the flight engineers had informed everyone that the N-9-M could not be rolled or looped.

I flew away from the base for a few minutes and practiced just that. Then I returned and put the plane through its paces.

Showing everyone maneuvers they didn't think possible with the wing provided me a bit of redemption, but I still ate humble pie for days on end after the incident. Especially when Jack and Chuck proceeded to make beautiful takeoffs in the N-9-M.

Jack Ridley was a technical whiz from the plains of Oklahoma. His native twang and squeaky, high-pitched voice were unmistakable. He wasn't a robust man, but with weathered skin and his ever-present cigarette, Jack had the appearance of a Western cowboy.

Ridley studied under a famous Hungarian aerodynamics expert, Theodore Von Karman. He knew the X-1 better than a mother knows her firstborn.

Despite his expertise, the research team from NACA tended to speak down to Jack. And to Chuck and me.

Chuck said it was because they were jealous of the Air Force and were used to working with civilian test pilots who were far more cautious. Compared to them, we were young, eager, enthusiastic test pilots who flew and lived balls out. And Ridley was a technical genius. We represented the Air Force flight-test division and were proud of it.

In the midst of our flying duties at Muroc, Colleen Humrickhouse and I got married. She became my wife on September 17, 1947.

The ceremony was held in a chapel at Patterson Field in Dayton. Fellow test pilot Jim Fitzgerald, who was later killed during an approach to landing in the first T-33 that Lockheed built, was my best man. Several other flying buddies attended as well. Even though Glennis Yeager was in California with their older son, Donald, Chuck joined us with the youngest boy, six-month-old Mickey, moments after we tied the knot.

The wedding was marked by a rather amusing incident that neither Colleen nor I have ever forgotten. As the minister was reading a special biblical passage, I detected a rather pungent odor. I sniffed a couple of times and then looked right into the eyes of Jim Fitzgerald. He had also gotten a whiff.

We both knew someone had cut a giant stinker. Fitz started to crack up, and I had a difficult time keeping a straight face. Colleen shot me a look that nearly brought me back to my senses. Then she smelled the odor as well.

There I was in the midst of holy matrimony, grinning along with my bride and the best man. Later, we decided the preacher had to be the culprit. Every time he moved with that large robe of his, the odor made another pass through the room.

Thanks to Chuck Yeager, Colleen and I had an interesting honeymoon, too. We drove across country from Dayton to Muroc with two chaperons, six-month-old Mickey and his father, Chuck. We were quite a foursome in Chuck's black '47 Ford coupe.

During my driving shift, I nearly fell asleep. Money was tight, so instead of finding a motel, I pulled the car off the road in a level, grassy area in the middle of Kansas. At the first ray of light, Colleen and I were surprised to learn that we had spent the first night of our honeymoon in a graveyard. I'm sure sleeping on a damp blanket in a graveyard wasn't quite what she envisioned as romantic.

But it was little Mickey who made the trip interesting. Colleen remembers, "He never caused us a bit of trouble. In fact I had never seen a happier, more cheerful baby. Later we learned the reason for the steady smile and the occasional stream of hiccups along the way. The Karo syrup Chuck's mom had mixed with water and canned milk for the trip had somehow fermented. The baby was sloshed!"

During this time, Chuck Yeager and I had the opportunity to meet Henry "Hap" Arnold, the chief of staff of the Air Corps in 1947. General Arnold was the big boss during World War II. He was the man who gave Jimmy Doolittle the assignment for the famous Tokyo raid.

Meeting Hap Arnold was like meeting God himself. I was so in awe of him that I could hardly speak the whole time we were together.

Listening to General Arnold inspired Chuck and me. His words of encouragement about the X-1 program made us even more determined to see it through to success.

The head of the NACA team at Muroc was a man named Walt Williams. He was a fast-talking, heavyset, medium-height fellow who wasn't all that thrilled to be working with us. He and the other NACA officials made life difficult for the three junior officers the military had brought into the fray.

We tried to ignore their snide comments. We were honored to be a part of the X-1 project and were determined to succeed.

The first nonpowered flights in the X-1 were designed to familiarize Chuck with the aircraft. After being dropped at twenty-five thousand feet, he was to glide back and land on the lake bed.

In early August, Chuck climbed into the aircraft and waited for the drop signal. I decided to see him up close and personal in my chase plane while he was dangling from the B-29 over the Mojave Desert. In a *Cleveland Magazine* article, Chuck is quoted as saying:

> I was going over my checklist when that damned Hoover buzzed me. He flew by so close that his jet exhaust almost knocked me loose from the B-29. I was rocking and swaying, scared to death.
>
> "Hoover, you bastard," I called out. I was really hot. I said, "If this thing carried guns, I'd shoot your ass out of the sky."
>
> Ol' Bob laughed. "Come and get me," he said. Well, I didn't try on this first glide flight. But on the third, when I saw him turning toward me, I turned into him, and we had a dogfight down to the deck, just like at Wright, except this time I almost stalled the damned X-1 waxing Bob's fanny true and good.

Several more test flights moved Chuck closer and closer to the magic Mach 1. As he increased his speeds, engineering problems surfaced. But Ridley and the others were able to resolve them.

It was the last day in August of 1947 when Chuck made the first powered flight in the X-1.

In *Yeager*, Chuck described his emotions:

> Anyone with brain cells would have to wonder what in hell he was doing in such a situation—strapped inside a live bomb that's about to be dropped out of a bomb bay. But risks are the spice of life, and this is the kind of moment that a test pilot lives for. The butterflies are fluttering, but you feed off fear as if it's a high energy candy bar.

After that flight, Chuck was rarin' to go. Unfortunately, everyone else wanted to take it slow.

While we were waiting for things to move on the X-1 program, I received another brief assignment.

I was to fly the new F-84 Thunderjet from Republic Aircraft Company's Long Island plant to Wright Field. My route was to have been over Pittsburgh and on into Dayton. Short of Pittsburgh, I realized that for some unknown reason I was short on fuel. I knew I couldn't make it to the Steel City.

I was flying over a mountainous and wooded area a hundred and fifty miles east of Pittsburgh when I had to attempt an emergency landing at a small airfield near Philipsburg, Pennsylvania. It had a very short landing area, but I was able to stop the plane safely.

I called Wright Field and explained that I was down, but the airplane was unscathed. A C-47 transport with fifty-gallon drums of fuel was flown in.

Because there was a light snow on the ground, I couldn't take on too much fuel because the weight would make takeoff difficult. My goal was to get to Pittsburgh, check everything thoroughly, and take on a full load of fuel.

The runway at Philipsburg was only about four thousand feet. This was far less than what is desirable for a "ground loving" F-84 airplane.

My biggest concern was with the drag I'd experience taking off in the snow. I knew I would have to put down just the right amount of flaps to manage it. My assessment was correct, and I was able to take off, but with little room to spare.

The plane ran out of fuel again after only about a hundred-mile distance. That forced me to land in Pittsburgh dead stick (without any power). Another load of fuel was added and I started to taxi away. I was still confused as to why I was running out of fuel until I glanced at the left wingtip. Fuel was pouring out of the wing of the airplane. It was pumping overboard as fast as it was going to the engine. I realized the pump had been reversed when it had been installed.

To achieve maximum mileage from my fuel, I took on fuel right at the edge of the runway. That worked and I made it to Wright Field where I still had power for landing.

Chuck Yeager and I met up there, and I accompanied him to see Colonel Boyd. Chuck wanted to vent his frustrations with the delays in the X-1 program. I wanted to talk about the F-84 flight.

That was necessary since I had heard that a fellow pilot told Colonel Boyd, "Hoover screwed up and got lost on the F-84 flight. That's why he ran out of fuel."

Clearing up the misunderstanding was important. If I got the chance, I'd give Colonel Boyd the true story.

At the proper time, Chuck and I stood before the colonel. Chuck was all set to relay his anger about the X-1 delays, but the colonel brought up my F-84 incident.

I attempted to correct his perception that I had gotten lost: "There was a fuel malfunction, sir. What you were told was false."

On and on I went. Chuck was impatient to grumble about the

X-1, but he couldn't get in a word edgewise. My words came fast and furious.

All at once I spit a false tooth that hit Colonel Boyd in the chest. Neither Chuck nor I dared grin. The colonel said nothing. I just reached down on the floor, picked up the tooth, put it in my pocket, and kept talking. The conversation ended shortly thereafter and Chuck never did get his chance to complain about the X-1 program.

Soon after that fruitless meeting with Colonel Boyd, Chuck reached .94 Mach. The X-1 experienced a loss of pitch control and the elevator ceased to be effective. Jack Ridley was able to design a controllable stabilizer, and Chuck was finally cleared to attempt faster speeds.

The flight on October 14, 1947, was a smooth one. I knew Chuck was pushing the envelope. He was ready to make history. In the chase plane, I listened carefully to Chuck's dialogue with Jack Ridley, who was flying nearby in the B-29 mother ship for the X-1.

"Hey, Ridley, that Machmeter is acting screwy. It just went off the scale."

As soon as Chuck said that, we all knew he had broken the sound barrier. I hadn't heard it, but those on the ground heard what they said sounded like thunder in the distance. Charles "Chuck" Yeager had flown into the history books. He had broken the sound barrier, traveling at more than 700 mph (1.07 Mach).

From my plane, I took the very first photographs of the diamond-shaped shock waves from the exhaust plume behind the X-1. Those pictures were on President Harry Truman's desk the next day.

That sharp, double crack as the X-1 broke through the sound barrier triggered the dawn of the space age. Other than Wilbur and Orville Wright's first flight and Charles Lindbergh's epic journey across the Atlantic, it was the most significant of aviation achievements. If not for that breakthrough, we would have been stymied in the quest to explore outer space. Neil Armstrong's voice may never have been heard on the surface of the moon twenty-two years later.

II

Broken Legs

One of the great disappointments in my life is that I never flew the X-1.

Just a month after Chuck Yeager's successful record-breaking flight, I got into serious trouble when the engine of an F-84 Thunderjet failed and caught fire high over the Antelope Valley. I called a Mayday and gave my location.

The aircraft was diving out of control because the push-pull rods to the flight controls had burned away. I would have to bail out with the plane in a steep dive at a high speed.

I pulled what we called the "next-of-kin handles" on the ejection seat, but they would not fire the seat. Quickly, I unfastened the safety harness and oxygen hose. Seconds later, after jettisoning the canopy, I was sucked out of the cockpit and my body slammed into the tail.

I hit with tremendous force on the back of my legs at the knees. My body buckled and my head hit my kneecaps. Fortunately, the rubber oxygen mask I was wearing gave my face some protection.

The blow to my head left me stunned, and only the rush of air from free-falling revived me to consciousness. I pulled the rip cord on the parachute. It was pure instinct.

My parachute was not damaged, but high winds were blowing dust. I floated to the ground miles away from the burning, crashed plane. Certain that my legs were broken, I dreaded impact with the ground. But by the time I touched down, the pain was so great that I must have been in shock. I did not even feel the brunt of the hard landing.

On the ground, the strong winds kept the parachute inflated and dragged me across the desert sagebrush. Each time I would try to pull the risers to spill the chute, a gust of wind would reinflate it. I'd be dragged across the ground. Each time the pain in my legs felt as if I were hit with a bullet. The parachute finally caught on a large sagebrush and collapsed.

I lay back on the ground, grateful to be alive. I soon realized, however, that I was alone in the desert with two broken legs and multiple facial injuries. I also knew that if I wasn't rescued before dark, I would have to deal with below-freezing temperatures.

I couldn't remember if Muroc ground control had acknowledged the Mayday prior to the bailout. I could see airplanes circling the smoke column from the burning wreckage. They had no way of knowing the plane was ten or fifteen miles east of my position. The base might have assumed that I hadn't been successful in getting out of the airplane. If that was the case, they would not even search for me.

The condition of my legs was frightening. I was sure I would lose both of them since the throbbing pain grew more unbearable as the hours passed.

I kept my eyes glued alternately to the sky and to the surrounding terrain. I also watched the sun sink farther into the western horizon while realizing that I couldn't even crawl to find protection from the cold when nightfall came.

I lay there on the desert sand, watching and waiting. Just before dark, I heard the sound of a truck approaching. A ranch hand in an old pickup had seen the burning airplane go down. Then he had seen my parachute. Because of the vast desert terrain it had taken him hours to find me. He was a welcome sight. I'll never forget his kindness.

The cowboy lifted me into the truck and drove me to the Antelope Valley Hospital. Despite my pleas, and a few choice curse words, the hospital staff wouldn't treat me. They were afraid they wouldn't get paid since I was military. Orderlies therefore placed me on a stretcher and wheeled me into an isolated hall without any treatment. By this time, I was in too much pain and too exhausted to protest their refusal to treat me.

Eventually an elderly nurse said to hell with the staff and gave me a shot of morphine. I was grateful for her kindness, but the pain was so intense that the medicine gave me no relief.

Officials at Muroc were notified of my condition and location. A War II ambulance was dispatched to transport me to the small hospital at the base. The trip was excruciating. Every little bump in the road sent searing pain to both legs.

After X rays were performed, I was told that only one leg was broken. I couldn't believe it because of the severe pain in both legs. Technicians did not share my concern. Only the left leg was placed in a cast from the ankle to the hip.

Colleen had been contacted and arrived shortly after I was brought in. I wasn't very good company since even the strongest narcotic gave me no relief from the extreme pain.

A short time later reinforcements arrived—Chuck Yeager and Pancho Barnes. Pancho was wearing a heavy black coat. "How are you feeling, you dumb SOB?" Pancho asked. "Pretty damn miserable," I replied. Pancho reached into her coat pocket and pulled out a bottle of whiskey. She thrust it into my hands: "The GD doctors don't know how to relieve pain; take a slug of this."

Colleen and I had only been married two months. I could tell she didn't know what to think about Pancho's raw language. I took a modest drink from the bottle. Pancho pushed the bottle back at me. I took another, more enthusiastic swig. She then put the bottle to her lips for a healthy drink and passed it to Chuck. We continued to pass it around until it was empty. By then, pain was a thing of the past. Colleen just looked on in amazement.

Colleen told me later that the accident made her more aware of the dangers of being a test pilot:

> "When Bob broke his legs, it really hit me that bad things could happen. Before that I didn't think too much about it. Test pilots don't look at the danger and never talk about it, but when he got hurt, I was really scared.
> "After that, I planned his funeral so that if something happened I would be ready. I never stood around by the door or sat near the phone waiting for bad news, but I was always prepared for the worst."

Dr. John Stapp was famous for his extensive research on high-speed acceleration and deceleration sled tests. He visited me while I was laid up at the hospital.

Those high-risk tests were conducted in the late 1940s and early 1950s to discover a means of producing safe ejection seats.

The sleds had rocket motors mounted on them for propulsion. Engineers would propel the sleds along railroad-track sections. The goal was to develop an ejection seat that had zero-altitude safety capability.

If a pilot who was about to crash ejected near the ground, the propulsion in the seat would send the pilot high enough to get a full-blossom opening of the parachute. We all respected John's courage because he rode the sleds himself.

I appreciated it when John stopped by the hospital. After looking over my injuries, he advised me to get on crutches and move about, fearing inaction would cause problems later on. Each time I tried walking, however, the leg not in a cast was so painful my knee would buckle.

Shortly thereafter, I was driven back across country to Wright Field in Dayton for more examinations. New X rays revealed that the right leg was indeed broken at the knee. I was put in a cast. After six weeks of rehabilitation, I was cleared to get back in the cockpit. By that time, I had been replaced by another pilot on the X-1 program.

After I was given a clean bill of health, I resumed my test-pilot duties at Wright Field.

I was assigned to a program that tested large ramjets on the wing-tips of a P-80. Since the ramjet engines performed more efficiently at high speeds, they could be ignited with much less chance of a backfire and fireball.

While testing the P-80, I wore a modified leather helmet. It protected against impact with the canopy when flying at high speeds in rough air.

That helmet was a result of a trip to a sporting goods store. There I bought a football helmet, one with holes in it. A visit to the parachute department at the base provided me with the snaps I needed, and I put those attach points on my regular leather helmet.

Before putting that helmet on, I snapped it to the football helmet so the top of my head would be well protected. I painted the helmet yellow.

When I was test-flying the P-80, I knew there had been several recent fatalities in the plane. For some unknown reason, canopies had come off at speeds above five hundred miles per hour. Pilots lost control and crashed without bailing out. Many of them were found decapitated.

On one particular flight in the P-80, I needed to turn on the valves that controlled the fuel flow to the ramjets. They were located down low on the floor of the cockpit, so I reached down to turn the valves.

At that very moment, the canopy blew off along with my helmet. The noise and buffeting were almost unbearable, but I managed to keep control of the P-80 and land safely.

When the ground crew located the canopy, they found yellow paint on it. The engineers realized that the canopy was dishing sidewise into the cockpit, striking the pilot's head. We lost my close friends Jim Little and Martin Smith that way. If my head had not been down, my scalp would have been where the yellow paint was. I would have been another fatality.

That near-miss experience was one in a long line of situations where luck prevailed. There was no other explanation.

Knowledge of the canopy problem prompted the engineers to study the situation further. A triangular piece of metal was fitted on each side of the windshield, preventing the canopy from dishing into the cockpit.

Not all of my time at Wright Field in 1948 was spent testing airplanes. Many evenings were spent at the officers' club.

Prior to War II, junior officers could socialize, but they weren't allowed to reserve certain tables. A directive from Gen. Jimmy Doolittle changed all that.

One Saturday evening, I called and requested a section normally reserved by generals. At eight o'clock sharp, a group of test pilots and I took our seats.

We encountered a few raised eyebrows and sour looks from those who wanted no change in the caste system. But one general came over to the table and commended us for our spirit. He even joined us for a drink.

In those days, we had to bring our own booze. Before the night was over, empty whiskey bottles were scattered everywhere. To intensify our fun, pilots would light a match, toss it into an empty bottle, reposition the cork, and then have a miniwar, shooting the loud, exploding corks at one another until it was closing time.

During this time I met General Doolittle. He landed at Wright Field in his own personal North American B-25 Mitchell.

It was a twin-engine bomber similar to the one he flew in the daring raid against Tokyo in April of 1942. It featured a paneled glass nose where the navigator and bombardier were positioned.

The view from there had to have been panoramic. To take it all in, General Doolittle had positioned a comfortable easy chair right in the middle of the nose.

Later on, I would be honored to become good friends with Jimmy Doolittle. The accomplishments of the great man were many, but four especially stand out.

American military efforts to advance aviation in the 1920s lagged behind other countries'. It was civilian pilots such as General Doolittle who made certain that aircraft flew at faster and faster speeds.

Air races provided rich opportunities for aviation advancement. In 1925, then Lieutenant Doolittle won the prestigious Schneider Trophy when he flew a Navy Curtiss R3C-2 biplane 232 miles per hour. The next day, he increased that speed to 245 miles per hour, a world record. That triggered national enthusiasm for aviation technology, a contribution that cannot be underestimated.

The general was the first pilot to successfully fly blind using instruments. That flight changed the course of aviation. Until that time, pilots couldn't fly in bad weather since their seat-of-the-pants technique wouldn't work.

Prior to the outbreak of World War II, Jimmy Doolittle had talked the Shell Oil Company into producing high-octane fuel. He used it in his racing ventures because it provided peak performances for his airplanes.

During the war, German and Italian pilots could not get maximum performance from their aircraft because they lacked high-octane fuel. Our pilots had a significant advantage since one-hundred-octane fuel provided maximum capability, and because of Doolittle, we had access to it.

Overshadowing these important feats was General Doolittle's remarkable adventure in leading a band of bombers over Tokyo in April of 1942. It came after our country's armed forces had been embarrassed at both Pearl Harbor and the Philippines.

Even though the damage inflicted on the enemy by Doolittle and his squadron was slight, the mission inspired U.S. fighting forces all over the world. Sixteen B-25 Mitchells had finally counterpunched the Japanese. There was no question now that the Americans were determined to win the war.

General Doolittle was a warm, friendly man, but his demeanor concealed a fierce inner drive that compelled him to be such a great leader. He commanded great respect even though he was slight in stature. On one occasion, he had his picture taken between Barry Goldwater and me, and I was amazed that we both towered over him. His size never bothered him. Doolittle's strong voice and authoritative nature made anyone who spoke with him pay close attention.

I saw General Doolittle frequently in later years. The Doolittle Raiders, who had been with him on the Tokyo raid, had a reunion every year. They kept a special bottle of brandy that they set aside for use in the future. Each Raider had a cup, and when one died, his cup was turned upside down. The understanding was that the last survivor would drink the bottle of brandy in tribute to his deceased comrades.

I was always invited to General Doolittle's birthday parties at his home in Monterey. They had a Doolittle chapter of the Quiet Birdman there, and I would attend those meetings. My friend John Myers and I would collect a group of Jimmy's friends and go up there just to see him. I never lost my appreciation for the opportunity to sit alongside my boyhood hero.

General Doolittle also kept an office near the Los Angeles airport until he was in his late seventies. We'd have lunch occasionally. He kept a little bound book in his pocket that he used for taking notes. He was as deaf then as I am now. He'd write down in that book what he *thought* people said and then what they *actually* said. I now know what he was talking about since the same thing has happened to me.

One time, Colleen was helping me learn to play tennis. I'd miss a shot, and she'd yell "dumbshit" at me. That went on for about fifteen minutes. I was getting madder by the minute. Finally, I was about to explode.

Colleen noticed my face was beet red. She called me up to the net.

"What's the matter, Bob, you all right?"

"I would be if you'd quit yelling at me."

"I'm just trying to help you. You really need to remember, bounce-hit, bounce-hit." General Doolittle loved that story.

Although he was honored many, many times, the general was especially proud that the highest award given by the Society of Experimental Test Pilots was the James Doolittle Award. I treasure a picture of him and me taken at one of the meetings of the Society. It hangs on my wall. Jimmy wrote, "To Bob Hoover, pilot extraordinaire and friend exemplary. Sincerely, J. H. Doolittle."

While based at Wright Field, I became acquainted with a great aviator named Jackie Cochran. She sent me a letter inviting me to fly a modified P-51 for her in the Thompson Trophy Unlimited Air Races in Cleveland. Jackie owned a cosmetics company, and she wanted publicity for her new line of perfume.

We never made a deal. Instead she hired Bill Odom, a pilot who had set some records and had a bit of a name with the media. He had told Jackie that he had a great deal of time in fighters. In fact, he had practically none.

Jackie's pilot won the Sohio pre-Thompson race the day before the main event. Prior to that race, he told me the Thompson race would be his finale. He would leave racing to "the fighter pilots."

I asked him point-blank how much time he had in fighters. "Thirteen hours" was the reply.

Not surprisingly, the Thompson race *was* the pilot's last. He was killed when he lost control at one of the pylons and crashed into a house.

In addition to Odom, two people in the house were killed in the accident. That tragedy ended air racing at Cleveland and other air shows for many years. They would not come back into prominence until the early 1960s at Reno.

I'm glad I had the chance to know Jackie Cochran. She was an amazing woman. An orphan who didn't even know her age, she became one of the great aviators of our time. Her unbridled courage and spirit of adventure were emblematic of many great aviators I have known.

Jackie Cochran and Amelia Earhart had been the first two women ever to enter the Bendix Transcontinental Air Race. Jackie won it in 1938. She held more speed, distance, and altitude records than any other man or woman during her career and was the first woman to fly faster than the speed of sound and then twice the speed of sound. She also was the founder of the WASPs (Women's Auxiliary Service Pilots) in War II.

I met up with Jackie again after I joined North American Aviation in 1951. She was married to former Howard Hughes financier Floyd Odlum. They invited Colleen and me over to their home near Palm Springs. Floyd owned the Atlas Corporation, which owned Convair, Canadair, and several other large corporations.

Colleen will never forget that first weekend:

> "The first time we were ever invited to Jackie Cochran's house in Indio [near Palm Springs], it was a big deal because we were in our twenties and there were all kinds of senators and important people there. It was New Year's Eve. She and her wealthy husband had quite a lavish estate complete with several guesthouses. Bob and I stayed in one, and when we went to dinner, I locked the doors. Later, I realized I'd forgotten the keys. When I asked Jackie about them, she laughed and told me there weren't any. 'You locked the door?' she said in her accent. 'Nobody locks the door in the desert.' I was so embarrassed when they had to get a locksmith to open the door."

In spite of our social bumble, Jackie Cochran remained a special friend, right up until her death in 1980. We visited their home often and each time was an adventure.

Chuck and Glennis Yeager were also frequent houseguests there. Chuck was Jackie's mentor and assisted her with many of her record flights.

I met Edward Teller, the father of the hydrogen bomb, at Jackie's home. Listening to him talk about the principles of nuclear engineering was mind-boggling.

Jack Ridley's mentor, aerodynamicist Theodore Von Karman, was also a guest when we were there. Ambassadors, cabinet members, and senators were frequent visitors. It was an exciting place where politics and world affairs were table talk.

One man who was well versed on these subjects was George Allen, a respected member of President Eisenhower's kitchen cabinet. He told me that he'd sit on the side of the bathtub in Ike's bathroom at the White House and listen to the president's woes while he shaved. George even took me over to his nearby home in a beautiful cove in La

Quinta. He had a swimming pool in his bedroom. He showed me the room where the president stayed when he came to relax and play golf.

On one occasion, Floyd Odlum invited me to attend one of the most unusual meetings I've ever experienced.

"I'm having a meeting of the board of directors for the Atlas Corporation," Floyd told me, "and I'd like for you to attend."

"I don't know much about corporate affairs," I responded.

"A young man like you could learn a lot. We'll have breakfast here in the dining room and then you'll stay for the meeting."

"But I'd be an outsider. The others might resent that."

However, realizing that his mind was made up, I headed for our guesthouse and a good night's rest.

"Oh, and wear your swimming suit," Floyd said as I was leaving.

I wondered whether he was kidding, but I came to breakfast the next morning in swimming trunks and a sport shirt. All the board members were dressed in similar attire. After breakfast, we stepped into the huge heated pool. Later I learned that many of the Atlas Corporation board meetings were held in the pool because the over-90-degree temperature soothed Floyd's debilitating arthritis.

The meeting dealt with questions about various oil leases that had been purchased in Argentina. Employees of the company stood on the deck beside the pool briefing the board with flow charts and graphs.

While all this was going on, the board members and I sat in inner tubes in the warm, crystal clear water. When refreshments were served, I decided then and there that this was how working in the corporate world ought to be.

Besides Jackie Cochran, another great aviator of that time was the irrepressible Mr. Hughes. I was never actually able to meet him, but that was my fault. I stood on the ramp at Edwards Air Force Base (formerly Muroc Air Force Base—renamed as of December 1949) not twenty feet from the legend when we were both preparing to launch in the late 1940s.

At that time, he was testing a twin-engine airplane of his own design. Even though he was the head of his aviation company, Howard Hughes was out there on the edge of high risk.

To this day, I wish I had walked over to his plane and introduced myself. I'm not a shy person by any means, but somehow I just couldn't bring myself to approach him.

Of all of Hughes's achievements, perhaps his design of the incredible Spruce Goose was the most ingenious. Later on I had an opportunity to tour that gargantuan flying boat, but it came under unusual circumstances.

After War II, Germany's Air Force was essentially extinct. When they resumed operations in the midfifties, their military sent a cadre of officers over to the United States to be checked out in the latest aircraft.

Many of the German officers were being trained at Williams Air Force Base near Phoenix. I was there to perform an aerobatic routine in connection with the preview of the film *The Hunters*, starring Robert Mitchum and Jill St. John.

I had some extra time prior to the preview, so I went to the officers' club dining room for breakfast. Sitting at a table was an officer in a German uniform. I couldn't help but notice him because the man's appearance was so disturbing. He had no eyelids, ears, or nose. His teeth were exposed because there were no lips to cover them. A lop-sided mustache had been fluffed in all directions in an effort to cover other facial scars.

I approached the man I would come to know as Macky Steinhoff. Later, I would find out he was a colonel in the German Air Force.

I asked if I could join him. He looked up at me and said, "I'd be pleased if you would."

Most people might think the last thing a man in his condition would want to do is talk about his injuries. I have seldom found that to be true.

"Boy, you must have been in one hell of a flamer," I said.

"I was," he said. "It happened while I was taking off in an Me 262 [German twin-engine jet]. Your bombers bombed the runway, and when one of my wheels hit a bomb crater, the jet engine on that side dragged on the runway and caught fire. I managed to get airborne, but crashed into a dense forest. There was a huge fireball when the plane exploded."

After the conversation, Macky Steinhoff and I became close friends. I learned that he was a decorated pilot who was credited with shooting down more than ninety Allied aircraft during the war.

Macky came to the Paris Air Show every other year, and he'd always come by the North American chalet for a visit. With each year, I could see an improvement in Macky's cosmetic condition. He finally got his lips rebuilt, and further plastic surgery resulted in reconstructed ears and finally a nose. But he still had no eyelids.

One year he didn't make it to the Paris Air Show. "There is a doctor in England, a plastic surgeon, who is the only man in the world who can reconstruct eyelids," he wrote. "He is going to retire and I'm going to be his last operation. It will take place at the same time as the Paris Air Show, and so I'll be in the hospital."

Sometime later Macky wrote me again. He was going to be in Los Angeles with Claudius Dornier, son of a famous German aircraft-company founder. They built airplanes during World War I and bombers and night fighters for the Luftwaffe all during World War II. They are still building commercial airplanes today. But in the old days they were most famous for designing and building huge flying boats. The DX-10 was one of them. It had ten engines, one of the largest planes at that time ever to get in the air.

Macky wrote me, "When we're in Los Angeles, could you arrange a visit to the Spruce Goose?"

The Spruce Goose had been built by Howard Hughes as part of an $18-million government contract awarded in the early to mid 1940s. German U-boats were blasting Allied shipping, and Hughes persuaded the military to permit him to build a flying boat under the code name HK-1 Hercules.

When the government refused to let Hughes use strategic materials (aluminum), he decided wood would work. He sent his engineers to forests all over the West.

The Goose would not be completed until 1946. Hughes finally flew it at an altitude of one hundred feet for some sixty seconds over the harbor at Long Beach, California. He was not happy with the two-hundred-ton seaplane's performance and never flew it again. Howard Hughes kept his prized Goose in a cloak of secrecy. Few people had ever seen it. I knew it would not be easy to arrange a visit.

Nevertheless, I called the president of Hughes Corporation. He said, "Bob, I have to tell you that *I've* never even seen the Spruce Goose."

I figured if the president of Hughes couldn't get in to see the plane, I didn't have a chance.

Nevertheless, I got a surprising phone call within a few days with specific instructions on how we would see the Spruce Goose. Macky, whose eyelids showed vast improvement, and Claudius Dornier accompanied me to the harbor at Long Beach where a black Buick was to pick us up.

It was clandestine mystery stuff. When I saw the car, the man behind the wheel simply gestured for me to follow him. Pretty soon we were in a maze of barbed-wire fences, headed for a huge warehouse.

The warehouse building was actually shaped like an airplane. When we arrived, we had to pass through a "clean" room. This was similar to the ones they had near the Apollo manufacturing areas and all the other space activities. We covered our heads and put on booties, gloves, and a smock.

Later, we laughed about the whole procedure. We were going to look at an airplane, not perform heart surgery.

My first glance at the Spruce Goose stunned me. The plane was huge. We saw that they were maintaining it so that it could still be flown. Warm oil ran through the idle engines twenty-four hours a day.

The one-of-a-kind plane was raised slightly out of the water. It was in immaculate condition.

All of us were permitted to sit where Hughes had sat when he piloted the plane. Macky, who later retired from the German Air Force as chief of staff with four stars, and Claudius were mesmerized.

Claudius simply couldn't believe how big the Spruce Goose was. "We've built some big planes," he explained, "but nothing close to this."

The size of that aircraft was astounding. I'm over six feet tall, and I could stand straight when I walked inside one of the *wings*.

PART

IV

TEST-PILOT TERROR

Bob Hoover starting the legendary Reno Air Show and Races competition. His words "Gentlemen, you have a race" are world-famous. *(Paul Neuman)*

Bob Hoover (fourth from right, front row) and fellow prisoners held at Stalag I near Barth, Germany, during World War II.

Bob Hoover stands in front of the Martin B-26 Marauder he rescued from the beach at the Messina Straights in Sicily during World War II. Hoover was awarded the Distinguished Flying Cross for his remarkable feat. *(Air Force, 1943)*

Bob Hoover and German aircraft designer Willy Messerschmitt. *(Aerospace Industry Association)*

Bob Hoover and German fighter pilot ace Eric Hartman. In World War II, Hartman shot down 352 Allied planes. *(Baron Volkmer)*

Members of the X-1 team that was responsible for the breaking of the sound barrier in 1947. They included flight engineer Ed Swindell, backup pilot Bob Hoover, B-29 pilot Bob Cardinas, X-1 pilot Chuck Yeager, Bell engineer Dick Frost, and Air Force engineer Jack Ridley. *(Air Force, 1947)*

Members of the Thunderbirds Air Force demonstration team salute
Bob Hoover before the start of his performance in the P-51. *(Air Force)*

Captain Bob Hoover, Charley Hillard, Art Scholl, Harold Krier, and
Bob Herrenden, members of the 1966 United States Aerobatic Team at
the Moscow Air Show.

General James Doolittle and former United States Senator Barry Goldwater present Bob Hoover with an Air Force Association award. *(Air Force Association)*

Bob and Colleen Hoover with Charles Lindbergh, the first man to fly across the Atlantic, and Neil Armstrong, the first man to land on the moon. This photo was taken shortly after Armstrong returned from space. Lindbergh was being inducted as an honorary member of the Society of Experimental Test Pilots. *(Tom Smith)*

Avid aviator and hotel tycoon Barron Hilton with Bob Hoover. He sponsored the Barron Hilton Cup, the largest soaring competition in the world. *(Dixie Walker)*

Bob Hoover with famous golfer and pilot Arnold Palmer. *(Rick Grissom)*

Bob Hoover, longtime friend and air-show announcer Jim Driskell, and actor Cliff Robertson. Robertson said Hoover performed aerobatic maneuvers "like a mad musician at the organ." *(Dixie Walker)*

The famous Bob Hoover P-51 on fire after a demonstration at Marysville, Ohio, in 1984.

Famed attorney F. Lee Bailey and Air Show aerobatic stars Steve
Oliver, Sean D. Tucker, Leo Loudenslager, and Dave Weimann show
support for Bob Hoover during his dogfight with the FAA.
(Dave Weimann, Oklahoma City, 1995)

Bob Hoover performing his famous one-wheel landing at the first Reno
National Air Races and Air Show in 1964. *(Paul Neuman)*

12

Civilian Bob

You can take this Allison time bomb and shove it right up your ****!''

That was my parting comment to the nonaviator general manager of flight test at the Allison Division of General Motors after twelve months on the job as a test pilot.

The position with Allison had begun in January of 1949, a year and a half before the Korean conflict broke out. However, the notion of trading the military way of life for civilian Skivvies had been on my mind for at least a year.

By the end of 1948, I was almost twenty-seven years old. I had served in my country's military for almost a decade. I was proud of my military service, but I was starting to consider what the future held for Colleen and me.

In those days, my salary of $420 a month stretched a lot further than it would today. Nevertheless, Colleen and I lived modestly.

Col. Albert Boyd told me in December of 1948 that Allison was in need of a test pilot. I was intrigued with the idea. Colonel Boyd recommended me to them.

After a brief round of interviews, we came to an agreement. I would become one of the two pilots testing Allison engines at Weir Cook Airport in Indianapolis, Indiana.

Leaving the military was not easy, but I would take a lot of it with me. The friendships I'd made would last a lifetime, and the training I'd received was first-rate. I had been able to fly many different types of aircraft, including captured German and Japanese planes, all the War

II aircraft, and the first jets our country manufactured. My days in the military were over, and I would sorely miss them.

Colleen and I said our good-byes, collected our belongings, and moved to Indianapolis, Indiana.

At that time, Allison manufactured engines for jet aircraft for the Air Force and Navy. I was responsible for testing those engines at all altitudes. The first tests involved the J-35 axial-flow turbine. It was being produced for use in the Air Force Republic F-84 Thunderjet. This plane was similar to the one that had bitten me just two year earlier.

When I took the job, I was told I would be the highest-paid twenty-seven-year-old at General Motors. The pay was $850 per month.

The other test pilot at Allison was Jim Youngins. He had joined Allison in 1944.

I was a replacement for Chuck Brown, a longtime friend from my Air Force days. He had left the company to join North American Aviation. Ironically, I would join North American about a year and a half later when Chuck Brown lost his life in an in-flight breakup of an AJ-1.

At first, I was delighted with the new job. Not only was I flying many of the same airplanes I flew in the military, but even newer aircraft as well. I was also getting paid more than twice the salary I'd received as a lieutenant in the Air Force. Colleen and I thought we were rich.

Three months in, however, I missed the military. Not having the camaraderie of fellow pilots bothered me since there was no one other than Jim Youngins, who was not very social, who could talk my language.

Colleen and I also missed the many friends we'd made during the years in the military. I therefore considered reenlisting. I even contacted the Ninth Air Force Headquarters, but since the military was cutting back on personnel at the time, the die was cast.

After about six months with Allison, I realized that I was earning every dime they paid me. Many factors convinced me of that, not the least of which was the necessity to land the jets dead-stick because of engine failures and fires on a runway that was only five thousand feet long without overruns on either end.

At one end of that runway was an area we called the "tank barrier," which contained the first experimental approach-lighting system developed in our country by the FAA. At the other was a large clump of trees. Between the tank barrier and the trees we actually had only forty-five hundred feet on which to land. Squeezing those jets in that space wasn't easy, but Allison officials ignored complaints about the short landing area.

That approach-lighting system was wonderful, but it was tricky since the lights were mounted on steel crossbars that sat at the end of the runway. This created an intimidating obstacle that meant certain death if the plane ran into them. If a tank couldn't get through that steel barrier, then how could a test pilot survive to tell about it?

We ran the engines at excessive temperatures, way above the standards that would be used in normal operations of the aircraft, in order to determine maximum capability. Many of the engines failed.

On one occasion, we had been having difficulty with oil pressure on a J-35 engine. Don Nolan, the senior engineer, said he wanted to check the pressure before I conducted the next flight. His maintenance people had installed a different oil-pressure gauge. This one would give a definite readout on the exact pressure that was flowing into the engine rather than through the transducers.

I was garbed in my G suit ready to go, but I sat on a fire truck running board with my fingers in my ears while Don made the engine run-up. I happened to glance in the direction of the cockpit where he was sitting with the engine running wide-open.

I stood up when I noticed that Don was as pale as a sliced potato and had both hands covering his face. Then I saw the blood trickling through his fingers. I screamed at the fire truck people as I rushed up the ladder to turn off the engine.

The oil-pressure gauge had exploded. Slivers of glass had penetrated Don's face and eyes. I managed to help him out of the cockpit and into a waiting ambulance.

I accompanied Don to the hospital in my G suit. They called in an eye surgeon, who managed to save one of his eyes. That was a sad day for all of us, and I knew that it could just as easily have been me in that cockpit when the disaster occurred.

Close calls were the rule rather than the exception at Allison. On another occasion, I was assigned to the test program for the prototype of the straight-wing Grumman F-9-F. Three of those experimental airplanes called the Cougar were built.

Of the three prototypes, one had already been lost in flight test. Grumman Aircraft brought the second one to Indianapolis. Allison installed a new engine, and I was asked to evaluate the actual performance of the airplane.

I was briefed by the engineers before climbing into the cockpit. When I was seated, the project engineer showed me the instrumentation switches to use to record data. He left for the control tower so we would be in direct communication while the flight was under way.

The test card dictated that I was to achieve maximum speed as close to the ground as possible. My mission was to obtain this at maximum exhaust temperature with full power.

As I started to taxi out in the F-9-F, I waved to my fellow test pilot Jim Youngins. He waved vigorously back at me. As I headed down the taxiway, other ground crew were waving just as enthusiastically.

I thought they were just giving me a great send-off, but then I happened to look back and see Jim. He had stopped waving and was sitting down on the taxiway. I knew something was wrong, so I stopped the plane. One of the maintenance people came over and told me that the external step was down. It could only be extended or retracted by ground personnel and could not be seen from the cockpit.

If the step had remained down, it could have ripped off and taken the tail with it, causing great tragedy. Jim probably saved my life that day.

After successfully completing the flight, I drove home. Just moments after entering our apartment, I received a phone call. Jim Youngins was dead. He had apparently suffered a heart attack shortly after returning home from Weir Cook Airport.

Two weeks earlier, Jim, who was just thirty-four years old, and I had undergone complete physicals. We had passed with flying colors. The physicians did warn us that flying at excessive altitudes could cause serious problems for us.

We didn't have pressurization in the test airplanes that we were flying, and we were using old oxygen masks from War II days. Those masks didn't have pressure breathing.

The altitudes we flew daily were in excess of forty thousand feet, and many times I was above forty-eight thousand feet. At the time, I wondered whether the high-altitude flying might have been a contributing factor in Jim's untimely death.

I regretted that I never had a chance to personally thank Jim for in all likelihood saving my life. He was a good man and I missed him.

I was now the only test pilot at Allison. I kept telling them the workload was too heavy, but my request that they hire another test pilot was never addressed.

During this time, I had an excessive number of dead-stick landings because of engine failure. I was flying high-risk missions with engines that were clearly experimental. Some of them were very scary rides. At times I would break out of an overcast with no power and feel fortunate even to find the airport. I'd shoot for it and then barely stop the plane before I crashed into one of the dreaded obstacles at the end.

Even though I was frustrated, I continued to accept every assignment given me. That included engine-testing for the Lockheed F-94 aircraft.

That plane was an Air Defense Command interceptor. It was a two-seater with room for a radar weapons technician in the backseat.

The F-94 was still in the design stages, so to simulate testing on their new engine, Allison engineers decided to take a T-33 and install an F-94 tail on it. The normal tail on a T-33 could not have handled the increased size and power, but the F-94 tail made that possible.

The flying G suit I wore to test the T-33 was constructed so that it inflated automatically. It pressed against my stomach, thighs, and calves whenever I went into a sharp turn or pulled out of a dive. Otherwise, centrifugal force would have pulled all the blood from my brain, causing a lack of oxygen. Blackout and unconsciousness would have followed.

Forced oxygen was critical when pilots got up around forty-five thousand feet and above. At that altitude, the oxygen supply could be a real problem. That's exactly what happened to me in the T-33 with the big engine.

On this particular flight, I remember talking to the control tower. They apparently could tell I was in trouble and needed assistance.

In command that day at Weir Cook Airport was a civilian by the name of Joe Clark:

> I remember Bob Hoover because he was a first-class pilot with a great deal of experience. On this particular occasion, we could tell in the squirrel cage [tower] that he was in trouble. His voice kept going in and out, and it was obvious that he was having a difficult time breathing. We kept him in sight with our binoculars [radar didn't come in until 1953] and then did our best to help him down. To his credit, he was able to land the plane safely even though he was very disoriented.

Over the years, Joe and men like him have saved my hide many times. There's not a test pilot alive who hasn't had a close call, and the men in the tower have helped us all dodge the bullet.

Shortly after that incident, I experienced engine failure in another airplane at very high altitude. I had a great deal of trouble saving it. That was followed closely by what would become my last test flight for Allison.

I was testing an F-9-F when I had a flameout (engine failure). The fire warning lights came on, and I didn't know if or when the plane might blow up.

I contemplated bailing out. That was no easy matter in those days since we still didn't have ejection seats that worked properly.

Since test pilots are paid to stay with the plane as long as possible and to save it at all costs, I shut down the engine. Fortunately the fire was extinguished.

As I approached the runway, I felt I was playing it awfully close. There's a thin line between having enough speed and altitude to bring the plane in and being able to stop it in a short distance.

That day I was very "short" and just barely able to get to the runway. Another close call had not left me in the best of moods.

That same afternoon, I tested a new engine in an Air Force prototype F-84. It called for having the fuel heated just as if it were involved in a desert operation where the outside temperature could be as high as 134 degrees. The temperature in the fuel tank would be considerably more. To simulate that condition, the fuel was heated to the exaggerated temperatures.

When the proper temperature was reached in the tanks, I took off. As soon as I reached my altitude above an overcast I climbed through at thirteen thousand feet, I began flying in one direction for a five-minute stretch to record the necessary data.

Suddenly, the engine failed. There were no navigational aids to tell me where I was, so I headed for the area where I thought Weir Cook was located. I flew down at a high rate of speed so that I would have a great deal of speed when I broke out of the overcast. This would permit me to extend the glide if I didn't find the airport immediately.

The plane popped out of the overcast at about ten thousand feet. I could see the airport. Remembering the morning's close call when I had just barely made it to the runway, I maintained the speed until I knew I could make the runway safely.

With that extra speed, I realized that if I braked any harder on the concrete surface, I would blow the tires and head right into the tank barrier. I made a millisecond decision to take the plane off the runway and onto the smooth grass. I could hit the brakes on that surface, not blow the tires, and hopefully get the plane stopped in time.

It worked like a charm. Relieved, I climbed down from the cockpit to a warm welcome from all of the members of the ground crew.

When I turned around, however, the dour-faced general manager of flight test was standing nose-to-nose with me. Without ever asking why I took the plane off the runway, he began to blast my performance.

"You realize the nosewheel tire is flat?" he began.

"Yes," I said, "It just went flat. I must have hit a rock in the grass after I took the plane off the runway."

"Well, that's what I want to talk to you about. That was terrible judgment on your part. Why didn't you stay there on the runway?"

At that moment, I knew that even if I explained my reasoning to the poor bastard, he would never understand. As he berated my judgment, I thought about the close call on the earlier flight, other recent near-disasters, and the loss of Jim Youngins and Allison's failure to replace him.

I had had enough. I wouldn't stand there and be persecuted by someone who had no idea of what test-flying was all about. His rude and unwarranted accusations ended up being the last straw for me at

Allison. I politely provided him with my "shove it right up your . . ." comment and walked away to an ovation from the ground crew.

Despite the problems with Allison, my time in Indianapolis was well spent. While living there, I renewed my acquaintance with the great aviator Roscoe Turner, whom I'd first met while a young, aspiring pilot at Berry Field in Nashville just prior to War II.

Turner was a legendary pilot who had performed in flying circuses, been a speed merchant, and raced in the Bendix and Thompson races. He also designed and built airplanes with enormous engines.

Always ones to experiment with aircraft, Roscoe Turner and Jimmy Doolittle and the other pioneers of racing were attaining more and more speed. The stock planes they raced may have been homebuilt or manufactured by small aircraft companies, but their planes flew faster than military airplanes. This contributed significantly to the advancement of aviation.

Roscoe Turner's flamboyance underscored his brilliance as an inventor. He was always experimenting with new designs for aircraft. I was amazed at his curiosity. He was always changing this or trying that in an effort to maximize the performance of an aircraft.

Mr. Turner was the first person to provide a parachute for an *airplane* instead of for the *pilot*. In the event of a failed engine, the parachute would open. The plane would simply fall from the sky to the ground in a straight vertical instead of gliding in for a landing.

During this time, Roscoe Turner had a fixed-base operation in Indianapolis where he serviced, leased, and chartered airplanes. He also had a flying school for would-be pilots.

C. F. "Fred" Roark, who worked at Allison welding aircraft engines and later founded his own engineering corporation, used to visit Mr. Turner's place of business. "He was a devil-may-care fellow, but he knew airplanes inside out," Fred says. "Everyone had huge respect for Roscoe Turner. He was a creative genius."

Turner was quite deaf by this time. Since there were no hearing aids in those days, people had to speak quite loudly for him to hear them.

Believing he had to respond in kind, Roscoe would literally yell. This became something of a problem, especially when he took Colleen and me out to his country club for dinner.

For the most part, we looked forward to visiting with him, but we would cringe when Roscoe began to tell dirty jokes. With his loud voice, everybody in the room was exposed to his off-color stories. We were embarrassed as could be, but if his jokes bothered anyone, they didn't show it.

In spite of that, I thoroughly enjoyed the time I spent with Roscoe. He was a flamboyant character right out of the adventure comic books. He drove a big old Packard with the spare wheels along the running board. His handlebar mustache was always waxed to perfection.

Roscoe Turner once asked me, "How many pilots have you known to have made a million dollars, lost it, and made it back?" I had to admit he was the only one I knew who could make that claim.

Roscoe Turner flew until an advanced age. He had a Douglas B-23, an old pre–World War II bomber, converted into a passenger airplane. He used it for charter work and his own personal use.

In my den at home, I have a picture of Roscoe Turner. He wrote, "To my fine feathered friend, Bob Hoover. May all your landings be good enough for you to walk away. Roscoe Turner."

After my altercation on the runway in Indianapolis with the Allison general manager of flight test, the company offered me the opportunity to move to Detroit and become a member of the corporate fleet of pilots for General Motors. The dollars and cents, future opportunities, and the potential to own an automobile dealership were certainly attractive. But I turned them down. I decided that I wanted to go to college and pursue not only an undergraduate degree, but a Ph.D. as well.

If, for some reason, I was unable to continue my work as a test pilot, I had no other career alternatives. With only a high school diploma, opportunities would be scarce. I therefore ventured back to my hometown of Nashville, Tennessee, and enrolled at George Peabody College, now a part of Vanderbilt University.

Peabody gave me credit for Air Force flight training as well as the test-pilot schools. That left me with just two years to complete the undergraduate studies. The president of the college expressed an interest in my teaching a new aviation course they had planned. Full professor's pay went with the teaching position. I could get my degree, teach a subject I enjoyed, live near my parents, and join my old Air National Guard squadron and continue flying military aircraft. I liked every aspect of this plan.

After a few months, however, I started to receive job offers to once again become a civilian test pilot.

I discussed those opportunities with Colleen. We both realized that if I took one of the jobs, I could still prepare myself for future employment. I would have to spend every waking hour studying engineering, manufacturing, and other facets of the aircraft industry, but I could do it.

Convair and Chance-Vaught were the first two companies to call, but I turned them down. Boeing Aircraft in Seattle was next to solicit my services. They had lost their chief test pilot when he was decapitated after the canopy came off during the testing of a B-47 bomber. I declined their offer since I didn't want to test bombers.

I recommended to them a friend of mine named Tex Johnston, who had been the chief test pilot at Bell Aircraft. He joined Boeing and was responsible for the success of many of their great airplanes. Tex brought fame to their first 707 transport and amazed the aviation world by "rolling" that huge aircraft over the skies of Seattle during the boat races at the Sea Fair.

When North American Aviation, located at Los Angeles International Airport, called, I was very enthused. Every one of their company's planes I had flown was top-notch. They included the T-6, the P-51, the P-82, and the B-25.

North American was looking for a test pilot because they had lost Al Conover and Chuck Brown during a test flight of the AJ-1 Navy bomber. Their offer for me to join them as an experimental engineering test pilot came in May of 1950.

That offer was one I simply could not ignore. Most aviation experts believed that North American was on the cutting edge of technology. I knew I would be flying the most advanced aircraft in the world.

Once again, Colleen and I packed our belongings. We headed west toward the promised land of sunny California. I was twenty-eight years old.

13

Forty Minutes of Stark Terror

The pay at North American was $850 per month plus bonuses based on the degree of risk with each test flight.

The bonus plan was quite complicated since it was based on a point system. Engineers assigned degree-of-risk points for each flight we took. They totaled the number of points at the end of the test program and calculated the bonus based on these numbers.

Six test pilots were assigned to engineering at North American. When one was killed, he was immediately replaced. Flights took place around the clock. When speed was the object of the test, each pilot would attempt to increase the previous speed by five knots and pull more g's or acceleration.

The pilots would rotate the missions, which were outlined on a test card. When a test program was completed, the senior test pilot brought us the news as to who had earned bonuses.

Before announcing those selected, our senior test pilot asked to meet with me.

"All these other test pilots," he began, "are just weenies. You and I are the only experienced test pilots here, and we are going to do the bulk of the high-risk tests."

Even though that was not my understanding of the way the system worked, I just gave him a qualified nod.

"All right then," he continued. "Even though you've been here less than a month, here's a big fat bonus for you."

I looked at the check and it was for almost four thousand dollars, nearly half a year's base pay.

"Wow," I said. "Great. What'd the other pilots get?"

"Like I told you. They aren't getting anything."

"But they assumed the same risks you and I did; that's not fair."

"It's fair in my book. And that's the way it is."

"Listen, I can't accept this. Let's just explain to management that we all shared the risks."

"No, I'm not going back to them."

"Okay. If you feel that strongly about it, I'll take my money and share it with the others."

"You do that and it will be the last bonus you'll ever get from this company as long as I'm alive."

I shared the bonus, and true to his word, that senior test pilot made certain I never received any other bonuses. I never said much about it. After all, he was in charge.

Only once, when I repeated a test dive in a Navy XFJ2 several times at great risk, did I receive a bonus. That came only because a vice president of engineering appreciated the high risk of the dives into known flutter conditions at supersonic speeds.

In addition, the senior test pilot purposely assigned me to every high-risk flight we had. He and I just never saw eye to eye.

I also thought he put the lives of fellow test pilots in jeopardy several times by exaggerating his exploits after testing certain aircraft. Since each test pilot based his test procedure on the previous flight, it was extremely important that he know accurately the data of the previous flight. Biting off more airspeed than was warranted could prove fatal, and if the pilot conducting the prior test inflated his figures, then the next pilot was doubling the risk.

One of the first test flights I flew at North American was in a great plane called the F-86 Sabre jet. It was a swept-wing, single-seat jet fighter that would achieve great fame in the Korean War. Its kill ratio (number of planes shot down versus number of F-86s lost) was almost unbelievable: fourteen to one.

In fact, an area near the Yalu River that separates Korea and Manchuria became known as MiG Alley. The F-86 battled its Russian counterpart over the skies there and established air superiority.

The F-86 would become best known for its agility. It was also an easy plane to fly. Astronaut Wally Schirra, who flew the F-86 during the Korean crisis, said it was a plane that a pilot "strapped on," as compared to being "strapped in."

A short time after I joined North American, I tested an F-86 D that had the horizontal tail located on the bottom of the fuselage. This was a test bed for the future F-100, which would feature a similar tail configuration.

As soon as I became airborne, the yaw damper failed, causing a full rudder deflection. At the same time, the fire warning light came on. My brain went on red alert. I focused on my options.

It's hard to imagine, but the Los Angeles International Airport had only two runways at the time. They were only five thousand feet long, ending on the west at Sepulveda Boulevard where a tunnel is now located, and at Aviation Boulevard on the east. The runway was so short that airport officials stopped traffic on Sepulveda Boulevard when big birds like the Pan American Boeing Stratocruisers took off for Hawaii.

When I developed problems in the F-86, my main concern was how much speed I would need to maintain control with the high yaw angle and no rudder control, and how to stop it on the short runway without blasting into evening rush-hour traffic. I concluded that because of the maximum gross weight I would lose control at normal approach speeds. Timing was critical because those fire warning lights were staring me in the face.

One of the design characteristics of the F-86 D test bed was that the dive brakes were located on the top of the fuselage instead of the lower section. When the brakes were extended, the plane pitched down and not up as would be the case with the conventional F-86s.

I called flight test and asked what kind of stall speed the engineers could recommend at maximum gross weight. That was important because I had to be way above that in order to land.

"Do you think one hundred forty knots will be acceptable for the approach speed?" I called out.

"It'll take at least that," was the reply.

With emergency equipment converging on the runway, I began the descent. I was concerned about landing with the nose of the plane yawed to the right because of the failed rudder. I extended the dive brakes instinctively over the railroad tracks parallel to Aviation Boulevard on the east end of the runway. It seemed as if the bottom fell out. The F-86 whammed into the ground two feet short of the lip of the runway.

Another test pilot, Dan Darnell, was sitting in an F-86 nearby. "Bob, get your canopy off. You just lost a wheel," he bellowed over the radio.

I knew I'd hit hard, but I couldn't believe one of the wheels had been torn off. Then the wheel bounced right up in front of me! The strut ran along the concrete. Witnesses would later tell me it was as red-hot as an old potbellied stove.

The F-86 was out of control and slid off the runway. The plane was clobbered.

A few hundred of the North American employees who were taking a work break got quite an eyeful watching it break up.

Fortunately, I was not hurt. A fine gentleman named Ray Rice was the vice president of engineering at the North American plant. I decided to face the music and went directly to his office.

"Ray," I said, "you're looking at the dumbest test pilot who ever lived. There was no excuse for losing that airplane. I knew those dive brakes pitched down. I just blew it."

Straightforwardness saved my job. Ray was understanding. He even tried to lessen my burden by pointing out that not only did I have a stuck rudder, but fire warning lights as well.

To my relief, both the company and the Air Force exonerated me with regard to the incident. I would fly another day for North American.

I was even more determined now to be the very best test pilot possible. I was just as determined to learn everything I could about each and every aircraft they built.

I even had visions of someday becoming president of the company. I went to see Lee Atwood, second-in-command, and told him what I had in mind. I wanted to be a test pilot for five years and then transfer into manufacturing and other divisions of the company to learn as much as I could about the whole operation.

I was twenty-nine years of age at the time. Lee recalls the visit:

> Bob came to me in 1951 and told me he loved being a test pilot but that he wanted to take over the company when he was through. He said he wanted to fly for five years and then learn all about the management of the company. He'd just joined us and I didn't know quite what to think, but I admired his gumption since he knew precisely what he wanted.

Those early days at North American were always eventful. I had a narrow squeak in an F-86 D when we were testing a new rocket system over the Inyo Kern rocket-firing range. The plane, dubbed the Sabre Dog, was equipped with twenty-four 2.75-inch rockets. These were in a pod that was recessed into the fuselage under the cockpit. The rocket pod extension was automatic when the rockets were fired.

The flight test called for firing all of the rockets at the same time. When I squeezed the trigger to fire the rockets, the pod did not extend. Bud Poage was flying the chase plane with high-speed cameras to capture the firing.

Even though the rockets were not loaded with warheads, they fired right through the nose of the plane. The plane became one big ball of fire. The nose was severely damaged. The engine fire-warning lights illuminated as the engine began to vibrate violently. Then it exploded.

I was at forty-two thousand feet above the desert. I called a Mayday and headed for the Inyo Kern China Lake Naval Air Station. The flight controls were operating on the emergency electrical system, but the battery power wouldn't last long. Then I'd have no way of controlling the F-86.

The bright blue sky tumbled past me as I tried to think clearly. To conserve battery power, I turned off everything except the emergency flight controls. Bud Poage confirmed the seriousness of the damage before a shortage of fuel required him to turn back.

Good fortune prevailed and I made it to Inyo Kern. I decided not to use the battery-powered flaps. Without the flaps extended, the landing speed would be higher, but I'd have to take that chance. I braced myself for a hard landing. Fortunately it was just the opposite on a dirt and sand road there in the desert.

After coming to a standstill, I snapped the electrical canopy switch to the open position and nothing happened. There was no battery power left. Had I used the flaps, there would not have been sufficient battery power to land the airplane.

My hands had had a viselike grip on the controls. I flexed them out as I relaxed and assessed my situation. I realized I had no radio communications, and I was stuck in the cockpit. I didn't even know if anyone had seen me land. Then I saw another F-86 overhead. I knew one of my fellow test pilots had reported my location.

For several minutes, I considered ejecting the canopy. However, I was concerned that the ejection seat might fire with it.

In the meantime, the heat from the greenhouse effect with the big bubble canopy and the hot sun built up the temperature in the cockpit. Had anyone been able to see me shed my flight clothing, they might have thought I was a contortionist. A Navy team arrived about an hour later. I was nearly naked when they rescued me, but they didn't seem to notice as they handed me a canteen. I don't remember when a drink of cold water tasted so good.

The first models of the F-86 were designed with boosted controls, which could be compared to the power steering in an automobile. However, when power steering goes out in a car, it is difficult to turn the wheels at low speed. It's the opposite in an airplane. It is easily controlled at low speed and runs out of control at high speed.

Engineers went to work on the problem. They fashioned a complicated system of electronics and hydraulics with spring bungees using a conventional stick in the cockpit to control the series of mechanisms.

This experimental system was scheduled to be incorporated into thousands of aircraft.

In November of 1950, engineering had designed and demonstrated a new flight-control system on the F-86. This was to be the first irreversible artificial "feel" system. The pilot control manipulations gave signals to the electric and hydraulic systems that moved the airplane's control surfaces.

We had adequate control at low speeds, but the aerodynamic forces increased the faster the airplane flew. As airspeeds increased, it became more difficult for the pilot to physically manipulate the flight controls.

I had taken a few rides in the airplane that featured the new systems, and everything seemed in order.

Two days later, I took another test flight. As soon as the landing gear was retracted, the nose of the airplane pitched straight up. The airplane was out of control. I pushed forward on the stick with all my strength, but it could not be moved fore or aft. Somehow both the normal and the emergency systems had failed.

The F-86 then pitched up, stalled, started to spin, and headed straight down. It was difficult to keep my bearings, but then the rudder control, which was mechanical, permitted me to stop the spin. The horizontal tail was free-floating and completely out of control, but the plane recovered, barely missing the ground. The plane climbed right back up, and the same process started again. I called a Mayday, unsure of what response would come next.

For the next forty minutes, it was stark terror. I was so certain that a crash was inevitable that I asked Los Angeles Airport to stop all air traffic. An airliner that was ready for takeoff on the other runway was told to hold his position, leaving one clear runway for me in the event I could regain control.

I went through all sorts of gyrations to figure a way to gain control. I played with the landing gear, the flaps, the speed brakes, and power settings, all to no avail. "What else is there?" I asked myself as precious minutes scurried by.

Rip Hewitt, a fellow test pilot who was flying an F-86 near LAX at the time, recalls my precarious predicament this way:

> After Bob took off on runway 25 left, that F-86 went straight up and I knew he was in deep trouble. Quickly, he tried a hammerhead stall in an effort to right the plane. That occurred near the old Pan American hangar and he missed that hangar by about twenty feet. Bob kept trying hammerhead stalls, and he would gain twenty to twenty-five feet each time, but it was touch and go over LAX until he decided he could fly off toward the desert.

A portion of the actual flight transcript illustrates the gravity of the situation:

HOOVER: Milt, talk to me. The airplane is completely out of control and I'm going to crash. The stabilizer is stuck full 10 degrees down and I've got over 150 pounds force on the stick and climbing straight up to the stall.

KUSKA: Use the alternate trimmer on the left-hand console.

HOOVER: I've tried that and it doesn't do any good. Is there anything I can do?

WELCH: Get out of the thing. Are you high enough?

HOOVER: No, and I'm headed right into a housing area.

WELCH: Have you tried to use your emergency system?

HOOVER: Yes. I've pushed everything in the cockpit. Can't anybody help?

KUSKA: Try your emergency switch on the left-hand console by the throttle. It should give some control.

HOOVER: Don't you think I've tried that? Is there anything else? Circuit breakers or anything?

KUSKA: It's either the one on the stick or the one beside the throttle. That's the only two that'll make it work.

HOOVER: I guess I've had it then.

WELCH: Where are you, Bob? Where are you?

HOOVER: I'm out over the water. I'm stalled. I'm starting to spin at this time.

WELCH: Get out of that thing, Hoover.

HOOVER: Is there anything I can do—anything? As soon as it stalls, I can hold it to 150. Then it goes right back to the stall again.

WELCH: Get out of it. If you can keep it flying, get it over the water or get it up here and bail out.

HOOVER: I can't do either one, George. I'm trying to get it away from the housing area here.

WELCH: Where are you?

HOOVER: I'm right off the end of the runway, just going around in circles, straight up and then straight down.

WELCH: Can you chop the power and belly it in?

HOOVER: No. Can't even control it—I've tried it. I've chopped the power and the stick has no control.

KUSKA: Hey, George, he's got the flying stabilizer there.

WELCH: I know it. Bob, are you high enough to get out, boy?

HOOVER: No, I'm not, George. I'm not at all.

HOOVER: Are there any circuit breakers? Anything I can pull on this right-hand panel?

WELCH: Throw your emergency switch on.

HOOVER: I've already tried that. I'm able to hold it though. Boy, I never saw anything like this in my life. I'm now going straight up.

WELCH: Try putting flaps down. That'll pitch your nose down.

HOOVER: Can anybody think of anything?

WELCH: Try putting your flaps down, Hoover. That'll drop your nose. Flaps and gears both, if you've got to.

KUSKA: Hoover, you have the elevator trimmer which will trim the
          elevator just forward of your throttle on your left-hand side. It
          should trim the elevator so you can put your elevator down.

HOOVER: Don't you think I've used that?

WELCH: Drop your gear and flaps, Hoover, that'll drop your nose.

HOOVER: Yeah, then it goes over vertically straight down. There's noth-
          ing I can do about that.

WELCH: There's a switch ahead of your throttle that will move the ele-
          vator itself. It's not the trim switch. Try that.

HOOVER: I'm climbing all the time—have to get out soon as I get enough
          altitude.

WELCH: How much you got?

HOOVER: I'm about 4,500 feet now.

WELCH: That's plenty if you get over the water or something.

KUSKA: Bob, what's your location?

HOOVER: I'm right over the beach section now. I'm over the edge of the
          water. If I leave it here, it might go back toward land though.
          It just goes straight up and then spins straight down, then I
          recover and then I go back into a complete nose-up attitude
          and the stick is uncontrollable throughout all of this. I'm just
          oscillating now.

WELCH: Don't worry about the airplane, hop out of it.

HOOVER: I'm going to keep trying.

WELCH: Has somebody got the crash boat alerted down there? The
          thing, Kuska, is to call the tower.

KUSKA: We can call the tower from here.

WELCH: Call them and tell them he's going to bail out over the water.

KUSKA: Roger. Lynch is taking off in 189 to see if he can get with him.

WELCH: I'm coming down there too. I'll be there in a minute.

KUSKA: Roger.

HOOVER: I've got a little control.

KUSKA: Bob, that's probably controlling your elevator alone. So possi-
          bly it'll be enough for you.

HOOVER: I've got it up to 180 now and it's tucking up, but not nearly as
          fast.

WELCH: I'm going to land at the factory, Milt.

HOOVER: Oh-oh, here we go again.

WELCH: Get that Coast Guard boat out there, Kuska. We want to pick
          him up before it gets foggy.

KUSKA: Roger, George. We'll get a boat out there.

HOOVER: [Recording is indistinguishable] just a slight nose-high alti-
          tude.

WELCH: Where are you?

HOOVER: I'm over the water and headed toward the mountains.

WELCH: What altitude?

HOOVER: Twelve thousand.

WELCH: I think I've got you in sight. Think you can make it to the lake?

HOOVER: I'm going to try, George, if we don't lose it again.

WELCH: All right, try to stay at the same power setting. Not touch any-
          thing.

HOOVER: Right, that's what I'm doing.
WELCH: I would touch—I'd bail out too at the lake.
HOOVER: Say again?
WELCH: I think I'd bail out at the lake if you are not worried at all about it, so that we won't disturb the trim.

Joe Lynch was flying formation with me as I approached the dry lake bed. It was eleven miles long and cracked in the early part of summer. Now, after the first rains, it was as smooth as a tabletop.

I had been increasing the power in an effort to get the nose up for landing. Joe had advised me to bail out before I set up the approach. Now he was telling me that I was going 240 knots and wouldn't survive the landing at that speed.

"Bob, you eager bastard. I begged you to get out of it," Joe bellowed. Those were the last words I thought I would ever hear. They came just before touchdown.

Instead of the hard landing I expected, the swept wings on the F-86 picked up ground effect (a cushion of air between the wings and the ground). To my surprise, I experienced one of the smoothest landings I've ever made even though I had no real control of the airplane.

The F-86 rolled completely across the lake bed and up to the main base. Jack Ridley, my old engineer buddy from the X-1 program, witnessed the landing and told me, "Bob that is the hardest flight I've ever listened to. What a miracle."

Jack also reached in the cockpit of the F-86 and felt the stick. "I can't believe it, Bob. It feels like it's in concrete."

The condition of my hand confirmed what Jack had said. I had torn the flesh between my index finger and thumb while pushing hard on the stick, trying to get the nose down.

Later, after some further inspection, I found that I couldn't have ejected even if I had wanted to. The ground crew had not pulled the safety pin on the ejection seat. I'd have gone down with the F-86.

People have asked me over the years what's the most terrifying ride I've ever had. There have been many, but none scarier than the one in that F-86.

During the years we were producing airplanes with this new flight-control system, I made numerous visits to fighter bases all over the world. In each case, I put on a flight demonstration to illustrate control of the aircraft at both high and low speeds.

Judging the risks when trouble developed in the F-86s was critical. We tried to inform all pilots flying the plane that if they had a flight-control-system failure, it was certainly not worth the risk of attempting to land. However, some felt they could handle it after learning of my success at Muroc Dry Lake.

Joe McConnell, one of our leading aces during the Korean War, was evaluating the F-86 H model. That model was a much larger airplane than the original, with considerably more power.

Joe had a situation similar to mine when he lost both systems, the normal and the emergency. The engineering people advised him to leave the plane, but Joe was determined to save the F-86.

His words to the tower were, "I'm sure I can make it."

Unfortunately, at about 500 feet, the airplane pitched over. Joe was too low to eject and went straight in. I felt awful when I heard about it.

Despite my earlier problems with the F-86, I later would become so confident with that airplane that I would perform a large loop and then a one-turn spin out of the top of the loop before recovering to land. Other aviators didn't believe that was possible, but seeing was believing.

In the mid-1950s, North American had designed and built an air defense model of the F-86. As I mentioned, I test fired the rockets on the all-weather fighter, which featured rockets instead of guns.

I had trouble in the F-86 D on one occasion while I was demonstrating it at the "William Tell" weapons meet that was put on by the Air Defense Command. The purpose of that event was to match up the best of the best in the military. The competition involved air-to-air firing of weapons against targets towed behind other aircraft.

This particular incident took place at Tyndall Air Force Base near Panama City, Florida. During the performance, I experienced a flameout. I was upside down and headed away from the airfield when it occurred.

Quickly I assessed my options. I could not pull up because of an overcast cloud deck.

By the time I got turned around, I knew I couldn't make it to the main runway. I spotted another one, but it had airplanes parked on both sides of it.

I realized that landing on that runway was the only way to save the plane and myself. I called the tower and told them my intentions. Then I crossed a deep ravine and nosed the F-86 right up to the lips of the runway and kissed it down. I squeezed in between the parked airplanes. Suddenly, not five hundred yards away, I saw a member of the ground crew walking across the runway in front of me.

I knew I couldn't possibly stop in time to miss the mechanic. He was a dead man unless he looked to his left. At the last instant, he did, and saw the F-86 bearing down on him. His face was filled with panic. He hit the deck, and the wing passed over, narrowly missing him. Years later I ran into the mechanic at an air show. He told me, "Mr. Hoover, you're looking at the luckiest man who ever lived."

After I was safely by him and regained my composure, I rolled out on the main runway and came to a stop. Ironically, the operations officer who came out to meet me was Daniel "Chappie" James. He later became our country's first Afro-American four-star general.

In the midst of the F-86 D test program, the Air Defense Command asked North American to produce a training film. It was to be shot at our North base Flight Test Hangar, where we had a half dozen or so of the D models.

The experimental test pilots were picked to play military air defense pilots. Among them was a real dandy of a character named Jay Ray Donahue, a relentless practical joker.

The script for the film called for us to come running out of the hangar in our G (antigravity) suits at the sound of the air-raid Klaxon horn. It signified scramble time, since the enemy was approaching. We were then to climb into the F-86s, start the engines, and launch in the shortest possible time in defense of the good ol' U.S. of A.

Production went smoothly, but none of us were aware that Jay Ray had done a little ad-libbing.

When the film was completed, all the pilots and the ultraconservative vice president of engineering for North American gathered in the projection room to see the footage. All eyes were glued to the screen as the film began. When the Klaxon horn sounded, here came the stampede of test pilots racing from the hangar. Everything looked great until we saw that the zipper was open in Jay Ray's G suit. His "talywacker" was flopping up and down in full view as he hustled toward the F-86.

Of course, the other test pilots and I roared in laughter with Jay Ray as we watched his shenanigans. Needless to say, the staunch vice president of engineering was not amused, and we had to reshoot the scene.

14

Living on the Edge

Flying experimental aircraft is addictive. Once it gets in the blood, there's no way to describe the rush of excitement that keeps a pilot going up day after day.

The feeling is similiar to that of a mountain climber who looks for new mountains to conquer. It's the challenge of the unknown, the quest to discover.

A test pilot understands and accepts the gamble even though he knows that most times the odds are against him. Writer Ward Lauren described the characteristics of a test pilot in the North American company magazine, *Skyline*, in the early 1950s:

> When men do things never done before with airplanes never before flown, anything can happen, it's true—the unexpected is always a positive factor. But always present to reduce its effect is the intense degree of skill which the modern test pilot must have to cope with today's increasingly complex airplanes.
>
> Contrary, possibly, to popular belief, Engineering Test Pilots are not white-scarved, leather-garbed barnstormers who fly for thrills and the chance to pass off a close call as "all in a day's work" (yawn).
>
> They have nerve, yes, but more than that they have years of flying experience, technical knowledge, and confidence in the aircraft they're flying, as well as in their own ability to cope with the unexpected, an awareness born of the combination of all three. They are, in effect, flying engineers: highly specialized, highly trained, but it must be admitted, with enough of the daredevil spirit of the baling wire and fabric days to push their luck a little now and then.

* * *

Some can handle the pressure Lauren talks about. Others cannot. Over the years, I have been asked for advice by several pilots who questioned whether they should continue flying. My answer was that if they were even asking the question, it was time for them to hang it up.

In the 1950s, military test pilots strongly felt that civilian test pilots usually were no more than hotshot, wild, and reckless showmen. This was certainly not accurate. I knew many qualified civilian test pilots who had been in the military and then worked for private aviation companies.

I must admit that when I was a test pilot in the service, I had the same prejudice. I felt we were much more qualified than civilian pilots because of our experience in War II and our firsthand knowledge of so many different types of aircraft. Military test pilots also resented that while we were overseas risking our lives in combat, the civilian test pilot was flying in friendly airspace, pocketing a good paycheck.

The disparity between the civilian test pilot's and military test pilot's pay was always an issue. I never made more than $420 per month in the service. We never received extra pay for risking our lives. Civilian test pilots were paid handsome salaries by comparison as well as high-risk bonuses. All of that provided fertile ground for jealousy between the two factions.

Even though I joined the "big bucks" pilots when I became a civilian test pilot, I never encountered resentment from the military test pilots. Civilian test pilots who worked for different aviation companies were fiercely competitive but a fraternal connection was just as evident.

During my days at North American, I became good friends with such respected test pilots as Lockheed's Tony LeVier and Herman "Fish" Salmon, and John Myers, the chief test pilot at Northrop.

I first met Tony in 1951 when he visited Wright Field. He had already been at Lockheed for more than ten years by then. He had risen from being a private pilot who taught himself to fly to an engineering test pilot in the Skunk Works program (secretly funded research aircraft—U-2 reconnaissance plane, SR-71 Blackbird Triple Sonic, and F117 Stealth fighter) run by the legendary aeronautical engineer Kelly Johnson. Tony remembers our first meeting:

> When I first met Bob, he was sitting on a windowsill looking up in the air from four stories above the ground. Open windows in tall buildings made me nervous, but Bob seemed quite at ease.
> I later saw him at the north base at Muroc where they tested all the experimental aircraft. He had a reputation for being a bit of a wild man. My longtime friend Albert Boyd told me one time, "I love Hoover, but he's too damn expensive." Apparently that meant he felt Bob had too

many crashes, but I doubted whether any were his fault because he had such a great reputation as a crack test pilot.

Tony LeVier's list of firsts included flights in such aircraft as the XP80A, the T-33 A and B, the F94C Starfire, the XF-90, the XF-104, and the controversial U-2. Like me, his ambition to be an aviator had been influenced by the flight of Charles Lindbergh.

Until recently, Tony kept a good story from me. He and some other Lockheed pilots pulled a practical joke on me at Palmdale Airport:

> We'd all heard how Hoover would do a roll on takeoff on almost every flight. One of us posed as an FAA inspector and called the tower to complain about his behavior.
>
> I happened to be in Flight Operations when Bob was notified. He was very upset and I rather wished we hadn't played the trick on him. After a while he must have figured out that somebody had played a fast one since he resumed his roll-after-takeoff routine.

Tony's and my competitive natures certainly increased when it came time to match up a North American plane against one of Lockheed's in a "my plane's better than your plane" rivalry. Tony says they were always trying to find out what test results we were getting. Their pilots and engineers even tuned in to our radio frequencies and listened to ground-to-air banter.

John Myers was a War II pilot who flew with Charles Lindbergh in the Pacific theater. Ironically, John never received his flight training in the military. He taught himself to fly back in the 1930s.

John started his civilian career at Lockheed as an attorney, but because he had an extensive flying background, he was called upon to test-fly the P-38 Lightning. Later, John hired Tony to help test the P-38.

John Myers later left Lockheed to become a corporate vice president and chief test pilot for Northrop. There, he tested the flying wing (no fuselage or tail assembly) along with every other plane they built.

Besides being a highly respected test pilot, Fish Salmon might be the greatest practical joker who ever lived. When ol' Fish was around, it was foolish to relax because it wasn't a matter of if but only when he'd somehow come after you.

Fish Salmon was a lifelong member of the prestigious aviation association called Quiet Birdman. Any pilot could join, but I was never able to since I couldn't attend the requisite number of consecutive meetings.

I did attend many times as a guest. Fish was always up to something at those meetings. I was always afraid he'd make me bear the brunt of one of his pranks.

He loved to initiate a panic and watch the reaction of the unsuspecting. Many times a Quiet Birdman banquet with a hundred members or more would become anything but quiet. If things got slow, Fish would set off a whole string of firecrackers under one of the tables.

Fish was especially lively when he worked in tandem with a Hollywood comedian named Vince Barnett. During a fancy banquet, Vince posed as a clumsy waiter who kept spilling food and drinks on chosen dignitaries. Fish would repeatedly apologize for the waiter's behavior. When Vince attempted to clear up the mess, his efforts just made matters worse.

On one occasion, Barnett spilled a whole tray of food on Fish and his brand-new tuxedo. A violent staged argument ensued. Finally Fish exploded and told Barnett if he spilled anything on him again, he'd blow his brains out.

A few minutes later Vince resumed his shenanigans and spilled a drink on Fish. True to their plan, Fish pulled out a gun and, as the dinner guests ducked for cover, shot the clumsy waiter. Barnett fell back as blood (ketchup) spilled from his guts. The banquet ended with people screaming and running for the exits.

Fish certainly never spared me. He'd tangle up the telephone cord in my office to where I could never unravel it. Using disguised voices, he and Tony LeVier also telephoned me one time in the early 1950s at Muroc. They informed me that the FAA was grounding me for some "unknown violations."

"But what are the allegations?" I asked.

"You mean you don't know what you've done wrong?" the mysterious voice responded.

"Well, I'm not sure," I said, trying to recall my most recent sins.

"You'll soon find out," I was told. All I could do was hang up the phone and wait for the worst.

Since this incident occurred just after I joined North American, I worried about losing my job. They had me going for two unsettling days before a friend clued me in on the prank.

Despite Fish's propensity to torment, I would later hire him to fly the maiden flight of an experimental plane designed by Pete Barto, who was with the Ball Aerospace Division of the Ball Corporation. On his sixty-fifth birthday, Fish flew the plane flawlessly.

Fish, who was killed in the tragic crash of a Constellation some years later, was also the first pilot to bail out of the F-104, which had a downward ejection seat. After the firing of the plane's guns caused an explosion, Fish ejected safely.

Lockheed wanted to find out what happened after the F-104 explosion, so they subjected Fish to Pentothal. That's the only time I ever heard of that happening. Fortunately ol' Fish's version matched the physical facts.

The F-104 was considered by some to be a treacherous aircraft.

Lockheed sold six hundred of them to the German Air Force in the mid-1950s.

Germany bought them despite a warning issued by German pilot Eric Hartman. He was their ace of all aces in World War II with 352 kills to his credit.

Then a full colonel, Hartman thought the inexperienced German Air Force pilots and maintenance crews could not handle such a sophisticated aircraft, especially in the bad weather that was prevalent in Germany.

Hartman's advice was ignored, but he was proven right when the German Air Force lost over one hundred and thirty of the six hundred F-104s they purchased. Even though his prediction came true, Hartman's fiery words to the Bonn government were not appreciated. They forced him into early retirement.

Without doubt, Eric Hartman was a brave man. He was safely away from his fighter base in Germany near the end of War II. Nevertheless, he flew back to be in command of his men knowing they would be captured by the Russians. When they marched through, they ignored his status as a living legend among pilots. They imprisoned him at hard labor for ten years in a salt mine.

I met Eric Hartman at a warbird show (exhibit of planes from War II) put on in 1971 by an aviator named Baron Volkmer in Alton, Illinois. It was a privilege to shake Hartman's hand. Like many of the great aviators I have known, he was humble and modest in spite of the many prestigious military decorations and other honors he'd received.

Baron had paid travel expenses to the show for Eric and a gentleman named Peter Townsend, who was an ace in the Battle of Britain. He later became famous right after War II for an abbreviated romance with Princess Margaret, the sister of the queen of England.

I'll always remember that air show. My good friend Paul Poberezny, who founded the Experimental Aircraft Association, came up with an interesting challenge. He wanted to see how many different aircraft I could fly in an hour. Paul rounded up at least fifteen War II–vintage planes, including the P-51 and the Spitfire. He lined them up one next to the other.

All the planes were running before I got in the cockpit. When I'd completed a tight flight around the airport in one, I'd just land, unbuckle, leap out, run to the next one, buckle up, and take off. That afternoon I took off and landed ten warbirds in one hour. Eric and Peter enjoyed the experience along with me. I have a wonderful picture of the three of us from that day.

Later on, they sent me a beautiful plaque that hangs on the wall in my den. At the top is the inscription: "To Bob Hoover, the greatest P-51 driver of all time." At the bottom Eric wrote: "From one jailbird to another. I'm glad we got you before they issued you a Mustang. Eric Hartman, Tomcat." Peter wrote: "Really, old chap, had you been flying a Hurricane rather than a Spitfire, you might have become famous a lot sooner. Peter Townsend."

During my years at North American, I avoided situations where pilots felt they were competing with me. On one occasion, however, I may have made a serious mistake in judgment. Looking back, though, I don't know how I could have prevented it.

The incident involved a friend of mine who had been a member of my outfit in War II. He flew Spitfires and was shot down. We ended up in the same German prison camp, Stalag I.

After the war, he stayed in the reserves and was later called to active duty in Korea. I saw him again when I was demonstrating the F-86 over there. He then returned from Korea and was assigned as an instructor at Williams Air Force Base near Phoenix, Arizona.

I received a letter from him stating that he would like to demonstrate the F-86 on Armed Forces Day at Williams. I would be there demonstrating an F-100. For some reason, his commanding officer told him to get my permission.

I called my friend and told him that I'd be pleased to see him fly the F-86. When time came for his flight, my wife, Colleen, was seated in the stands next to four-star general Oppy Wyland, commander of the Tactical Air Command. They watched as the pilot taxied the F-86 to the end of the runway.

Just as he took off, he attempted a favorite routine of mine, a roll on takeoff. Wham! The plane dished out of the roll and hit the ground. I saw the ball of fire. Then the smoke plume.

Colleen remembers the moment: "I didn't know when Bob was going to fly, so when a plane crashed right in front of me, I wondered whether it might be his. Just then, Bob walked up behind me. I hugged him tightly. I have never been so relieved in my life."

By the looks of the crash, it appeared as if my friend was a goner.

General Wyland asked me what I wanted to do. "We need to divert the attention away from the tragedy," I said. "I'm ready to go."

I couldn't get my friend off my mind all the time I was flying that day. I also couldn't help but wonder whether I could have done anything to have prevented the tragedy. I finished my flight demonstration and then went by the officers' club with the general. Everyone there was still in shock over the accident.

To our amazement, word came through that my friend was still alive. When he hit the ground, the plane was almost level. The impact didn't hurt him seriously. The plane slid to a halt just a few feet from the fire marshal's jeep. Rescuers pulled him out of the cockpit before he was consumed by fire.

One of the base physicians called me shortly after I'd arrived at the officers' club. He asked me to come to the hospital. "Except for smoke inhalation, he's okay physically," the doctor told me. "But I'm afraid he's going to will himself to death."

Knowing that pilot's personality, I was prepared to help him ease the embarrassment. I knew how he felt. When I got to the hospital, I told him, "Gee whiz, I heard the engine quit. I even told General Wyland I heard the engine quit. In fact, everybody on this base thinks the engine quit because I yelled, 'He's lost his engine.' "

Fortunately, my words broke the ice. He finally decided in his own mind that was what happened. Whether that engine quit or not doesn't matter because that pilot was an extremely courageous man. He just tried to push the F-86 beyond its capabilities.

That pilot's near-fatal accident made me keenly aware once again of the need to warn those who fly demonstrations or perform at air shows not to try aerobatic maneuvers they haven't practiced hundreds of times. I frequently remind pilots of this and their responsibility to respect an airplane's limitations and above all to know their own.

Flying conditions for testing North American aircraft at Los Angeles International Airport were usually acceptable. Except when the fog moved in. When that happened, it was like plunging through mud. My old flying buddy Jim Driskell describes the conditions this way:

> At one time, the fog was even worse than it is now at LAX. I've even seen a fog ball move from one section of the airport to another. To try to solve the problem, they came up with a series of lighted gas pipes and spaced them all along the sides of the final approach area on the runway. The experiment never proved successful since you could only see about two feet on either side of the pipes.

The fog at LAX was selective. It could be terrible at the west end of the airport and perfectly clear on the east end. The control tower was sixty-three feet high, and sometimes it was not visible even when you were right next to it.

I used the foggy conditions to impress the flight-test crew. After a landing, I'd taxi down to the flight-test hangar where the fog was so dense you couldn't see the taxiway. What they didn't know was that the area I'd landed on at the east end of the runway was sunshine and blue skies.

I'd hear them say, "Boy, that Hoover can fly in any kind of weather." I never let them think it was any other way.

All the company's experimental test pilots had offices, locker rooms, and shower facilities on the second floor of the flight-test hangar. We each had a desk, and there was a Spartan lounge area where we could pass the time between flights.

A real sense of camaraderie existed between the pilots in those days. Near the middle of the airport was a small homey restaurant called Red's where all the pilots would gather for breakfast every morning. We would eat, drink coffee, and find out who was scheduled to fly what and where.

We never indulged pilots after they'd had a near miss. I remember when Dan Darnell ambled into the Patmars Restaurant and Bar near LAX looking as if he'd just been on a combat mission. Actually, he had lost part of the tail dive-testing an F-86H. He expected sympathy or at least acknowledgment of the incident. He got none. We all had plenty of close calls. Danger was part of the job.

The test pilots wore G suits, which were zipped on like cowboy chaps. The suits had a hose attachment with bladders located on the abdomen and on the upper and lower legs. When the pilot pulled the g's, the bladders would inflate with air and swell up enough to block the flow of blood to the lower extremities, which permitted the pilot to pull more g's before the onset of blacking out.

By this time, significant research had been done on protective helmets. Even a two-hundred-pounds-per-square-inch blow couldn't penetrate some of the new helmets. A high-pressure oxygen mask completed our headgear even though we had partial pressurization and heat in the jets by this time.

Test-flying was scattered all across California. In addition to operations at LAX, we flew out of Downey, south and east of Los Angeles where we built T-28s and the Navy AJ-1 atom bomber. Flights were also scheduled to the north of Los Angeles at Muroc (Edwards) Air Force Base in the Mojave Desert and later at Palmdale Airport.

A typical day involved four to five flights. Most flights were short: make a dive to a certain Mach number, pull so many g's, and then land. After the flight-test data were processed, engineering would give the clearance to increase the speed and g forces.

North American had a "secret" hangar on the north Muroc dry lake bed. It was next to a six-thousand-foot blacktop runway that we used when the lake was wet. Most of our flying there was high priority, and so we operated separately from the rest of the Air Force base and other aircraft companies.

Each morning upon arrival at engineering at LAX or at breakfast, we'd learn where the six experimental test pilots were assigned for that day. If the assignment for a flight test was at Muroc, we would depart either in a DC-3 transport plane or in a Navion four-place plane that had been built by North American.

All those flights would terminate at the north base on the Muroc dry lake bed. There we would huddle with the engineers and receive briefings on what type of data they wanted us to obtain for that particular flight. We would then be given our flight-test card.

Armed with this information, the pilots would alternate in taking different aircraft through their paces. If the test called for spins, that meant the airplane would be deliberately stalled and forced into a spin so we could determine how quickly it could be recovered.

That type of test would involve a clean airplane, which meant no external stores, tanks, bombs, racks, or rockets. Later, we would conduct additional tests using various configurations of external stores, which included tanks on one side only, bombs on one side only, rockets on one side only, and so forth, so that we could obtain data for spin recovery for all configurations.

While testing F-86s out of that north base, some of us decided that we would conduct our dive tests directly over the hangar. The F-86 would not exceed the speed of sound (Mach 1) unless it was dived straight down. As the plane reached sonic speed, it would release a wham or boom-boom sound that would rattle windows and shake the hangar.

The faster the pilot went above the speed of sound, the greater the intensity of the shock-wave sonic boom. Lowering the altitude for recovery would also increase its intensity. During the dive testing, it became a contest between the pilots to see who could produce the loudest boom and provide the most shake to the hangar.

This contest went on for weeks. After every flight, each of us was anxious to know the intensity of our noise signature. The competition was fierce, but we did play a joke on Joe Lynch. After each of his dives, he would inquire about the effect of his boom. All the pilots would look at one another and say, "What boom?" We even had the flight engineers and the maintenance people in on the plot. In the end, Joe had the last laugh. The instrumentation proved that he had gone faster than the rest of us.

Later on, we would test an F-86 to see the effect of Stuka-fin damage. This occurred after an Air Force pilot, attempting to set a new speed record in an F-86 with external fuel tanks, crashed while flying at a high rate of speed near the ground. No one knew for sure what had happened, but speculation was that the fins, which guided the tanks away from the airplane when they came off, flew off unexpectedly. A flight engineer came up with a theory. He suggested that the Stuka stabilizer fins (named after the JU-87 German dive bomber) on the streamlined watermelon-shaped tank had blown off.

Those fins were set horizontally, with small vertical fins fitted on the end of the tanks. The air flow that hit that surface when the tanks were released forced the tanks to drop straight and away from the aircraft.

The engineers surmised that if one of those fins blew off, it could strike the tail, the ailerons, or the wing. This could cause severe damage and veer the plane out of control. To test that possibility, I was assigned to a program that would blow the fins off intentionally. We would see firsthand what could happen by using high-speed cameras to record the release.

While the pilot who had been killed was flying near the deck, the first time I blew the fins off, it was at a comfortable altitude. I was able to recover, but everyone had underestimated the destruction a missing fin could cause to the F-86.

On one occasion, we inspected the aileron and it was gashed badly. During another test, the flying fin cut off part of the tail. Even though the fin was small, at high speed it was like a projectile when it hit any part of the plane.

The test program convinced us that the pilot who was killed experienced that destruction. I was fortunate to have survived the fin's damage. On each occasion, my plane looked as if it had been in combat.

In effect, we were taking experimental aircraft and putting them through the worst conditions they might ever experience. Our job then was not only to save the plane and ourselves, but to record the recovery procedure for those who would fly the aircraft later on.

I was never hesitant to refuse to fly when I felt the danger was excessive. If a pilot was killed, I wanted to know what went wrong. If a defect in the plane caused a fatality or loss of aircraft, I didn't want to fly it until we had some answers.

Test results from harried flights weren't known right away. While everything today is telemetered, providing an instantaneous readout of all test data, such was not the case then. Sometimes we would have to wait several days for the results. Engineers in data reduction would check the tapes frame by frame so they could plot the data.

Exchange of information among test pilots was thus critical to staying alive. We all paid attention when a previous flight was discussed so we would know what to expect.

A number of test pilots lost their lives, both with civilian companies and the military. To appreciate the military losses alone, the many streets at Edwards Air Force Base are named after pilots who were killed testing planes.

To alleviate the tension of the high-risk profession, test pilots were what I would term "socially active" after hours.

The crown prince of good times in our engineering flight test was Joe Lynch. He could have made a living as a stand-up comedian.

Joe was also an outstanding test pilot. He was interviewed by Ward Lauren for the North American Aviation magazine, *Skyline*, in the early 1950s. A more serious side of Joe emerged as he described what it was like to be a test pilot:

> Our job is to run engines and airplanes as hard as anyone says they can be run. This sometimes includes flying the plane to its breaking point and then bringing it back so it can be studied, and its automatic recording instruments interpreted. The number of things we do to test a plane is almost endless, and new things are always coming up.

We referred to Joe as the original "anthropoid" since he had a large body and short legs. He didn't object to the kidding about his physique. In fact, he frequently joked about it himself.

Joe's one-liners were classic. I've laughed until my sides ached at his hilarious stories and commentaries.

"That stick felt like a garden hose in a pickle barrel," Joe would say, meaning the airplane would not respond to the stick control. Referring to the danger of test-flying, he said, "You stack up the money high enough, and I'll jump off the hangar with my ass on fire."

On another occasion, Joe arrived at Patmars, the watering hole we frequented, and asked if any of the pilots had heard an F-86 crash on runway 25 left. It ran parallel to the corner of Imperial Highway and Sepulveda Boulevard, which was close by. I told him that as I had left the hangar, an F-86 was taking off. I watched it head into the fog and didn't know it had clobbered.

Joe said that right after the pilot retracted the landing gear, the plane hit the runway, crashed, and burned. "That pilot wasn't very good at flying instruments," Joe bellowed, "but he sure could hold a heading. Hell, he was sitting right in the middle of the runway."

I have wonderful memories of time spent with Joe. He was a treasured friend who loved the sound of laughter. That made it even more devastating when the flight-test manager at North American received a phone call while I was in his office one morning. Joe had been killed demonstrating a dual-control F-86 at Nellis Air Force Base while performing a roll on takeoff.

Joe would frequently remind me when I was out performing in air shows, "If someone gets killed in front of you, don't even bother taking off. The dead pilot has already stolen the show." Recalling his way of looking at tragedy helped me deal with the loss. Joe had finally stolen the show.

The head of the flight test and I drove to La Canada to Joe's residence. We had to tell his wife, Serene. It was one of the most difficult and painful things I've ever had to do. I dreaded it.

No one was home upon our arrival. We sat in a station wagon across the street and waited.

When Serene finally drove up, I suggested we wait a few minutes until she got settled in. Instead, the head of flight test bolted up to the door. When Serene answered, he blurted out, "Joe's been killed." I could not believe the cruel insensitivity of his remark. He offered her nothing to cushion the devastating blow.

Joe Lynch was the genuine article. He had as much courage as any pilot I have ever known.

Dan Darnell was a fellow pilot during my early years at Wright Field.

He used to kid me about who shot me down during the war in southern France. "Hell, Hoover," he'd say, "every time I went to Marseilles, I'd shoot down a cadet. I think it was a damn cadet who shot you down over there."

I really wanted to shut Darnell up for good so I asked Macky Steinhoff, the German war ace I'd met in the midfifties, to see if he could find out who was responsible for shooting me down. "I'll see what I can do," he said, "but if it was a cadet, I'm not going to embarrass you. I just won't say anything."

After that, every time I'd see Macky he'd gesture to me with open palms as if to say, "Nothing yet." Of course, I never knew if he hadn't discovered anything or if I'd been shot down by a cadet and he wasn't saying so.

We laughed about that situation for years. When Bob Anderson, president of Rockwell, put Macky on a European advisory board for North American Rockwell, Macky told the whole group that story. Later on, I was relieved to discover that a very distinguished pilot had shot me down.

Since Dan had ragged me for so long, I jumped at the opportunity to get back at him.

When we finished up the dive-test program on the F-86 at El Centro, California, everybody went across the Mexican border to celebrate. Unfortunately for Dan, someone snapped a picture of him in a conga line with a pair of panties draped over his head.

I had a large number of copies made of that picture, and I numbered them one through fifty. When Dan opened his locker in our hangar at LAX, there was the incriminating snapshot with #1 on the back. Above his bunk at the north base, I posted another copy of the photo with #10 on it. Week after week, Dan would find the photos with different numbers on them, all the while trying to find who was the culprit.

"There are only five of you bastards," he'd say. "Now who's tryin' to drive me nuts?"

I finally had the infamous picture of Dan blown up to life size. We displayed it in the middle of the room at a going-away party we had for him before he joined Northrop.

Of course, Dan tore it to shreds, cussing a blue streak all the while. Near the end of the party, I approached Dan.

"All right," I told him, "I confess."

"Hoover, you son of a bitch," he said, "I knew it was you."

"Well, it's over now, Dan. Here's the negative."

He was relieved. Little did he know I'd kept a copy of the negative.

I was in the Philippines in the early 1960s performing demonstrations for North American. I knew Dan, now a customer relations representative for Northrop, was coming down. I arranged with the general at Clark Air Force Base to have the negative printed and blown up to billboard size.

When Dan arrived at a party at the officers' club, I told him, "Dan, they sure think a lot of you out here!" Looking puzzled, he said, "What do you mean?" I answered by pointing to a billboard that was visible from the officers' club. There was Dan's picture.

Dan almost had a stroke. "You son of a bitch," he cried out. "I'll get you."

And he almost did. At the party, he brought a cameraman and had a naked prostitute plop down on my lap. The camera clicked away, but ol' Dan's retribution was denied when the flash didn't work.

15

Diving at the Deck

In 1951, I had made my first landing on an aircraft carrier. I was twenty-nine years old at the time.

We've had aircraft carriers or flattops since World War I. During World War II, they were largely responsible for our successes as our military regained territories captured by the Japanese.

Supported by fuel tankers and supply ships, flattops could stay at sea for extended periods. Since they did not have the protection of armor plates like battleships, however, they were susceptible to attack from torpedo bombers, submarines, and dive bombers. Antiaircraft guns were their only defensive weapon.

Although I had only been with North American Aviation for a short while, I was selected along with six civilian pilots from other aviation companies to attend the Navy Test Pilots School at Patuxent River, Maryland. That would be followed by carrier training at Pensacola, Florida.

There, I flew a Bearcat (Grumman F-8-F single-seat, single-engine fighter). I was assigned to be flight leader for the group of planes heading for the carrier, which meant I would be the last one to land.

We steamed out into the Gulf of Mexico and the pilots began to circle in for their first landing. Of course not everyone succeeded on the first try. They got a wave-off because of poor positioning or other factors.

On this day, many of the pilots were getting wave-offs, and the delays were eating into my fuel reserves. Finally, everybody got down safely except the plane in front of me.

As I readied myself for my first attempt, I noted with frustration that the pilot in front of me had fouled the deck. He went up on his nose. He wasn't hurt, but the plane was severely damaged.

I was in a serious situation. I couldn't land on the carrier, and I didn't have enough fuel to fly back to the base at Pensacola.

I continued circling and called out, "Bingo," which signaled my dilemma—almost no fuel. If they didn't clear the deck soon, my choices were to ditch (belly in the water) next to the carrier or gain some altitude to bail out before the fuel was exhausted.

On board the carrier, they realized my precarious situation and solved the problem. They pushed the airplane that had just landed and fouled the deck overboard. They'd learned how to clear the deck quickly during War II days, and they did it at pit-stop speed.

I didn't think I would have enough fuel to take a wave-off. I felt that I had to make it on the first pass. I held the plane steady, caught the first wire, and landed safely.

The old Monterey carrier had a straight deck, not the canted decks we have on aircraft carriers these days. On the canted decks, the pilot lands and never takes the power off. They just come in, touch their wheels, and if the hook catches a cable, take the power off. With the power on, they can keep on flying if they miss a cable. They just hit the deck and take off for another go-around.

On a straight deck, landing was considerably more difficult. The landing signal officers (called paddle-wavers) gave pilots signals to assist in landing.

The hardest thing about landing on a carrier was staying in the groove. The pilot had to be in a turn all the time coming in toward a straight deck. Unless they were at a turning angle, they couldn't see the carrier since they couldn't look out the front of the aircraft. The engine was so big it blocked sight of the deck.

Hitting the right groove was critical, and gauging and timing the landing the main challenge. The pilot was completely dependent on the landing signal officer and his paddle signals. If the pilot did not obey the two mandatory signals that indicated wave-off (pull up, do not land, or cut power off and land), he was subject to immediate dismissal.

Once I recovered from the anxiety of the first landing, I completed eight or ten more that day. When I came in for the last one, I knew they wanted the airplanes positioned for the next morning's operation.

When they positioned the airplanes, the last pilot to land went to the very forward left or port side of the deck. From the cockpit, the pilot couldn't see anything but water out to the left side, and nothing but water over the nose. Faint lines painted on the deck couldn't be seen from the cockpit. "Come on, come one," the chief petty officer kept saying as he guided me into position.

Of course, I'd never been on a carrier before, and I was afraid I'd dump the airplane over the side. The chief had no sympathy for me, and he kept motioning me forward.

Per regulations, I had the cockpit open and the noise was deafening. I could read the chief's lips, and he was saying, "You stupid civilian SOB, keep moving forward, you're not in position." I kept creeping, and he kept calling me a stupid SOB. I was in an absolute panic. I couldn't see any deck; all I could see was water. I thought he was going to guide me right off the bow. And then of course I'd be run over by the ship.

I continued to inch forward and finally got the Bearcat positioned where he wanted it. I was afraid to get out on the left-hand side because I still couldn't see anything but water down there. The wheels were that close to the edge of the deck. I climbed out the right side, never glancing at the man who thought I was an idiot. I was hoping my knees wouldn't buckle as I walked gratefully away from the plane.

While I had no serious difficulty with the flying portion of the test pilots school, I had a real battle with a calculus course at Patuxent River. Tom Connolly, commandant of the test pilot training, finally got me a tutor, and it wasn't a moment too soon. By the grace of God, I received a passing grade on the final exam and graduated from the Navy Test Pilots School.

At North American Aviation, I was the first pilot to fly the Navy XFJ-2. Part of flight testing involved carrier suitability, catapult take-offs, and arrested landings.

We tested the FJ-2 at Inyo Kern Naval Air Station and at the north base at Muroc. One test was to determine the airplane's capability to withstand enormous side loads on the landing gear.

To perform the test, I landed on a simulated carrier deck. On one occasion, the A-frame tail hook of the FJ-2 grabbed the arresting cable at 135 knots while I was executing a twenty-seven-foot off-center engagement that could be encountered on an aircraft carrier.

The seven-eighths-inch pierced steel snapped and danced across the simulated carrier deck like an electric snake. I scrambled out of the cockpit and raced toward the carnage, all the while thinking, "How many people have I killed?"

The first person I saw was the landing signal officer. He was screaming in agony, and I saw half his buttocks had been severed. Other technicians were lying on the bloodstained concrete cradling legs and arms that had been severely injured from the whiplash of the cable.

Fortunately, no one was killed. Warnings given to those on the deck to stay clear in case the cable snapped had been ignored. I used to watch old World War II movies where deck personnel would stand on the deck as a landing occurred. In real life that could mean disaster, so the ship crews always dove for the catwalk just below the deck to avoid being hit by a snapped cable.

Proving to the Navy that the F-86 clone Fury jet could land safely on an aircraft carrier was a great challenge. Many times I had my helmet and oxygen mask jerked from my head. They rolled across the simulated deck due to the violent eyeballs-out landing decelerations as the cable stopped the aircraft abruptly.

We also tested the structural integrity of the FJ-2. The Navy wanted to determine if it could withstand enormous loads when landing on a pitching deck in high seas. Hard landings were made to discover how the plane could withstand the resulting high loads.

To provide an instant measurement of the sink rate (hard or soft landing), the Trody system was developed. It could give a visual readout to the flight-test engineer. Eighteen feet per second was the magic number we were after. To pass muster, we needed to achieve that rate several times.

The Navy provided a landing signal officer who would give the signal to chop the power and land. I would take the "cut" (power off) and make the landing at so many feet per second. Then I'd repeat that routine time after time.

The ideal way to land on a carrier was to touch down in the middle of the deck so the cables would reel out equally from both sides of the deck. This would arrest the plane without pulling it significantly to one side or the other. A Davis webbing was in place in case the cable snapped or the tail hook of the plane bounced over and missed the cables.

To prove to the Navy that a plane could land safely even if it hit the deck off center, we would simulate landings to one side or the other. That way if an inexperienced ensign misjudged his landing point and hit off center, the Navy knew the plane could withstand the punishment.

I was assigned one test that required me to perform a twenty-seven-foot off-center deck landing. When the tail hook engaged the cable, the FJ-2 jerked violently to the side, causing an eyeballs-out deceleration of six g's.

The amount of cable run out was then adjusted for different speeds and different engagements off center. The tests were performed with an open canopy in case the plane skidded over the side of the deck into the water.

We simulated the hard landings at Muroc and Inyo Kern, and each was like a crash landing. Getting the high sink rate was difficult because of the air cushion (ground effect prevalent with the swept wings) that we encountered close to the ground or near the carrier deck.

Time and time again, we repeated those landing tests without attaining the required sink rates. Finally, I recalled that during War II some pilots landed using a technique called diving for the deck. The nose of the aircraft was forced down, slamming onto the deck of the carrier. That prevented the wings from encountering the air cushion from ground effect.

When I hit the runway using this procedure, the plane was almost level, and the severe jolt caused my helmet to come down over my eyes. I would quickly push it back up, add power, and go around for another landing. These tests were required with different fuel loads and with external stores.

During one landing, the flight-test engineer notified me that I'd lost the tires. Damage to the aircraft was the last thing I wanted since the FJ-2 we were testing was a one-of-a-kind airplane. Once the tests were completed, it was headed straight for the Navy carrier trials and serious competition with the Grumman F-9-F swept-wing fighter. That wouldn't be possible if the FJ-2 was wounded.

Since debris was scattered on the runway, the engineer was right to assume I had lost the tires. Now I was faced with trying to land the FJ-2 as smoothly as possible after having spent hours of making nothing but hard landings. If the plane veered off the runway because the tires were blown, it could sustain severe damage.

The landing was relatively gentle. I was surprised to find that the tires had in fact not blown. When I got out of the cockpit, I could not believe that the tires had stayed on the wheels and were still inflated since the rims were missing.

The landing that had busted the rims had not seemed any more severe than the others. To my surprise, the feet-per-second readout was 22.8, much higher than the Navy design requirement of 18.

Besides the broken rims, the only damage to the plane was a small wrinkle on the outside of the fuselage. One of the ground crew painted a big white X over the wrinkle. It was the perfect camouflage.

I was also required to demonstrate the FJ-2's capacity to be launched by catapult. First, I demonstrated on a number of hydraulic catapults and then ones powered by steam, which accelerated the aircraft to 125 knots in approximately two hundred feet.

This produced an eyeballs-back effect that required the pilots, before launch, to brace themselves and place their heads firmly against the headrests. Then they'd lock the throttle open, give the signal for release after achieving full power, and grab the controls before the plane became airborne.

A pilot's first catapult shot, like the first solo flight, becomes indelibly etched in his or her memory. It could be extremely dangerous on a carrier. If the catapult didn't accelerate the aircraft enough to get airborne, it was called a cold shot, and the plane dumped into the sea off the bow, most times resulting in a fatality.

The AJ-1 Navy bomber was capable of carrying atomic weapons. It had a jet engine in the center of the fuselage and two R-2800 propeller-driven reciprocating engines on each side. That made it virtually impossible to see the wings from the cockpit.

While we were service-testing the airplane around the clock, two of my test-pilot friends, Joe Lynch and Bud Poage, were approaching the runway at Muroc. The landing was proceeding normally when all at once Joe looked over at his copilot and calmly said, "Bud, I didn't know they put landing lights on this plane." Bud Poage, a mild-mannered gent, took a quick glance outside the plane and nervously replied, "Those aren't landing lights Joe—we're on fire!"

Somehow Bud and Joe were able to land the wounded bird without an explosion. They scampered out of the cockpit and ground emergency personnel put out the fire.

Built by North American in 1949, the AJ-1 was the first atom bomber that the Navy bought. Chuck Brown, the pilot I replaced when I was recruited by North American, had been killed testing one. The tail of the airplane came off. The plane dove out of control into the Pacific right off the west end of the airport.

I never felt comfortable flying the AJ-1. None of the fifteen to twenty production pilots who checked out new airplanes were even allowed to fly it, and it gave all six of the experimental test pilots a lot of headaches.

When I took it up, several "squawks" (complaints) were listed on the test card attached to my kneepad. The plane ultimately had to be squawk-free; each complaint had to be resolved through testing.

All the pilots flew the AJ-1 out of Downey, which is south and east of Los Angeles. Adjacent to the runway was the Red Star Manure Factory. Mountains of manure two hundred feet high attracted gigantic horse-flies. On one hot summer day, three of the AJ-1s were covered with thousands of flies. Joe Lynch told the factory manager, "My God, John, look at those horseflies. They don't know one pile of shit from another."

At that time, the plane was the largest and heaviest (52,000 pounds) Navy plane to be landed on an aircraft carrier. It was also involved in a large number of emergencies and deaths. I remember my friend Jim Pierce losing his flight-control hydraulic power just before landing. He was fortunate to have made it.

Brown and Conover weren't so lucky. When the tail came off, both were killed. My friends Dan Darnell and Bud Poage had trouble when they were conducting a time-to-climb test at full power. At twenty-nine thousand feet, Dan called a Mayday. He was in a spin and unable to recover. The AJ-1 did not have ejection seats. To abandon the airplane, the crew had to climb out of the cockpit, go through a bulkhead, and down steps to the exit door. Opening the emergency door in a gyrating plane was difficult. Each time they got near the door, they were violently thrown back against the bulkhead.

Finally Dan put his feet against Bud's back and shoved him out the door. Dan finally got out at minimum safe altitude. He was so low that he almost landed in the fireball from the crashed airplane.

The reason the AJ-1 went into a spin and then out of control was a mystery until Chuck Yeager, who was flying an F-86 nearby, explained what happened. He saw the wing come off. Then one of the engines. We later learned that a fuel line ruptured and sprayed fuel onto the red-hot exhaust system, which burned off the wing.

Two days later, a flight test engineer and former test pilot handed me a flight-test card. I was to repeat Bud and Dan's flight. I told him it was suicide and refused to conduct the test. I wanted engineering to determine why the fuel line failed and to correct the problem. He suggested that I was gutless, but the chief engineer agreed with me.

In all fairness to the flight test engineer, when I later repeated the test, he rode with me. He took a high-risk ride in an airplane that only had one set of controls.

At North American, most of the pilots owned jazzy sports automobiles. To fit in, I decided I had to have a sports car. My desire was to find one of the last two-man race cars that raced in Indianapolis.

Joe Lynch loved automobiles and I told him about my interest. He said he'd keep an eye out for one. A few weeks later, he called and told me, "Bob, I've found just what you're looking for."

I met him at a Buick dealership over in Santa Monica. When I saw the beautiful, sleek Bugatti sitting in the showroom, I knew I had to own it.

Back in the thirties, that car cost more than $200,000. It was one of the last two-man race cars to compete at the Indianapolis 500. This one was especially rare because it had holes bored in the metal chassis on both sides to make it lighter.

That car had a large number 2 on the side. I ended up buying it for less than $1,000.

I couldn't convince the motor vehicle department in California to let me drive it the way it was, so I had to start making changes. I bought some motorcycle fenders, had them built up and installed. It needed a windshield and wipers. They were added. A transmission was next since I didn't want to keep pushing it to get it started.

The only brake the Bugatti had when I got it was on the driver's side, a hand-pump brake. That was replaced.

The car also had a spherical cylinder fuel tank. The only way the driver kept the McDowell engine running was to keep pumping it gas. Another fuel pump was on the passenger side. If the driver was busy steering after getting up to high speeds, the passenger could keep pumping fuel. That permitted them to race the car at Indianapolis. A big chrome exhaust pipe on the passenger side that stretched past the back fender kept the fumes away.

I tried to get Colleen interested in my new toy, but she didn't care for it much. "It bounced around a lot. I never felt safe in it," she recalls.

I loved that car. A stretch of road that paralleled the beach called the Esplanade didn't have stop signs. On several occasions, I had the Bugatti up to more than 125 miles an hour on the way home from the airport.

I kept the car for several years before finally selling it. I remember one time taking the car over to a neighbor's house to show it off. A gaggle of neighborhood kids surrounded it, oohing and aahing as I sat in the driver's seat.

I noticed one little six-year-old staring at me. Assuming he was admiring the Bugatti, I said, "Well, what do you think?" He looked at me and said with the kind of honesty that disappears in adulthood, "I think you've got the biggest nose I've ever seen."

PART

V

FLYING OVER KOREA

16

Bombs over Korea

As the test of wills escalated in Korea in early 1950, everyone knew a heated conflict was potentially imminent.

Finally, at 0400 hours on June 25, 1950, North Korea attacked the Republic of Korea. Assisted by Soviet-built tanks, thousands of their infantry streaked across the thirty-eighth parallel in an act of war.

The U.N. Security Council quickly denounced the invasion and called upon its members to join the fray. U.S. Air Force and Navy planes joined an air battle that would last the better part of three years.

North American Aviation had built several hundred F-86s for the Air Force. When the Korean conflict escalated, our plane was by far the best fighter used against the North Koreans.

While we knew the F-86 was a superior air-to-air fighter, word filtered back from Korea that we should develop a dive-bombing technique to gain more accuracy.

We all knew that dropping a bomb could be a tricky business. The F-86 was the pride of the company, and we believed in its capability to fly its missions against the enemy. Yet, in response to a request from the Air Force, engineers at North American began talking to me about how we could get more dive-bombing accuracy out of the fighters.

Many of the Air Force fighter bombers were using saturation-bombing techniques. Large formations of fighters would fly over a target and release their bombs. This did some damage, but was mostly harassment. What was needed was pinpoint accuracy to destroy precise targets such as bridges, roads, and troop convoys. That would disrupt enemy supply lines. Less exposure to ground weapons could be guaranteed if the bombs could be dropped from higher altitudes.

Jack Cover, an engineer at North American, came up with some innovative ideas on how to improve accuracy. He calculated that many errors were caused by not having a precise dive angle. Other errors were associated with release altitude and release airspeed.

After several days of around-the-clock meetings, I suggested that we mount a small cabin altimeter right next to the gun sight. We would then run a white line from the airspeed indicator so the pilot's eye could trip right down to it. In addition, we put grease-pencil lines on the canopy so the pilots would know what dive angles they had been making. This would make it easier to line up with the horizon. These lines were to familiarize the pilots with dive attitude. The grease-pencil lines would be used for training only since the pilot needed maximum visibility in combat.

To test the new mechanism, I dropped at least a hundred bombs from the F-86 over the Edwards Air Force Base bombing range. Using the new sighting system, I put most of them squarely in the center of the target.

My former commanding officer at Wright Field, Gen. Albert Boyd, flew in to see the demonstration. He was so confident of my accuracy that he wanted to stand at the thousand-foot line. We talked him out of that.

General Boyd stayed around and watched me drop a great many bombs flight after flight. Then he suggested that I travel to Korea and pass this information along to our fighter-bomber squadrons.

My feeling was that we needed to do anything we could to help our pilots drop the bombs in the right place. They were exposing themselves to the risk of being shot down over enemy territory, and yet they were missing many strategic targets.

After overcoming the customary government red tape, I flew from Los Angeles to Tokyo. There I gave briefings to Gen. Pat Partridge, commander of Far Eastern Air Forces. I also briefed his staff before departing for Seoul, South Korea, where I briefed Gen. Glen Barkus and Col. George Brown.

Before I left California, I had been given express orders to stay out of combat. I still hoped the opportunity might present itself. If at all possible, I wanted a chance to fight in MiG Alley.

When I first arrived in Korea, I was invited to the officers' club at the K-52, an American and South African base. While visiting with one of my friends, I overheard a young pilot talking to one of his buddies:

"There's that old guy Hoover. Hell, he won't even fly combat with us. Bet he's not much of a drinker either."

Attacking my combat capability was one thing. Questioning my drinking prowess quite another. Drinks were fifteen cents. I told the bartender to set up one for everybody at the bar.

In the midst of the race to the bar, I said loudly, "I'll have three straight shots." When they were set down before me, I held up a jigger of straight whiskey and toasted everybody before I downed it. Then I toasted their health again, and again.

I drained my three shots while the fighter pilots were still working on their first one. "I thought this was a fun-lovin' outfit," I bellowed, "but I don't see much drinkin' around here."

While those young pilots were trying to figure out what to make of the "old guy" (I hadn't even hit thirty yet), I excused myself and went to the men's room, where I tossed my cookies. Then I returned to the bar and ordered three more straight shots before returning to the men's room.

I continued that ritual until I had everybody snockered. Late in the evening, most of the young pilots fell by the wayside. Even though I had a sore throat from gagging, I managed to escape without so much as a hangover the next day.

I never did let on what I had done. After I'd left the base, other pilots told me word got around that no one should ever consider getting in a flying *or* drinking contest with the "old man."

Being in Korea brought back many memories of my War II days. Seeing the young pilots suit up reminded me of the courage I had seen in so many fighter pilots.

Shortly after I arrived at Wright Field in Dayton, Ohio, after War II, when the weather was not suitable for flying, we used to go down to the film library at the base and watch combat gun-camera footage. It made me regret all the more that I did not have more combat missions. I had wanted to be among the aces.

I remember one film in particular. It captured the bravery shown by two friends of mine, Don Gentile and John Godfrey. I watched as they dived two P-51 Mustangs down on more than a hundred Me-109s. Not transports or bombers; 109 fighters.

Against those odds, Don and John rolled their planes over. They headed straight down and fired as they flew right through the middle of the formation of 109s. The pilots of the enemy planes scrambled after them. Don and John were going so fast the 109s couldn't catch them.

Another time I saw footage of Don taking on a formation of six 109s.

He slipped underneath them and shot down three of the enemy planes before the pilots knew what happened. He was so close to the 109s that pieces from the debris damaged his plane. When he returned to base, his Mustang looked as if he were the loser, but just the opposite was true.

We also watched footage of a friend named Jerry Johnson, who ended the war with eighteen kills. He would later become a three-star general, but I remember Jerry as a pilot who absolutely hit every plane he shot at. He was deadly. There was never any question of the number of kills Jerry had. Each plane he hit turned into a fireball.

Both Jerry Johnson and another pilot named John Jaraudo were in prison camp with me in Germany. John got shot down a second time in an F-86 while I was in Korea. When he refused to talk, the communists threatened to kill him. When he refused again, his captors shot him just below the left shoulder.

Undaunted, John unwrapped a scarf he was wearing and plugged up the large bullet hole. How he survived, I don't know. Years later when I saw him, he had full use of both his arm and shoulder and had become a two-star general.

My mission in Korea was to brief pilots on the latest technical information regarding operation of the F-86 and to demonstrate that plane's dive-bombing capability. We wanted the pilots to see firsthand what a significant weapon it could be in eliminating enemy targets.

One of my first flight demonstrations was before the Eighteenth Fighter Bomber Wing. I talked to the pilots about the flying characteristics of the F-86 with solid leading edges and the difficulties pilots were having when taking off with heavy loads.

During the early part of the Korean War, the external fuel tanks on the F-86 were jettisoned once pilots entered the combat arena. The expense and logistics for external-tank replacement were costly.

North American decided to store fuel in the leading edge of the wing. That would provide the plane with a capacity of approximately seventy gallons for each of the two wings.

We tested the plane with this new leading edge on the wing and found a problem. At heavy weight the airplane would not take off if the nose was prematurely raised.

That didn't seem too serious at the time. We could instruct fighter pilots to keep the nose down until they got well above their normal takeoff speeds.

A large part of my message in Korea would be to brief all of the pilots about this potential problem. All they had to do was to push the stick forward and let the airplane accelerate another ten knots before raising the nose.

My instructions, however, went against a pilot's normal instincts about the control of the airplane on takeoff. I knew it would take a great deal of discipline for them to push the nose back down. Failure to do so would result in disaster since the plane would not stay airborne heavily loaded.

Pilots learned firsthand when I visited the Fourth Fighter Group how important my message was about keeping the nose down.

After we had our briefing in the base theater, I walked out toward the runway. Looking to the west, I saw a huge fireball. Somebody hadn't gotten the message.

The pilot had been unable to lift off and crashed into a barrier at the end of the runway. Five people on the ground were killed along with the pilot.

After the war, a pilot taking off from the Sacramento Airport made exactly the same mistake that caused the deaths in Korea. Dozens of children and their parents in an ice cream parlor were killed when the out-of-control F-86 veered off the end of the runway. Ironically, the pilot, who was not qualified to fly the aircraft in the first place, survived without a scratch.

I always talked to the fighter pilots before doing my demonstrations at various bases. I told them I had a great deal of respect for their versatility as pilots. "You have to fly in tactical situations, bad weather, and unfamiliar territory," I said. "All I have to do is make this airplane look good and find the feathered edge of its capability. I can't do your mission; don't try mine."

One pilot who was stationed with the Fourth Fighter Group was future astronaut Jim McDivitt, who later copiloted Gemini 4 during 62 orbits and Apollo 9 during 151 orbits around the earth.

Although I didn't meet Jim until a few years later when he was a test pilot in California, he recalls my visit to his base:

> All the pilots were called into the briefing room. In came Bob Hoover, a civilian official from North American. We all looked forward to a technical briefing that would bore us to death. We listened . . . but the message really didn't register all that much. Then all the pilots followed Hoover out to the airfield.
>
> What impressed me and the other pilots was when Hoover said to the commander, "I'll take any plane you choose." Instead of wanting to fly a special plane, he just wanted to fly any one off the flight line.
>
> Somebody chose one for him and away he went in just his straw hat and business suit. He borrowed a parachute and for the next half hour,

the rest of the pilots and I watched the damnedest air show I ever saw as Bob Hoover flew that F-86 every which way but loose.

I never imagined that the plane could be flown like that, but I took to the air on my next combat mission with renewed faith in my ability. I think all of us came away feeling like we could lick the whole Chinese Air Force by ourselves!

I had a strong reason for letting those in charge pick any plane for me to fly. I wanted to fly an F-86 just like the one the pilots would be taking up so they would realize the great capability of the plane.

My demonstration for the pilots was also described by Ward Lauren in the North American company magazine, *Skyline*, in 1951:

> Hoover opens their eyes with a demonstration that begins with two rolls immediately after takeoff, followed by an inverted pass at about 150 feet, followed by a precision 16-point hesitation slow roll. Besides demonstrating particular abilities of the Sabre Jet in these maneuvers, Hoover constantly illustrates his complete confidence in his airplane—a confidence based upon the fact that having helped design them, he knows their limitations and accomplishments.
>
> His maneuvers demonstrate the surprising controllability of the Sabre Jet at all speeds and altitudes, its ability to twist, turn, roll, and climb about the sky at near-sonic speeds or "crawling" at 120. . . .
>
> It's a tame pack of tigers that comes in for the indoctrination lecture after witnessing this flying testimony to the Sabre Jet's capabilities.

I continued briefing the pilots about the leading-edge situation, but discussing the new bombing procedures for the F-86 was also a priority. When I brought up the idea about the lines on the canopy, one fellow said, "Hell, there'll be a MiG behind every one of those wax-pencil lines."

I explained that the lines, which represented ten-degree dive angles from zero to ninety, would be there only during training. After a while the pilots wouldn't need them because they would develop a feel for the dive angles.

My belief was that if the pilots followed instructions, they would eliminate at least three hundred feet of error. Many were skeptical of the device, which was dubbed the Moving Pipper Target Indicator.

Even though North American had instructed me not to fly in combat, it became clear that I needed to. It was the only way to prove the validity of the new bombing procedures.

Gaining clearance was not a problem. When I spoke to General Barkus, commanding officer of the Fifth Air Force headquarters, after I first arrived in Seoul, he told me, "Hoover, if you're not willing to fly and fight, pack your bags and head home. Other test pilots have visited for a day or so and spent the rest of their time living it up in Tokyo."

Before I left, George Brown, who later became chairman of the Joint Chiefs of Staff, told General Barkus I wasn't like that. When my request to go on combat missions was forwarded to General Barkus, he approved it immediately.

Since I would be flying combat, my fellow pilots were briefed to shoot me if for any reason I had to go down over enemy territory. My knowledge of the new supersonic F-100, which I would soon be testing, made me a potential liability if I fell into the hands of the enemy. I understood and accepted the order.

During my first mission, I was in the number two position behind Col. Marty Martin, the group commander. Sixteen airplanes made up the formation.

The squadron headed up into enemy territory in North Korea. Unfortunately, we came out of an overcast so low that we never had a chance to find the priority targets on an enemy airfield. I pulled back up into the overcast and out on top.

I finally spotted Marty and moved back into a trail formation. We headed for our secondary target, a bridge connecting the enemy supply route to the front lines. Deep craters surrounded the target, clear evidence that our pilots had not been able to hit the bridge.

Marty dove in with me right behind him. I got all lined up on the bridge and then pickled (dropped the bomb). After a pullout from the dive, I looked over my shoulder and the bridge was gone. I knew I had a direct hit.

Through my radio I heard number three in the formation yell, "Hey, boss [meaning Marty], you've got a direct hit." I looked down and saw only one blast, but I heard another pilot say, "Cheers, boss, a direct hit."

When we joined formation, I looked over at Marty's plane and he still had his two bombs. Soon everyone in the squadron realized what had happened. Marty's bomb release had malfunctioned. When the fact got around that I had hit the target, the younger pilots were more willing to listen to the "old guy."

Aviation writer Lou Davis, a weapons evaluator during the conflict, wrote an article in *Air Line Pilot* magazine about my days in Korea:

> Bob Hoover not only performed loops and spins with the F-86 [in Korea], but flew bombing missions with fighter-bomber units and demonstrated his prowess as a bombardier by putting two bombs on a bridge in the first pass. The man I've come to regard as the greatest

pilot confidence builder to ever fly a plane changed pilot attitude overnight. . . .

Pilot morale wasn't the best. But, there were some reasons for it. . . .

The day before I arrived at K-14, four Sabrejets, caught in a violent weather front, suffered high-speed stalls and screamed to the ground with their helpless low-time pilots.

Just a week before that, I stood at a hillside radar shack near Kimpo and watched another Sabrejet roll into the overrun and explode into a ball of flame. . . .

Too many pilots, playing it safe with more airspeed than they needed on the final approach, landed long, burned out tires and often, when lucky, wound up in the crash barrier, called Brentnall's Rabbit Catcher after the general who pressed for the nylon rope and Japanese anchor chain rig to save airplanes and lives.

In fact, the night before the meeting, a few hours of yakking with jet jockeys at the officers' club bar convinced me that North American's man was not coming too soon.

The next morning was clear and sunny. That man from North American Aviation arrived dressed in a green Eisenhower jacket, a white shirt and black tie. He looked and acted more like a misplaced Madison Avenue advertising executive than a test pilot. It was Robert A. (Bob) Hoover.

The pilots figured this would be another dull, GI-type lecture. . . . The time could be better spent in the sack.

Interest picked up when Bob started talking. He told them he could land their jets within 2,500 feet without burning rubber. He further stated that he'd show them how to get the F-86 off the ground with plenty of concrete to spare. Interest raised another level higher when he told them about a mechanically operated bombsight that would provide more reliability than they were currently getting from an unpredictable electronic A4 gunsight, then installed in the birds.

They and I were totally unprepared for what was to come next.

In completing his general remarks . . . he said, "Okay! You've listened to my story. I suspect some of you don't believe me. [Nearly all heads nodded in the affirmative.] Now let me show you that I meant what I said." Continuing, he asked: "Give me any Sabrejet on your line. The oldest dog you have, if you wish. All I ask is that you put on a new set of tires."

The flight line crowd suddenly grew in size. Instead of 150 pilots, there must have been 1,000 jet jockeys and GI's on planes, bomb carts, work stands.

From the time Bob started the engine, until the Sabrejet was back on the line with a stilled engine and barely a mark on the new tires, that gang of MiG hunters and bridge busters had never seen such flying before. Hoover rolled at takeoff, looped, flew upside down just a few feet above the runway. The "Hey, look's" . . . "Wow's" and "Man, that's for me's" . . . chorused by the pilots were unmistakable evidence that Doctor Hoover's medicine was having effect. The payoff came on the landing approach when he used what was then an extended landing approach of 110 knots at the threshold. And within 2,500 feet of the point of the gentle touchdown screech on the blacktop, he stopped.

It's needless to say more. Hoover stayed in Korea for many days. He flew bombing missions with fighter-bomber units and demonstrated his prowess as a bombardier by putting two bombs on a bridge in the first pass, with his manual PIP control sight. There was no need for the rest of the flight to drop. Pilot attitude changed almost overnight. Wherever I went in Korea and Japan, F-86 units showed that Hoover had been there.

In all, I spent six weeks in Korea. Assisting those pilots was a great experience. While I felt I made a contribution, my biggest disappointment during my short tour of duty was that I did not have an opportunity to fly the F-86 in air-to-air combat. My request to fly air-to-air missions had been turned down.

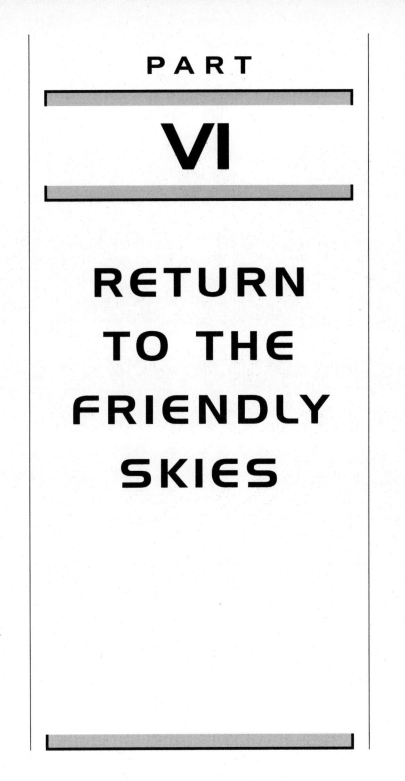

PART

VI

RETURN TO THE FRIENDLY SKIES

17

Feuding over the F-100

I like to fly alone. When critical decisions have to be made, I want them to affect only me. That was part of the appeal of being a fighter pilot during World War II and later a test pilot.

Shortly after arriving at North American, I was surprised to find my name listed on a test card to get checked out in the B-45 bomber, which required two pilots. However, in this case, I didn't mind sharing the cockpit since Joe Lynch would be conducting a test while checking me out.

The B-45 Tornado was developed by North American because the Air Force realized they needed a jet-age bomber. All of the major aircraft companies competed for the multimillion-dollar contract.

The B-45 made its first flight in 1947. Its configuration was similar to North American's B-28 except the pilot sat ahead of the copilot, not beside him.

The Tornado was the first four-jet aircraft flown in the United States, and its internal bomb bay could hold more than twenty thousand pounds of conventional as well as nuclear weapons. North American later dubbed the B-45 the "flying cartographer" since its five cameras made the plane a useful reconnaissance weapon in Korea.

The test we were assigned called for opening the bomb bay doors at 550 mph. Those doors had to be extremely large to permit the plane to drop any size bomb. They also were well built in case the bombs needed to be dropped at maximum speeds.

Conducting this type of test was dangerous because the doors under pressure from the high wind velocity could separate from the plane. If the doors came off, they could take part of the tail with them.

That's exactly what happened on the B-45 test flight where I was the copilot behind Joe Lynch in my checkout flight. Just prior to opening the doors, Joe said, "Bob, put your hands on the next of kin [ejection-seat handles]." I braced myself and got ready to eject if disaster occurred.

When Joe opened the doors, that B-45 shook like a dog excreting a peach seed. Seconds later, one of the doors snapped with a whoosh and headed straight at the tail. It clipped the top edge and then zipped across the sky.

The plane continued to shake, but Joe kept it under control. We landed safely, but another airborne pilot took a picture of the damaged B-45 that I still have today.

North American also designed and manufactured another bomber in the mid-1950s, the B-70 Valkyrie. This enormous airplane was capable of speeds in excess of Mach 3. It traveled at the speed of a bullet fired from a thirty-aught-six rifle.

The triple-sonic B-70 could fly at seventy thousand feet. In-flight refueling enabled it to fly nonstop from our coasts to the Soviet Union. That was enough to panic them into action. Its incredible capability forced the Soviets to almost bankrupt their economy by manufacturing hundreds of SAM (surface-to-air) missiles designed to knock out invading B-70s.

With the B-70's incredible speed, it was capable of actually outrunning most missiles. If the missile wasn't launched in time, it could end up tail-chasing the B-70 and never catching it.

The Mach 3 speed produced over five-hundred-degree temperatures. Water jackets had to be installed in the wheel wells to keep the rubber from melting on the tires. During tests, our test pilots discovered that the high temperatures caused another problem. Continuous explosions took place inside the fuel tanks. To prevent this, a head of inert nitrogen gas was pumped into the fuel tanks.

Ironically, the Soviets' expensive defensive efforts were not necessary. The B-70 program was canceled by Secretary of Defense Robert McNamara.

In the late 1950s, the great aviator Eddie Rickenbacker came to North American Aviation to review the B-70 program. He was a tall, distinguished man. I was extremely impressed with his intelligent questions.

Mr. Rickenbacker was a true Renaissance man. He developed an early fascination with internal combustion engines and the automobile. He was a race driver before World War I and became one of the finest automobile race drivers of his time. He even owned the famous Indianapolis Motor Speedway for a time.

Eddie Rickenbacker was a man of principle. He was successful at nearly every venture he attempted. His work ethic was demonstrated in a booklet that was given to members of his automobile racing team. He included a portion of it in his autobiography, *Rickenbacker:*

> If you don't like the way we do business, if you don't like your team-mates, don't grouse and don't go around with a long face. Quit this job and get another one somewhere else. The trouble with a lot of people is that they are not willing to begin anywhere in order to get a fighting chance. My advice is: Throw away that false pride. No honest work is beneath you. Jump in and demonstrate your superiority. Once you get on the pay roll, make up your mind to master everything about your own job, and get ready for the job at the top. Your particular task is merely one end of a trail that leads to the driver's seat. That is my philosophy of success. It works, I have tried it and proved it.

Captain Rickenbacker was also a man of immense courage. He started as an ambulance driver in World War I. He then became a chauffeur for Gen. Black Jack Pershing, who got him an assignment as a pilot.

Eddie Rickenbacker went on to become a member of the Ninety-fourth Aero Pursuit Squadron. He became our leading ace in World War I with twenty-six kills, which earned him the Congressional Medal of Honor.

After the war, Rickenbacker joined American Airways and then became involved with the North American Aviation holding company in 1933. He later was president of Eastern Airlines, the position he held when he visited our North American plant.

Captain Rickenbacker was in his sixties at the time we met. I hadn't turned forty yet and was honored to spend time with such an honored aviator.

I escorted him through our facilities and showed him mock-ups of experimental planes. The engineers briefed him on the B-70 program.

Captain Rickenbacker's vast knowledge of engineering and incredible stature as an aviator made him an intimidating figure in the eyes of the North American engineers. But they were encouraged by his support and challenged by his insightful and forthright questions.

Chief competitors for North American during the 1950s were Boeing, Republic Aviation, Northrop, Lockheed, and McDonnell.

The first generation of jet fighters had been built shortly after War

II. North American's F-86 series had clearly dominated the field. Now America's foremost aviation companies sought to build a second generation of fighters that would signal the U.S. air superiority for the 1950s and beyond.

Intense competition between the aviation companies for the multi-million-dollar contract ensued. North American was finally selected to build the very first aircraft for what would become known as the Century Series. That plane was ordered by the Air Force under the test designation YF-100A. It would later be called the F-100 Super Sabre.

The F-100 was a single-seat day fighter. Its armament consisted of four 20-mm M39-E cannons plus external stores on six underwing hard points on later models.

The F-100 was eagerly awaited. It had the potential to be the first airplane to fly supersonic in level flight. The government was anxious to add it to their fleet. They knew the Soviets were developing a successor supersonic aircraft to the MiG-15 and MiG-17.

Intense pressure from the Air Force to deliver the F-100 resulted in a test program that was rushed from beginning to end. I felt the aircraft was superb in many ways, but the prototype had problems that needed to be corrected. Among other squawks was the tail design. It was too small, which caused directional instability.

Before the extent of the tail-design flaw was recognized, the F-100 was given the go-ahead for flight test. In the North American company magazine, *Skyline*, writer Ward Lauren describes the atmosphere surrounding the very first flight:

> A nervous platoon of ants scurrying along the bare floor of the Mojave Desert was roasted and swept from sight by a sudden scorching blast of air.
>
> Small stones and chunks of earth were torn from the ground. They bounced and rolled down the earthen runway as if hurrying to get out of the way. A growing cloud of dust rose into the air to protest this disturbance of the unusual quiet, sun-baked calm of Rogers Dry Lake bed.
>
> In front of the roaring air stream, looking for all the world like some strange, science-fiction grasshopper about to leap off, the first North American YF-100 Super Sabre made ready to take its first flight.
>
> Company engineers, flight test mechanics, Air Force personnel, and photographers stood about in small groups, talking, checking data, completing last minute preparations. Crash trucks from the Edwards Air Force Base test center waited, like patient Saint Bernard dogs, off the runway.

The F-100 was originally designed as a fighter and an interceptor, but not to carry bombs. Later, the F-100C was designed with a multi-role, fighter-bomber capability.

The extra weight of the bombs and tanks reduced its performance level and destabilized its control. That change in performance was typical of all fighters when external stores were added.

For one of the few times in my career as a test pilot, I felt very much in the middle of a controversy over the performance of an airplane. Since the F-100 had so much performance speed and rate of climb, there was little concern with the directional stability problem.

It became quite obvious that I was bothered more by this than the engineering department. Some of the engineers were concerned because they understood the fighter's purpose was to have a stable gun platform and to intercept enemy aircraft. If the plane yawed during a gunnery pass, the uneven spray pattern of the bullets would render the weapons system less effective.

I knew the aircraft needed more vertical tail. When I was test-flying the YF-100 and dove at supersonic speeds, the plane would yaw out severely. The nose would swing to the left or right. When the pilot tried to straighten the flight path, it would swing in the opposite direction until the speed was reduced.

To quell the furor, two experienced tactical air command military pilots were permitted to evaluate the F-100. They came back with glowing reports to the effect that "Wow, that's the greatest thing I've ever strapped on."

The fighter pilots were so fascinated with its speed and rate of climb that they failed to focus on whether the plane experienced handling problems that could prevent them from hitting their targets as effectively as they would like.

The "gee whiz" report from the pilots and visits by Dutch Kindelberger, head of North American, to the Pentagon resulted in the delivery of two hundred F-100s to the Air Force in 1954. Shortly thereafter, chief test pilot George Welch, known as Wheaties after he appeared in a commercial for the breakfast cereal, was killed in a test flight. The planes were grounded until modifications could be made.

I was in the pilots' office and lounge when I heard the engineers brief George on taking the F-100 to 7.33 g's at 1.4 Mach. After the discussion was over, I warned him against it.

"Hey, George," I said. "Hold on a second. They are asking you to exceed the design limits on the yaw-angle side loads for the vertical tail of your airplane. The tail could come off."

I knew that was possible from firsthand experience. On my last dive at that speed, the airplane yawed to the left. When I tried to make a correction, it went to the right.

In spite of his knowledge of that incident, George replied, "Hoover, you are overeducated in grade. Why don't you quit being a test pilot and become an engineer?"

I said, "George, we've got to be as smart as the engineers to stay alive. I wouldn't accept that flight-test card for anything in the world."

George said, "Hell, that's because you're a g – – d – – – coward."

George Welch's unfortunate death supported my conviction that to stay alive, test pilots had to know their aircraft. They had to be knowledgeable enough to challenge what they considered to be inappropriate risks. Accepting the occupational risks of being a test pilot was one thing, stupidity was quite another.

I was convinced that George's death could have been prevented. Shortly thereafter, I was offered a $10,000 bonus to continue the test program on the F-100. I declined. I knew ten grand wouldn't buy very many groceries for a widow.

Another test pilot, Ray Morris, was offered the same deal, but after some thought and conversations with me, he declined as well.

The assignment to complete the test bounced around between different pilots, many of whom were reluctant to participate. Based on all the data from those tests, engineering finally realized that the tail on the F-100 did indeed need more vertical area. High-speed testing was delayed until the new design was ready for flight.

In January of 1993, aviation writer Dick Hefton recalled the F-100 controversy in an article entitled "Hoover Deserves Better Than Stunt Pilot Label":

> His candidness nearly cost Hoover his job at North American . . . when he alone called for grounding of the F-100 Super Sabre on the eve of its release to Air Force operational units. Hoover's popularity within the sprawling aviation company located at Los Angeles International hit rock bottom. Supervisors and riveters alike scorned him and he became a persona non grata in the assembly plant. Even his best friends and fellow test pilots lined up to discredit Hoover's contention that the F-100 had serious design flaws. . . .
>
> The great new supersonic fighter was now a "hangar queen." Those shiny new birds sat unmoved on the tarmac for days while officials determined a fix which became a major modification to the vertical stability. This was a fix that needed factory attention, not repair. So rather than take off the wings and truck 24 planes back to LAX, a "one-time" landing . . . was approved at the lowest practical altitude.
>
> It was quite a sight to watch as that string of our nation's first supersonic fighters lumbered uncertain between the gap of Cajon Pass on their way home toward major surgery.
>
> Ironically, Hoover became no instant hero. Animosities lingered for a long time. But over the years, the respect he so richly deserved became his reward. Especially a respect he had for the lives of untold numbers of young fighter pilots who might have fallen victim to the ill-advised attempt to rush the process.

* * *

Dick exaggerates my role somewhat. It was the fighter pilots who un-wittingly made my task difficult. They couldn't see beyond the aircraft's performance. They continued to tout it as the greatest plane ever to take to the sky. Those were my feelings too, but corrections needed to be made. That's why I continued to file daily flight-test reports contain-ing criticisms about the aircraft.

On one occasion, I performed a spin test in the F-100, forcing the airplane into an uncontrollable flat spin at forty-two thousand feet. The drama was enhanced since none of us knew whether the plane would recover at all from a flat spin. The airplane had already been through conventional spin tests without difficulty.

When I attempted the textbook spin entry, I decreased the airspeed no greater than one knot per second and then held it until the airplane completely stalled. Some aircraft will drop off abruptly and start rotat-ing wildly while others will drop straight through or fall off to one side into a conventional spin. In most cases, the F-100 had to be forced into a spin but recovered easily.

To simulate the worst scenario that could occur, the moment the F-100 stalled, I went to cross-controls, which is analogous to purposely throwing an automobile into a skid to the left and then turning the wheels to the right to keep it skidding. In the F-100, I had the stick all the way back and put the ailerons to the left with full right rudder. This cross-control application was used to force the plane into a flat spin.

The technique we had planned on using for recovery was four turns with each different type of control-recovery application. As soon as the plane went flat, I went into the first application of recovery controls, all the while talking to the flight test engineer on the ground. After four more turns, I applied the next set of control applications, but nothing worked.

I was spinning uncontrollably. I knew I had just a short time to recover and only so many options available to me.

I decided to select the afterburner, believing it might power the plane out of the flat spin. But the afterburner wouldn't ignite. Nothing happened.

I then deployed the drag chute to see if that would dump the nose and effect a recovery. No luck.

After twenty-two turns and five different control applications, jetti-soning the canopy was my last hope. That might change the air flow sufficiently to effect a recovery. It didn't. I was surprised to be sitting in calm air with no wind in the cockpit even though I was falling like a rock.

Ejection was initiated and seat separation took place. I pulled the rip cord. The parachute opened.

As I floated down in the parachute, I had a fleeting feeling.

"Don't stop spinning now," I thought to myself as I looked at the plane, wondering if the weight change might somehow brake the gyroscopic effect. It didn't. The F-100 continued to spin until it splattered into the desert floor. I hated that sight and a part of me went down every time that occurred.

I had notified flight test control that I was ejecting. As I neared the ground, I was gravely concerned that I would land on top of a Joshua tree and be filled with needles. I narrowly missed them, but the parachute was so close it was draped over the limbs.

Within a very short time, a rescue helicopter was on the scene. I was strapped into a litter basket for the trip back to Palmdale where the test had been initiated.

Upon arrival there, everyone was interested in precisely what had happened. They were anxious to hear whether I had had any difficulty in getting out of the airplane. When I told them I'd had no problem whatsoever, they asked me, "Why are you holding your right arm as you are?" I looked down to see that I was cradling it at an odd angle. Apparently the adrenaline disguised the discomfort.

As I'd exited the airplane in the ejection seat, my shoulder had apparently banged against the canopy rail on the side of the cockpit due to the centrifugal forces from the spin. It was nothing serious at the time, but it bothered me for a long time. Years later, I learned that my shoulder rotary cuff had been severely injured during that incident, and an operation was necessary to rebuild it.

We lost another F-100 a few months later as a result of tests involving a flat spin. On other occasions after that, I successfully managed a recovery with the use of the afterburner. It was still a scary experience, but the plane did recover.

While George Welch had great credentials as a test pilot, he and I crossed swords many times before he was killed in the F-100. On one occasion, I came back from a test flight and reported a problem with the hydraulic pump. It did not have the capacity to handle full-duty cycles of the flight controls at low speed upon landing.

I explained that during a crosswind landing with rough air, the pilot was forced to manipulate the controls to such an extent that the hydraulic flow would be used up. The plane then wouldn't have the required hydraulic-control power it needed to perform under these weather conditions.

To my amazement, one of the engineers stood up at a flight-test meeting and said, "Well, the answer is to just keep people like Hoover away from the aircraft."

That response was meant as some sort of backhanded compliment. It clearly was not a solution.

My detractors seemed to be saying that the average pilot would not be manipulating the controls that precisely and wouldn't experience these hydraulic problems. I pointed out that pilots needed to fly planes every second without ever letting the aircraft get out of kilter.

The heated debate ended rather abruptly when fellow test pilot Jay Ray Donahue broke into the meeting. He had just experienced a loss of hydraulic pressure and control lockup on landing. But, engineering still wouldn't budge.

In one of the early flights in the prototype YF-100, I had been flying up to the gunnery range at Inyo Kern to fire the guns for the first time. At forty-two thousand feet I experienced a violent, soul-shaking explosion and fireball that belched out of the engine air inlet. It lasted only a millisecond, yet it was terrifying.

With each subsequent explosion, the flames streaked by the cockpit. I had to do something or the F-100 was going to blow up. My mind was racing as I throttled back and then cut the engine. Finally, after shutdown, the explosions ceased. I thought a fuel line had ruptured and due to lack of oxygen at forty-two thousand feet the engine couldn't sustain burning except intermittently.

Ground control told me to bail out. They sent fire trucks and ambulances racing across the desert lake bed to meet me. I was reluctant to give up on the airplane, especially since it was still flying well enough.

I made a split-second decision to try to make it back to the dry lake bed. I wanted to try to prove that the F-100 could be landed without power. Many thought its wing loading was so high that it would take a great deal of speed to stop the sink rate on landing.

I had turned back toward the north base after the first explosion and arrived overhead with plenty of altitude. I planned to execute a circling approach for a lake bed landing. I advised flight test of my intentions to land. They suggested abandoning the plane and then asked if I had used the emergency ram-air-turbine handle, which provided additional hydraulic pressure to the flight controls for landing.

It was on the right side of the cockpit by the seat. When I reached for it, I realized I had already released the handle instinctively.

As the final turn for landing was completed, a landing flare was initiated, and the flight controls began to stiffen. I was losing control of the airplane as I neared the lake bed.

To keep the plane steady, I pulled on the control stick with both hands. The F-100 slammed into the lake bed at 322 mph.

I was momentarily stunned from the impact, which sheared the landing gear. When my vision recovered, the airplane was airborne at a steep bank angle. The rudder control was manual, and I pushed full left rudder in an attempt to get the wings level before hitting the lake bed again. I didn't quite make it. When the right wing hit the lake bed, the plane slithered around its axis twice before sliding to a stop.

The spinning disoriented me. The instrument panel had broken loose on impact and was resting on my legs. I had sharp pain in my legs and severe midback muscle spasms. Despite the discomfort, I tried to collect myself and hoped that help would quickly arrive.

It did. The rescue squad chopped the canopy open. "Be careful," I told them. "Besides the injuries to my legs, I think I've broken my back."

I asked that I be lifted out in the seat by a crane. I also told them I didn't want to be moved until a doctor arrived. Despite some resistance, the rescuers agreed to my demands.

There was good reason for the requests. Just a week before my accident, fellow test pilot Richard L. "Johnny" Johnson had been hospitalized after he'd crash-landed in a Convair F-102 on takeoff. He had a broken vertebra. I visited him in the hospital and he told me what it felt like when he'd landed. He said muscle spasms occurred around the fracture as nature's way of protecting the spinal cord.

I told the doctor who arrived about my concerns. The rescue crew did extricate me in the seat from the cockpit with a crane. Medics kept my body in a stable position on the ride to the hospital.

I continued to experience back spasms, but when we arrived at the hospital, the X rays did not indicate a fracture.

My refusal to accept the X-ray findings was not appreciated by the doctor in residence. In spite of his protestations, my request that I be transferred to the Good Samaritan Hospital in Los Angeles was granted.

The set of X rays taken there revealed a diagonal fracture. This type of fracture only showed up when X rays were taken from shoulder to shoulder. I was told that I could have become a paraplegic had I accepted the first X-ray reading and walked out as suggested.

I ended up in a cast. When it came off, I was confined day and night to a rigid brace. Six weeks later, I was back in action.

This had been our experience with the violent compressor stalls with the J-57 engine. But it was not the last by a long shot. They did become less intense with new developments, but were still an occasional nuisance for years to come.

During my career, I've had my nose, teeth, jaw, and both legs broken. Fortunately, nothing has ever diminished my capability to fly.

After recovering from those types of injuries, it's never easy to get back in the same plane responsible for the accident. Shortly after I recovered from my fractured back, however, I was back in the F-100 performing a similar program of tests involving rapid throttle shifts from idle power to wide open.

Those compressor stalls that caused the F-100 accident became as common as flying at altitude. At times, I felt as if I were sitting on top of a 75-mm cannon. Every time a blast occurred, my feet would come right off the floor. If I had done those tests a thousand times without incident, I would never have been comfortable with it.

Ground control and a group of engineers seemed reluctant to believe that the compressor-stall explosions in the F-100 were so violent. To convince them, I left the microphone switch on open so they could listen in. After that, they decided on further modifications to the fuel control.

That series of tests resulted in alterations to the hydraulic system for the F-100. When the engineers finalized the specs, the capacity for the system was nearly doubled.

The F-100 was only the latest in a series of innovative aircraft designed and manufactured by North American Aviation. Head man at the company during this time was a West Virginian named James H. "Dutch" Kindelberger. Next in command was Lee Atwood, a quiet, unassuming civil engineer from the University of Texas.

The two men worked well together in spite of their far different personalities. On one occasion we were all together in a conference room at North American, briefing Secretary of the Air Force Gene Zuckert on the development of a new plane. Dutch preferred the conference room warm while Lee wanted it cooler. They kept asking me separately to turn the thermostat up or down, and so the temperature changed dramatically every fifteen minutes or so.

Finally, Secretary Zuckert had apparently tired of being too cool one minute and too warm the next: "How can we trust you guys to build airplanes for us? You can't even agree on the climate in a conference room."

Regardless of any differences, both these men loved aviation. Together they propelled North American forward to the point where it was the premier aviation company in the world.

Dutch Kindelberger was very innovative in creating mass production techniques for the assembly of aircraft. This accomplishment earned him the title "the Henry Ford of aviation."

Lee Atwood joined North American along with Kindelberger in

1930. His engineering skills enabled him to assist in the design of many of the company's most innovative aircraft over the next decade.

Lee was called the "dean of aerospace" for his many contributions. Bob Cattoi, vice president of engineering for Rockwell, told me he thought Lee was "one of the top ten technical geniuses of the century."

Both men were committed to designing and manufacturing aircraft for the defense of the United States. Kindelberger was quoted as saying, "Our responsibilities to the nation are as direct and vital as those of the United States government." Atwood added, "At North American, we turn square corners when we deal with the government . . . for it is not just the customer, but the sovereign law of the land."

I was proud and honored to be friends with such fine leaders as Dutch and Lee. In the 1940s and 1950s, North American built nearly sixty thousand trainers, fighters, and attack and bombing aircraft. This is an accomplishment unmatched in the history of aviation.

Those numbers pale in comparison to the incredible diversity of their later aviation projects. By the 1960s, they included the development of the Hound Dog missile system—the nuclear strike weapon of the Strategic Air Command (SAC)—the guidance system and electronics for the Minuteman intercontinental ballistic missile, and the inertial navigation systems for the Polaris (armed nuclear submarine fleet). The B-70, which was the most powerful strategic bomber ever designed, and the rocket engines for Thor intermediate missiles were also North American projects. They developed the A-5 Vigilante attack aircraft for the Navy and the combat electronics for first-line defense aircraft for most of the free world.

In future years, North American would design, build, and flight-test the X-15 aerospace research rocket plane, develop power reactors, and build rocket engines.

I believe the success of the company was due to many factors, but one stood out above everything else. Dutch Kindelberger and Lee Atwood shared a common love, understanding, and vision of the aviation industry and its future.

During this time, executives at North American were anxious to get members of the Thunderbirds, the crack Air Force demonstration team, to switch from flying the F-84 to the F-100.

One of the goals of the Thunderbirds, like the Navy's Blue Angels, is to motivate young men and women into joining the military. I always enjoyed watching them and admired their precision flight.

Word reached us that the Thunderbird pilots didn't have confidence in the F-100. I flew to Randolph Field in Texas where the colonel in charge of the Thunderbirds told me, "Bob, they don't want to fly the

F-100. They don't believe it will show well. It takes too much room for a turnaround."

With his permission, I visited the home of the Thunderbirds at Nellis Air Force Base near Las Vegas. I talked up the F-100 and then performed an aerobatic show so they could witness its capability firsthand.

The demonstration paid off. The Thunderbirds' team leader took the F-100 up shortly thereafter. His laudations echoed mine and thoroughly convinced them of the plane's capability.

At no cost to the government, North American modified the F-100s with smoke tanks. The Thunderbirds proudly flew them for thirteen years.

Demonstrating the F-100 was the purest of pleasures. In 1970, aviation writer Lou Davis described one of my performances for *Air Line Pilot* magazine:

> The North American F-100 streaked across the hot airbase runway upside down. The canopy and the pilot's head were but a few feet above the concrete. At 400 ATS [knots], the pace was furious. For a split second, the nose pitched down in tribute to a stubborn thermal. Just as quickly, it was back up, zeroed-in on the precise flight path. By the time my heart started to pound and my head-born computer told me that the jet was dangerously close to trouble, the threat was gone. So was the F-100.
>
> With afterburner blazing, it was passing through 1,000 feet, headed for the color blue, executing a superbly timed eight-point vertical roll before the roll-out on top. More rapid-fire maneuvers followed: loops, more rolls, slow and max speed passes and then the soft squeal of the touchdown and the short roll to the parking ramp. Applause from the 20,000 Air Force personnel, friends and families was deafening.

18

Japanese Masseuse Torture

Even though my days of flying experimental aircraft at North American were over, I still performed in numerous air shows for them.

Flying demonstrations at events around the world balanced my life. Working in corporate America had its advantages and challenges, but I still loved being in the air as much as possible.

When I wasn't flying, I concentrated my efforts on learning everything I could about North American Aviation. The company was fairly small in the early 1950s, but Lee Atwood envisioned it with advanced-technology divisions including electronics, rocket propulsion, and atomic energy.

When Lee reorganized and expanded the company, design and manufacture of all aircraft ended up in the aircraft divisions. A marketing department was started, and I was appointed director of customer relations. I would also be assistant to the marketing director.

My new position began in 1955, but before long Lee Atwood altered my destiny once again. He appointed Gen. Austin Davis, an old friend who had flown unarmed reconnaissance P-38s during War II, to head the North American Aircraft Divisions in Los Angeles, Tulsa, and Columbus, Ohio. When Austin took the job, he asked Lee if I could become his executive assistant.

I was flattered by Austin's request, and when he accepted his position, I accepted mine. This was a great opportunity. I now saw the entire operation of the company from the catbird seat.

During this time, North American was developing the OV-10 Bronco, an observation plane being built for the Navy, Air Force, and the Marine Corps at the Columbus, Ohio, facility. Developed during the Vietnam War, the OV-10 was built first for the Navy. Designated a LARA (light armed reconnaissance airplane), it could be utilized for counterinsurgency missions.

Lee Atwood sent me back to Columbus to evaluate the plane, which was about to undergo an NPE (Navy Performance Evaluation). Forty people were going to descend upon the plant, evaluate its performance, and decide whether it met the Navy's requirements.

When I arrived back at Columbus, the division president met me personally. "We think we've got a good airplane, Bob," he boasted. He then asked me what I wanted to do first. "I want to see every flight test report that has been prepared. Then I want to talk to your test pilots one by one," I said.

After I went through the flight reports, I sat down with Ed Gillespie, the project test pilot. He was a man I really admired.

I told him, "You squawked about this point in the report, then again in the next one, and so forth. How come that wasn't fixed? That was ten months ago."

Ed was a company man and quite loyal and chose his words carefully: "Bob, I reported it again and again. Unfortunately, nothing happened."

Ed and I then continued on through the reports. More squawks appeared, but no corrections were made.

After taking time to fly with Ed and the other test pilots, I finally went to the head of the division.

"You know there's one thing I can't understand. Don't you realize that your test pilots are former Navy test pilots? When they tell you something is wrong, it's extremely likely that their counterpart in the Navy will find the same problems when they evaluate the plane."

Ignoring my remarks, the executive proclaimed, somewhat disgruntled, "What's your report going to be?"

"I will suggest that the NPE be delayed. I don't believe any inspection should occur until all the squawks the test pilots have reported are corrected."

The evaluation was delayed after Lee Atwood saw my report. Then the corrections were made, one by one. Later, the OV-10 ended up passing the NPE with flying colors. It was flown extensively in Southeast Asia and had a good combat record.

Months later, North American management honored me with a special dinner one night at the Palladium in Los Angeles. Lee Atwood brought in Jimmy Doolittle, Chuck Yeager, and astronaut Gordon Cooper, among others. NBC's Roy Neal was the master of ceremonies.

What was most enjoyable about the evening was that guests were kept hidden backstage. They surprised me with their appearance when the festivities began. Lee Atwood addressed the crowd. He talked about my work on the OV-10 and other contributions to the company. It was a special evening.

When I flew aerobatic demonstrations for the military, they would send planes to Los Angeles to fly me to bases all over the country. At the time, I was the only civilian test pilot allowed to fly Navy and Air Force aircraft for this purpose.

Later on, due to liability concerns, I had to discontinue flying military planes. Lee Atwood suggested we look for an F-86 to buy so that I could continue my demonstrations on behalf of the company.

Since the military had not declared them surplus, none were available. I then started looking for a P-51 Mustang. A gentleman named Dave Lindsey was rebuilding them at his Cavalier Company in Sarasota, Florida. North American purchased one from him for my use.

The P-51 we bought had a rich history. It may well be the greatest piston-engined fighter of all time. Like the Spitfires, P-47s, P-38s, and Zeros before it, the Mustangs became legendary for their exploits in World War II.

The P-51 was born of the need to fulfill the British RAF's insatiable appetite for fighter aircraft. It made its first appearance in 1943 when it accompanied B-17s and B-24s on their long-range bombing missions. What the Spitfire had done to protect the bombers for forty-five minutes, the P-51 could do for several hours.

The P-51 performed admirably, and many believe it established Allied air superiority. In all, the P-51 brought down nearly five thousand enemy aircraft during the war. It is no wonder the Luftwaffe chief, Reichsmarschall Hermann Göring, told colleagues he knew the war was over when the P-51 entered the fray.

The P-51 we bought was designated N2251D since North American purchased it twenty-two years after its first flight. Its aerobatic capability was just what I was looking for. That plane and I were made for one another.

Most flights were completed without a hitch. However, while on a flight-safety tour with the Air Force in 1961, I lost the engine during a demonstration at Myrtle Beach Air Force Base in South Carolina. It failed during a landing out of a roll when the P-51 was inverted. I was just barely able to get rightside up before touching down several hundred yards short of the runway. The P-51 hit in a creek bed, and the plane and I were submerged in mud. I was covered from head to toe and couldn't momentarily determine where I was.

The plane's nose section and one wing had been sheared. Rescue crews responded at once with a fire-suppressant helicopter. I was finally able to climb out of the cockpit, unhurt except for a sore back and a bruised ego.

After I clobbered the P-51, my insurance rates skyrocketed from $350 per flight to $5,000. My recommendation to Lee Atwood was to collect the insurance money and discontinue my demonstrations. To my amazement, however, he wanted the plane rebuilt and flown back to California.

While the P-51 was being rebuilt, I received a number of requests to perform aerobatic routines across the country. When I explained that the insurance premiums were prohibitive, promoters shocked me by agreeing to pick up the $5,000-per-flight cost.

Later, we discovered from insurance agent Joe DeBona, who was also the pilot for motion-picture star James Stewart, that our agent was gouging us with those exorbitant rates.

Joe said he knew that because of his relationship with Lloyds of London. He told me that every year at their London insurance conference, my safety record was brought up as a symbol of excellence. "Your premiums should be as low as any in the aviation industry," he told me. When the smoke cleared, Joe handled my insurance at a cost of $50 a flight!

I flew the P-51 at nearly every Air Force and Navy base across the country and in North America. In addition, we hit the major air shows in Dallas–Ft. Worth; Reading, Pennsylvania; Vancouver; Toronto; Winnipeg; and upstate New York. The promotional value to North American far outweighed the cost.

My travel adventures for North American in production aircraft took me to Mexico, Guatemala, Venezuela, Okinawa, the Philippines, Taiwan, and all over Japan. Since the bases were so close together in Japan, I once performed at seven different locations in one day.

At the base in Iizuka, Japan, the host commander planned a big party in my honor. I tried to beg off since I had been on the road for several days straight. I was simply exhausted.

The commander insisted, however, and told me he had just the remedy for my weary bones.

"Iizuka is the home for the training academy for masseuse," he informed me. "You will have the best of the best, the one who trains all the others." Bowing to his wishes, I descended upon the plush massage academy where a muscular Japanese woman greeted me.

After a tour of the facility, several women bathed me with sponges while I sat on a stool. The women then escorted me to a hot pool. From there I was led to a massage room.

The expert masseuse approached, bowed, and went to work. She was massaging my back and shoulders. All at once I felt a rather pointed object in the small of my back. When I craned my head around, I saw that she was using her chin to massage my vertebrae.

The massage continued for fifteen minutes or so. Then I heard what sounded like weeping. Raising my head, I saw that my talented and famous masseuse was crying.

I was concerned that I had offended her in some way. Since I didn't speak Japanese and she didn't speak English, I had no idea what I might have done for her to be so upset. As it turned out, the masseuse was so distraught because I was the first person that she could not get to relax.

I apologized and explained that I had just returned from days of multiple air-show performances. My explanations were of little help and I left still very concerned for her feelings.

After that experience, I had a better understanding of how much pure physical effort went into performing multiple aerobatic routines in one day. Manipulating the controls and pulling heavy g's along with insufficient rest tightened up the body like a bowstring.

In those days, I didn't wear a G suit, but instead flew in a business suit and a wide-brimmed straw hat. The formal dress had become my trademark. Every time I pulled g's, I would take a deep breath and then tighten the muscles in my neck and stomach. That kept the blood from going below my waist and causing a blackout.

I was often asked about my preference for wearing the dark business suit. I'd explain that by wearing it, I never had to change clothes for a business meeting, cocktail hour, or an evening on the town. If that explanation didn't work, I'd say that if I stubbed my toe and busted my buttons, I would save the undertaker a lot of time and trouble.

Wearing that suit came in handy one time when I was demonstrating the F-100 over in Guam. Astronaut Wally Schirra tells the story better than I do.

> Bob stepped off the plane in his tailored three-piece suit. Immediately some of his buddies told him they wanted to pull one over on some of the pilots and their wives. They took him to a party and introduced Bob as "Dr. Hoover, a physician with a specialty in breast cancer." One thing led to another, and before long Bob was back in the cloakroom, "examining" several of the young wives. The next day, they and their husbands were quite startled when "Dr. Bob" was announced as a great test pilot. Several of the wives turned beet red as Bob climbed in an F-100 to perform his demonstration.

*   *   *

Robby Risner was a friend of mine who was a gifted aviator. He had always been promoted at the earliest time possible all the way up the line.

Later, Robby was shot down over Vietnam. He survived repeated torture during his seven years in the Hanoi prison camp.

Prior to that time, Robby was assigned as my escort officer. We flew around the Pacific arena and performed at various air bases. He had just been promoted to major when we flew to Taipei to put on an air show for the Chinese Air Force.

I flew with a Chinese general who was their chief of staff in his transport plane to the next stop on the tour. There I was to demonstrate both the F-86 and the F-100, which the Chinese had purchased from our government.

Either too much food or drink caused me terrible diarrhea that day. Extreme one-hundred-degree temperatures and equally high humidity compounded my discomfort.

I was asked to first fly the F-100, the newer of the two planes, in front of the Chinese Air Force. Then I would fly the F-86 so the pilots wouldn't get the idea that it was in any way obsolete.

The F-86 had a sliding canopy. When flying at low speeds, I generally left it open. Because of my touchy gastrointestinal condition and the extreme heat, I left the canopy open to perform one particular maneuver.

I'd done rolls at a lower speed on takeoff many times with all different types of airplanes. The maneuver consisted of taking off, rolling the airplane 360 degrees, coming in and touching on one wheel, rolling, and touching on the other wheel before completing a standard landing. The tricky part was not to let a wing drag even though it came close to the ground during the maneuver.

When the canopy was open and the airplane upside down, the fuselage did not get the same air flow or lift over it as it did with the canopy closed. At the low speeds I utilized while rolling, that suddenly was critical. The plane started to lose lift.

I recognized the problem right away, but recovering was another matter. Suddenly, the F-86 was in a stall, and to get back control, I had to play the stall from upside down to rightside up. That maneuver paid off. Even though I hit hard on landing, I didn't damage the airplane.

I was disappointed in my judgment. I should have provided more room for safety. I'd almost paid the ultimate price for carelessness. I was lucky to have survived.

The Chinese pilots and fans who crowded the airfield had never seen this kind of performance. They had no idea I had been in danger when they rushed the F-86 in mass and boosted me up in the air. My feet never touched the ground for several minutes. If they had dropped me on that concrete ramp, my head would have split like a ripe water-melon.

This enthusiastic demonstration went on for some time until guards rescued me. Robby helped get me to safety, but the heat, my lower-intestinal malady, the brush with tragedy, and the rush of humanity made that day at the Chinese base one I never forgot.

19

Waterskiing with Yuri

From my point of view, Defense Secretary Robert McNamara could not have hurt our country's aviation research and development effort more if he had been president of the Communist Party. The X-15, XB-70, and many other research programs existed because of government funding.

Presidents Kennedy and Johnson's defense policies, implemented by McNamara in the early 1960s, cut that funding. This destroyed the enormous advantage the United States had built up in the fifteen years after World War II.

This was especially disheartening to me because of the constant threat from the Soviets during the Cold War battle for air supremacy and space exploration. McNamara's defense-budget scissors slowed our progress and allowed the Soviets to catch up.

Prior to the clampdown, our government spent millions of dollars funding research and development. These programs propelled the United States to the leading edge of technology. Our country had a further boost when Wernher von Braun and his German colleagues joined our design team after World War II. They were brought over as part of Project Paperclip, which was designed to capitalize on the talents of German rocketeers.

Germany's V-1 work in rocket research had put them way ahead of our country. We had virtually no test programs in rocket research at that time.

Von Braun's expertise combined with good old American ingenuity spurred the United States back into the technological fray. He was the father of our rocket program. Without his work at Huntsville, Alabama, we would have been left in the dust.

During my stay at Wright Field in Dayton, I was introduced to Mr. von Braun. I also talked with him when he visited the North American plant in Los Angeles. A former pilot, he was a pleasant, unpretentious man who was unmistakably a genius.

The Soviets finally caught up with us when they produced the MiG-21. The development of that aircraft elevated military stakes between the two countries.

By 1965, the Cold War tension between the Soviet Union and the United States was at its peak. Neither side trusted the other.

Lyndon Johnson was the president of the United States, having taken his oath of office two years earlier when John Kennedy was assassinated. His vice president was Hubert Humphrey, the former senator from Minnesota.

The first secretary of the Communist Party in the Soviet Union was Leonid Brezhnev. He had replaced Nikita Khrushchev when he was dismissed from office in 1964.

Besides waging a battle in development of retaliatory military weapons, the Soviet Union and the United States volleyed back and forth with achievements in outer space. A number of unmanned space launches earmarked the late 1950s. When the Soviets launched *Vostok 1*, carrying cosmonaut Yuri A. Gagarin, into space on April 12, 1961, they scored a major victory.

Needless to say, the White House and our space agencies were disappointed to learn of the Soviets' achievement. Besides its research and development value, Gagarin's single-orbit space voyage was a huge public relations coup for the Soviet Union.

Twenty-three days later, on May 5, 1961, Comdr. Alan Shepard became the first American in space. It may have been a suborbital flight for only fifteen minutes in *Freedom 7*, but the United States was on the map.

American Virgil I. "Gus" Grissom duplicated Shepard's suborbital feat in *Liberty Bell* in July of that year. Gherman Titov, another Soviet cosmonaut, retaliated with seventeen orbits the following month in *Vostok 2*.

Not until February of 1962 did the future U.S. senator from Ohio, John Glenn, become the first American to orbit the earth. Astronauts Scott Carpenter, Wally Schirra, and Gordon Cooper followed Glenn into space. Cooper completed twenty-two orbits on May 15, 1963.

The United States and the Soviet Union continued to alternate achievements in space for the next two years. Gus Grissom and John

Young were our first tandem to orbit around the earth on March 23, 1965.

In June of that year, Jim McDivitt and Ed White completed sixty-two orbits in *Gemini 4*. As soon as they returned in *Gemini 4*, the two astronauts were thrown into one of the biggest Cold War public relations battles of the decade.

The Soviet Union had kept a lid on its military warfare and space capability since the end of World War II. Our government's intelligence operation knew generally about Soviet weaponry. For the most part, however, their potential firepower was kept top secret.

Every other year, on the odd year, the French have held an eleven-day gala Air Show and Aviation Exposition at Le Bourget Field outside Paris. To the surprise and delight of the 1965 Paris Air Show organizers, the Soviet Union agreed to participate for the first time. The Soviet Union's accomplishment of putting the first man in space had probably triggered their desire to showcase not only their space prowess, but military capability as well.

The "Super Bowl of the aviation industry" would be a coming-out party for the Soviets. They came dressed for the occasion. The Soviets sent Yuri Gagarin and his *Vostok 1* spacecraft. *Vostok 3*, which had carried a cosmonaut, a physician, and a physicist into space, was also there. Several high-ranking military officials showed up in Paris just for good measure.

The United States, still embarrassed that the Soviets had beaten them into space with Gagarin's flight, now geared toward recouping our global image by putting the first man on the moon. That would ultimately occur some four years later. On July 20, 1969, Neil Armstrong stirred up the dust on the moon's surface and uttered the famous words, "That's one small step for man, one giant leap for mankind."

In the summer of 1965, however, we were not in a position to grandstand in Paris. No Americans were even scheduled to participate at the air extravaganza. Certainly companies such as North American would have an exhibit booth and chalet, but no flying display. In addition, no American astronauts, spacecraft, nor dignitaries were expected to cross the Atlantic and make an appearance.

Chet Bolin, the U.S. ambassador to France, got wind of the Soviets' intention to impress the world with their space-age achievements. He decided to take action. He called me shortly after my arrival in Paris. I was there as a part of North American's corporate delegation to Paris, but after a fifteen-minute phone call with Chet, my plans changed drastically.

To counteract all the publicity the Soviets were getting, Chet thought I should perform my aerobatic routine in a P-51 at the air show. I would not be in competition, but Chet hoped that my performance would shed some positive light on the American side.

After checking out Chet's request with the folks at North American, I agreed to perform in Paris. Somehow Chet located a P-51 in Belgium, and everything was set.

Little did I know that my trip there would end up involving espionage and international relations.

Upon arrival in Paris, I made the rounds in my corporate capacity. All the while Chet was publicizing my upcoming routine in the P-51. Right from the beginning, the world press picked up on the intense rivalry between the United States and the Soviet Union. This competition would form a basic undercurrent for the air show. I was thrown right in the middle of the melee when a French television producer asked if I would appear on a program with cosmonaut Yuri Gagarin.

Although they wanted to publicize Gagarin as the first man in space, Russian authorities kept their star virtually under lock and key. He was hidden away and protected from the media. When he did make a public appearance, he could not take a step or say a word without permission of Soviet officials.

Later talks with his Soviet colleagues explained why. Gagarin was an inexperienced aviator, one who was apparently chosen more for his personality than his flying prowess. They did not want him to embarrass the Soviet Union with his answers to technical questions from the media. Therefore, they did not allow him to participate in any interviews or activities where they could not have complete control.

He was treated like a petted prisoner. From the lobby of the hotel, we saw that a rather obese Soviet soldier always stood guard outside Gagarin's door. In some ways, I felt sorry for him since he appeared to be little more than a puppet under the control of his Soviet taskmasters.

When the French producer first asked that Gagarin and I be featured on one of their television programs, the Soviets refused. The producer told the Soviets I was going to do the program even if Gagarin didn't. They had a quick change of heart. Gagarin would appear.

In addition to interviews and shots of us beside both American and Russian aircraft, they actually filmed Gagarin and me waterskiing. We were skimming along in the water-sport version of the Cold War. No one kept score, but neither of us wanted to be outdone. I'm not sure who won, but I think my long legs gave me better form!

Gagarin spoke no English. We used an interpreter to communicate. Even though our discussions were superficial, I had a lot of respect for him. It took a great deal of guts and determination to face the dangerous challenge of being the first man put into orbit.

Sergie Mikoyan, the Soviet general accompanying Gagarin, spoke fluent English. I was therefore able to discuss more aspects of aviation with him.

I found General Mikoyan to be friendly and intelligent. His brother Aren designed the MiG, and we were able to debate the pros and cons of that plane in depth.

After my meetings with these men, U.S. government officials asked me to relay any pertinent information gained from them. I was also asked to provide any data I could about the I-266 (later called the MiG-21), which Mikoyan was testing.

I gave them all the information I'd gathered. I suspected my news was old news to our government's intelligence.

The P-51 flight demonstration went well, but Chet Bolin decided to call in reinforcements for the international war of images. He telephoned Vice President Hubert Humphrey and asked whether astronauts James McDivitt and Ed White could attend the Paris show.

McDivitt and White were former test pilots. Jim was the commander of the *Gemini 4* mission while Ed was the first American to take a walk in space, on June 3, 1965.

The Paris Air Show was held just a week after their return from space. The White House initially refused Bolin's request, but Chet was persistent. He argued that the show would be a major event in the eyes of the world since the Soviets had never made an appearance like this before. Chet's tenacity paid off. The White House finally relented.

Jim McDivitt remembers when he was told he might be heading for the Paris Air Show:

> After our Gemini mission, we completed the debriefing on the aircraft carrier on my birthday. We went back to Houston and then participated in a parade or two. At the one in Chicago Vice President Humphrey told Ed and me we might be going to the Paris Air Show. This would be the first time an astronaut had ever made appearances overseas.
>
> We then flew to Washington to meet with President Johnson. We had the Rose Garden ceremony where we received our medals. The ceremony was followed by a reception for congressmen and senators. While we were in the receiving line, Vice President Humphrey told us we were definitely going to Paris.
>
> The only problem was that neither Ed nor I had a passport. Neither did our wives. It was rather hilarious. I remember that a photographer stood our wives against a wall and took their pictures. He then raced over and developed them. Ed and I were spared the photo session since

they used our NASA pictures. Finally, our diplomatic passports were in order.

We were told that we were going to leave right after the reception along with Vice President Humphrey. We were staying at the White House. In fact, the President's daughter Lucy Johnson had been baby-sitting with Ed's and my kids while we were attending all the ceremonies.

Mrs. Humphrey was even flying down from Minnesota to meet us. My wife was concerned about not having an evening dress in case she needed it in Paris. While this is hard to believe, Mrs. Johnson actually loaned both of our wives some of her clothes.

At two or three in the morning, the whole entourage was whisked off to Andrews Air Force Base in the President's helicopter. Then we were off to Paris in *Air Force II*.

Jim's impressions of the Paris Air Show remain vivid in his mind today:

It was quite an extravaganza. If you love airplanes as I do, that was the place to be. I remember being impressed with the sheer number of planes. There was no way you could have seen them all if you'd stayed there a month.

Before leaving for Paris, the astronauts had been briefed by State Department officials. Jim McDivitt remembers their mission:

We were told that the Russians were sending Gagarin to Paris. Before we left, President Johnson told us that our mission was one of peace, so we made a special effort to seek out the Russians and be cordial to them. When I saw Gagarin, I made it a point to go over and talk to him. I knew our countries were caught up in the so-called Cold War, but I wanted to show everyone that Americans were friendly.

Jim McDivitt had an interesting impression of Gagarin:

Many thought Gagarin wasn't much of an aviator, and that other, more experienced pilots could have been chosen by the Russians. I found that talk pure malarkey. Regardless of his background, here was a guy who had the guts to go on that dangerous mission in space. I for one had a lot of respect for him.

After finally making the decision to send the astronauts and Vice President Humphrey to Paris, the State Department opened its checkbook, sparing no expense in promoting their visibility.

The desire for a media triumph involved attention to the smallest detail. I had noticed on an earlier visit that the American embassy lawn was uncut and pockmarked with bare spots. After it was confirmed that the astronauts and Vice President Humphrey were coming, a reception was planned honoring them. The next day the enormous embassy lawn had been completely resodded and spruced up for the occasion.

At the reception, a long receiving line numbered into the hundreds. As I neared the spot where Vice President Humphrey was standing with Jim McDivitt and Ed White, I wondered whether the vice president would remember meeting me. We had been introduced a year earlier at the unveiling of a new North American plane.

Jim McDivitt recalls the reception:

> There were thousands of people at the reception. Ed and I stood in line with Vice President Humphrey and shook so many hands mine were sore afterwards. I knew Bob Hoover was at the show, but when he came through the reception line, we had a warm hug for one another. Bob was a real hero to me. He wasn't a guy to shoot his mouth off about his accomplishments. His reputation came from being a guy who had been there, had taken the risks, and was an inspiration to others.

After I shook hands with Jim and Ed, they introduced me to Vice President Humphrey. It was an emotional moment. He took the time to pull me aside for a brief chat, which caused quite a snag in the receiving line.

Jim and I got together years later in Paris and talked about our experience at the 1965 event. He and his son Mike and Colleen and I got together at our hotel. Jim says it's an evening he will never forget:

> My son Mike recently reminded me that what he remembers about the evening in Paris is that Bob Hoover asked him if he would like to taste some French wine and cheese. Of course he said yes, and expected Bob to bring out a glass of wine and a slice or two of cheese.
>
> What Mike saw next astounded him. Here came Bob with a tray stacked with every cheese imaginable. It was about four feet in diameter. He also brought several bottles of fine French wine and champagne. We all sat in the lobby of the George V Hotel in Paris and thoroughly enjoyed ourselves. What Bob did still amazes Mike to this day.

20

Rockwell's Bandit

In 1968, the most famous merger in aviation history took place. Rockwell and North American Aviation combined to form North American Rockwell.

The merger was the result of Lee Atwood's belief that North American was too dependent on government contracts. He knew the company needed diversification to survive. His hope, and one that proved true, was that in lean times, Rockwell's assortment of products could pull the new company through.

The merger brought together two entirely different companies. North American was the premier aerospace company in the industry. It boasted research advancements that left competitors gasping. Rockwell on the other hand was a smokestack organization that was only peripherally involved in the aviation industry.

At the time of the merger, North American was a $3-billion aerospace giant and the largest producer of military aircraft in the country. Rockwell, the world's largest supplier of automotive mechanical parts, was a $200-million concern.

Rockwell's corporate offices were in Pittsburgh, but it also had an axle factory in Oshkosh, Wisconsin. Ol' Col. Willard Rockwell and his brother had started the business there. Since Willard was quite an aviation buff, he often attended air shows where I performed.

Printing presses, textile machinery, chains, and gas meters were just some of the products manufactured by Rockwell. They also had an Aero Commander division in Oklahoma City, but it was losing more than $13 million a year.

Early on after the merger, I was sent down to evaluate that division's aircraft. I flew the latest model of the twin-engine, cantilevered, high-wing monoplane and checked out its future upgrading design plan on the drawing boards. I also toured the manufacturing operations.

I was surprised to find dozens of unsold airplanes sitting on the ramps outside the hangars. In disrepair, many had discolored or fading paint and flat tires. It was somewhat like an abandoned used-car lot.

Dick Robinson, vice president of sales and later president of the division, asked me if I thought I could develop an aerobatic routine that would instill confidence in and gain attention for the airplane. After spending time with the engineering department and in manufacturing, I was convinced that the airplane was well designed and structurally capable. I concluded that if I could duplicate my P-38 demonstrations from War II, we could accomplish the sales objectives.

The key was to see whether I could perform the P-38 maneuvers within the structural design limits of the Aero Commander. The P-38 was a fighter capable of pulling 7.33 g's, whereas the Shrike Commander was limited to 4.4 g's as a utility design.

We had an accelerometer installed so that I would know the exact number of g's for each maneuver. For the first flight, I gave myself a limit of 3.5 g's and began to lower the g's after a few practice flights.

The first public demonstration was during the annual National Business Aircraft Maintenance Show in Reading, Pennsylvania. All of the aircraft manufacturers as well as a sizable gathering of the media attended this event.

The demonstration went quite well and the North American salespeople were pleased with the reaction. It also gained a great deal of media attention, which didn't set too well with the competition.

The next morning, Dick Robinson and I discussed ways to improve the demonstration. He pointed out that I might consider flying closer to the ground since I didn't have any big propeller to worry about as was the case with the P-51.

That afternoon, I concentrated on flying as close to the ground as possible. On one high-speed flyby, the belly of the plane actually scraped the pavement. I was totally unaware of that happening. The propeller's arc is above the bottom of the plane. In fact, if the landing gear was not or could not be extended, the propellers and engines were not damaged.

When Dick Robinson told me I had scraped the bottom of the plane, I asked what the damage was. We towed the plane behind a hangar away from the crowd to take a look. I lay down in the grass and looked up to see that there was no structural damage. A four-inch radio antenna had been ground down about two inches, and the exposed heads of some of the rivets were sanded down. We used white spray paint to cover the damage and I was back in the air.

Ironically, much of the viewing public thought the scraping of the bottom of the Shrike was part of the act. Since that time, however, I have not pressed my luck to see how low I could fly that plane.

Once these performances in the Shrike demonstrated its capability and intrigued the buying public, it started selling. Within a few months, all the Aero Commanders in the parking lot had been sold. Production increased from one a month, to two, and then eventually to eight a month, quite a significant number.

To promote the Aero Commander, I flew the plane all over the globe. One memorable trip took me to Venezuela, where the city of Caracas had been built around the airport. Fifteen- to twenty-story buildings in the downtown area surrounded the airfield. At either end was a narrow approach where pilots could take off and land.

It was not a runway to be used in bad weather. Danger lurked on either side of the small airfield since one-way expressways ran parallel on each side of the landing strip.

An administration building was located at the end of a runway, and the president of Venezuela was waiting to receive me there when I completed my aerobatic maneuvers. I was to roll the Aero Commander right up in front of the president. I planned to shake hands and then present a North American Rockwell pen-and-pencil set to him.

Once I got airborne and began my air show, I noticed that literally tens of thousands of people had gathered to watch. More than that, traffic on the expressways had stopped. People were standing outside their cars with eyes skyward. There were spectators not only on the expressways and on all the other streets, but shoulder to shoulder on the runway as well. I knew that at some point I would need to land where all those people now stood watching me. From above, it looked like swarms of ants had taken over the airport and all of the downtown area.

When flying the aerobatic routines, I always carried just enough fuel for the performance. This was no exception, and I didn't have enough fuel to get me to another airport.

During the performance, I tried to communicate to ground control that they needed to clear the people off the runway, but the language barrier deterred my efforts. Eventually, however, I saw police attempting to move the cheering crowd back.

The police could only move the spectators back as far as the edge of the concrete runway. Despite their assistance, I feared that some overzealous spectator might run out in front of the Aero Commander as I was landing. If I left the engines running and hit someone, he or she would be chopped to pieces. If I was performing my Energy Management Maneuver, the propellers would be feathered and the result would be like hitting someone with a car.

I chose the latter and lined up for the runway with the engines shut down. Just as I had anticipated, people started running all over the place. I slammed on the brakes and stopped as quickly as possible.

Fortunately, no one was hit, but the crowd swarmed the Commander as it rolled to a stop. I looked out at all the curious faces. The fans were waving their arms and beating on the side of the airplane.

I had come to a stop a thousand feet away from where the president was waiting. "How am I going to get through that crowd?" I asked myself.

All at once I saw military police and guards pulling the spectators away from the plane and creating a path to the president's platform. I expected a great big, warm handshake, but instead, the president ignored me and turned toward an aide.

I stood there wondering what was going on. Later I learned that the president told the aide, "I don't want to meet the president of the company. I want to meet Bob Hoover." Since I was dressed in a business suit and straw hat instead of a flight suit, he assumed I couldn't possibly be the pilot.

The president did finally greet me after the aide explained who I was. I had been warned not to reach into my jacket for the pen-and-pencil set since an excitable bodyguard could misinterpret the gesture as an attempt to assassinate the president.

I therefore asked an aide to retrieve the present from my pocket. I smiled and nodded as I gave the pen-and-pencil set to my host.

The crowd at Caracas was mild-mannered in comparison to the reception I once received in Rio. Over a million people turned out and the event was chaotic.

After the performance was over, the crowd rushed my plane. When the police finally got to me, patches of my suit had been cut away by frenzied spectators wanting a souvenir.

In the late 1970s, Rockwell came out with the 112 and the 114 Commander. These were single-engine, four-seater, private aircraft. Their cruising speed was approximately 150 miles an hour.

The unveiling of the 114 Commander was as dramatic as a Cecil B. DeMille production. At this highly publicized event, the press, celebrities, and dignitaries from all over the world flocked to see the new plane. They sat in theater-style seating inside a huge hangar at Rockwell's facility in Oklahoma City.

Behind dark blue velvet drapes, the new 114 Commander was

perched on a raised platform. It had been painted a dramatic gold color and the interior was outfitted in luxurious, light tan leather.

To complete the ensemble, an attractive brunette model clad in a tight gold flight suit sat smartly on the left wing. After an announcer had lauded the plane in Hollywood style, huge movie-premiere spotlights focused in on the drapes. To popping flashbulbs and oohs and aahs, the drapes opened to reveal the beautiful new Commander 114.

I flew that gold airplane on sales tours and in air shows all over the country and in Europe, Central and South America, Canada, and Mexico to increase its recognition. Most places I went, the company hired a lovely model to sit on the wing. She was always outfitted in a gold flight suit. It was grueling work, but someone had to do it.

North American had manufactured the T-39 for both the Air Force and the Navy. It became the first American-built business jet and was called the Sabreliner. It was given that name to take advantage of the Sabre designation associated with the great military fighters built by North American.

A Sabreliner division was established, and the Pet Milk Company bought the first one for just under a million dollars. That sale was a forecast of things to come since the Sabreliner became a multimillion-dollar success for the company.

Although the Sabreliner, which held a crew of two and eight to ten passengers, was never intended for aerobatics, it had great maneuverability. I could put it through many of the same routines I performed in the P-51. The two Pratt and Whitney JT 12A-8 engines gave it .8 Mach capability and an altitude capability of forty-five thousand feet.

That plane was very dependable. And a pleasure to fly. I did, however, experience an unfortunate incident in a Sabreliner at the Hannover Air Show in Germany in 1968. It was owned by a gentleman named Mondavi, who owned the largest publishing company in Italy. He also operated a sales outlet for the Sabreliner in Europe.

Mondavi asked me if I would like to perform in his Sabreliner. North American Rockwell did not want me to perform aerobatics, but I agreed to demonstrate the plane because I enjoyed flying it so much.

Two of Mondavi's pilots sat with me in the cockpit (one in the jump seat), but I handled the controls for the entire flight. It had been raining throughout the performance, but the weather would be the least of my concerns. As I started to land, the red warning light for the right landing gear illuminated. When I pointed that out to my two companions, I was amazed when they said, "Oh, don't worry about that. The red light has been flashing intermittently for some time."

Such an incredible disregard for safety was unimaginable to me. I couldn't believe the pilots had flown several flights with an intermittent red landing-gear warning light indicating an unsafe landing gear. I didn't even know whether I had a real emergency or not.

Years of experience, however, had conditioned me to treat any type of warning as an actual emergency. I explained that to the pilots as I pulled the emergency lanyard, which releases the uplocks that keep the landing gear locked up. The red light was still on, however, leaving me wondering whether the gear was up or down.

I flew by the control tower and asked them to use their binoculars and tell me whether the landing gear was down. "It appears to be down and locked," was their response.

Since the red light was still on, I told the control tower that I intended to touch down on the left wheel first. I would then ease down on the right wheel to see if it was in fact locked. When I did that, I could tell that the right landing gear was "walking" inward on me. It was not locked down securely.

I flew by the tower again. This time they informed me that my observation was correct. To attempt to get the gear down and locked, I flew by and landed on the left wheel and bounced it. That did no good. I then flew to three thousand feet and tried cycling the landing gear handle up and down while pulling g's. That didn't work either.

By this time another red warning light was on, telling me I was extremely low on fuel. I had to land. I informed the tower that I'd belly the Sabreliner in on the grass.

By this time one of the pilots had panicked. "We're going to die. We're going to be killed," he yelled. I was shocked, since he was an experienced pilot.

I calmed him down some when I told him that I had experienced this type of problem many times before. But, his fear was compounded when I put the gear handle in the up position and there was no reaction. The left gear and nose gear remained down and locked. At that point, I knew both engines were going to quit at any moment because the fuel gauge indicated empty and the low-level red light had been on for some time.

I changed my strategy. I informed the tower that I would need to land on the left side of the runway. The landing was going smoothly as I eased the plane down on the left wheel and held the right wing up as long as I could. Shortly after that, it made contact with the runway. We were all starting to relax when suddenly an explosion occurred on the right wing.

The friction from dragging the right wing had caused a spark that ignited fumes that had built up in the fuel tank. When the explosion took place, I lost directional control of the airplane. The Sabreliner went off the runway onto the soft ground. The left landing gear and nose gear were sheared off instantly, and the airplane went up on its nose and then flopped back down.

Fortunately no one was injured. Later on, I expressed my displeasure to Mondavi. I'm sure he gave his pilots an earful.

Three years after the merger of North American and Rockwell, Colleen and I were vacationing in Monterey, California. I received a phone call from Frank Jameson, the president of Ryan Corporation. He was calling from the home of Moshe Dayan, who was the defense minister of Israel at that time.

The Ryan Corporation was famous for having built the *Spirit of St. Louis,* the aircraft that Charles Lindbergh flew across the Atlantic.

I had known Frank for a long time and had a great deal of admiration for his accomplishments. A self-made millionaire, his rise to success began shortly after his release from the Navy.

Frank was calling to tell me that he had been offered the number three position at North American Rockwell. Just as was the situation with Austin Davis before, Frank would only take the position if I agreed to work for him. We would be responsible for corporate marketing plus the field offices that were located in Huntsville, Alabama (for NASA), Colorado Springs (for the Air Defense Command), Omaha, Nebraska (for the Strategic Air Command), Langley, Virginia (for the Tactical Air Command), and Washington, D.C.

In addition to my corporate responsibilities, Frank, himself a pilot, encouraged me to fly more than ever. I stepped up my schedule as a roving ambassador for North American Rockwell.

Frank Jameson was one of the most flamboyant and innately aristocratic men I've ever known. He had one of those old rail cars like the railroad magnates used to own. It had crystal chandeliers that were held in place with piano wire to prevent movement when traveling. The railroad car was also magnificently appointed with the works of famous artists. A guest in the rail car experienced luxury such as the Vanderbilts and the Du Ponts enjoyed back in their day.

Frank was gracious to all the employees at North American Rockwell. His cousin raised fresh fruits and vegetables, and Frank would have truckloads brought to the street outside our corporate offices. The employees were given the fresh produce to take home to their families, free of charge.

One day, Frank showed me a newspaper clipping featuring him at a gala Hollywood party with Eva Gabor. She was the star of the *Green Acres* television show at the time, but had the less attractive reputation of attempting to take advantage of wealthy men she became involved with.

Eva was an exotic lady whose beauty and rich Hungarian-accented "yes, dahling" made her hard for anyone to resist. Sticking my nose into that situation was a mistake to begin with, but Frank asked my opinion of the affair. I gave him what I thought was a pretty strong dose of good common sense.

"Frank, it is generally known in Hollywood and Beverly Hills that the Gabor sisters are fortune hunters. They take everybody they marry to the cleaners," I told him.

A week later, I picked up the *Los Angeles Times* and saw another cozy picture of Eva and Frank on the society page. This time, I said nothing.

"You really don't like the Gabor sisters, do you?" Frank asked me soon after that.

"The whole damn family is the same," I answered. "The mother included. Hell, they'll have their hands in your pocket before you know it."

A few months went by, and I continued to see Frank and Eva on the front pages of the society section. Finally, Frank stopped me cold one morning by telling me, "Bob, I want you to be the first person to know that I've asked Eva to marry me."

My face registered the shock as I congratulated Frank. I decided, however, to take a wait-and-see attitude.

Later, Frank brought Eva, who died in 1995, to our home in Palos Verdes. She was indeed a charming lady, and my son Rob was mesmerized by Eva's wit and friendly manner. In fact, when Rob said his schoolmates would never believe she was there, she asked him to call them. Eva told each of them how much she was enjoying her visit with Rob.

Frank's argument that Eva was not a fortune hunter was right. She was making almost three-quarters of a million dollars a year with her wig company. She didn't need Frank's money. His instincts were correct, and he and Eva had many wonderful years together.

During this time in the early 1970s, I met and became friends with another film celebrity, the great actor James Stewart. He had been a B-17 pilot in World War II and was a great fan of aviation. He would often attend air shows where I was performing and be in attendance when our company unveiled a new airplane.

As I've mentioned, unveilings were a big deal in those days, similar to the opening of a Broadway play or a new motion picture. Roscoe Turner and Jimmy Doolittle frequently attended, as did celebrities, aviation executives, and government leaders from around the country. I met Richard Nixon for the first time when we rolled out the X-15.

President Johnson was known to have a fear of flying. When one of his pilots went off the side of the runway in a Sabreliner, he panicked and vowed never again to set foot in that aircraft. He never did.

21

Airplanes Big and Small

Air show performances and demonstrations as well as attending to North American Rockwell corporate matters kept me quite busy as I turned the ripe old age of fifty-one in 1973. Shortly after my birthday, the company's name was changed to Rockwell.

That year I received an unusual call from Welko Gasich, president of the aircraft division of the rival Northrop Aircraft Company.

"Bob, would you be interested in flying our new F-5E Tiger II at the Paris Air Show this year?" he inquired. "We want to show it off. We think you're just the pilot to do that."

"But, Welko," I said, "you've got a number of capable pilots there at Northrop."

"I know, but we need someone with an international reputation to call attention to the plane."

While I was honored by the invitation, I wondered how their pilots would feel about my flying their plane. I was especially concerned because I had twice been president of the Society of Experimental Test Pilots, an organization composed of pilots who had flown experimental aircraft. Most of the Northrop pilots were members, and I didn't want to create a conflict.

"What about offending your pilots?" I asked.

"We've already cleared this with them. They agree that your celebrity status at the Paris Air Show will enhance our chances to sell the airplane all over the world."

"Well, you're very kind. Let me see how my company feels about it."

I contacted Bob Anderson, CEO and president of Rockwell. His first reaction was predictable.

"Why the hell would we want you to fly a plane built by our competitors?" he bellowed.

I had anticipated Bob's response, so I chose my words carefully. "We have no direct competition with the F-5E. I also think that if we do Northrop this favor, somewhere down the line they'll scratch our back."

Bob's expression told me he was still dubious.

"Listen," I continued, "if they're successful in selling the twin-engine tactical fighter to third-world countries, that will cause offshore gold flow into this country. This helps with national employment and other economic factors. Otherwise those third-world countries are going to buy their planes outside the country. The U.S. will lose the revenue."

Bob Anderson reluctantly agreed to permit me to fly the F-5E. Before doing so, however, I ran into another obstacle.

The resident colonel in charge of the Air Force Northrop Plant Representation Office was strongly opposed to my flying the plane since I did not have reserve status with the military and had never flown a T-38 Talon trainer. That plane was similar in construction and design to the F-5A aircraft, the predecessor to the new F-5E.

I bypassed him by calling my old friend George Brown, who had been promoted a number of times since I had last seen him in Korea. He was now a four-star general, commander in chief of the Air Force. George told me to forget the red tape and go fly. I really appreciated his support, but it dawned on me that if I had any type of trouble with the one-of-a-kind F-5E, it might cast an adverse reflection on his decision.

Because of my concern, I flew a T-38 at Williams Air Force Base outside Phoenix. Then I flew to Edwards Air Force Base and took the high-altitude pressure-chamber test.

That behind me, I took two rides in the F-5E at Palmdale and was impressed with its superior performance. My friend Bob Elder, a famous Navy test pilot, assisted me by critiquing my practice flights. I also knew one of the Northrop test pilots had been killed demonstrating the T-38 in Spain, so I studied the F-5E from stem to stern before arriving in France.

Every test pilot knew that the Paris Air Show had a high accident rate, so the desire to make the plane look spectacular had to be tempered with caution. Over the years, I had witnessed several fatal accidents, including the crash of a B-58 that dished out of a barrel roll.

I had also seen an Italian G-91 fighter crash on its landing ap-

proach. The pilot and eleven spectators were killed. The French aerobatic team also lost one of their members in a tragic accident.

In spite of the risks associated with the Paris Air Show, I was intent
on putting on the finest demonstration possible. I stayed awake at night
deciding how I could make the plane look good so interested parties
with third-world air forces would want to buy it.

My favorite response to people who asked how I determined the
aerobatic routines for a particular aircraft was, "You can't pull a rabbit
out of a hat unless you put it there first." I felt it was impossible to
show off an airplane if I didn't have the capability to push the envelope
and put it through maneuvers at the highest possible level of performance.

To that end, I went to the engineering department at Northrop. I
discussed the fact that the airplane was designed for 7.33 g's. Realizing
I would be flying the aircraft with minimal fuel in order to lighten the
load, I requested they clear me for eleven days at 8.5 g's.

I knew if I could fly the plane at those numbers, the aerobatic routines would appear more spectacular. After some discussion, I got the
go-ahead. I was off to Paris.

I would also be flying the Shrike Aero Commander, which Rockwell
was showcasing at Paris. I wanted both planes to look their very best.
I would therefore need a set of maneuvers that would make both of
them look better than the competition. How could we demonstrate
good low-speed handling qualities? What could be done at very low
speeds to make the airplane look great? What could we do at moderate
speeds? High speeds?

The Aero Commander routine surpassed the competition easily and
quickly. I thus focused my attention on the F-5E.

I had already figured out what maneuvers I could demonstrate to
prove that it was the best fighter plane in the show. I felt the main thing
I needed to demonstrate was maneuverability—how tight could it turn,
how steep could it climb?

I knew that performing the best maneuvers possible in a minimum
amount of time was the key to success. Since they were in charge, the
French would already have an advantage. They always put their aviation companies in the best time slots when the audience was at its peak.

The F-5E I was flying was one of a kind with no backup except
spare wheels and brakes. On every flight for eleven straight days, the
landing-gear warning light came on when the gear was extended for
landing. I never knew whether the left main gear was locked down
or not. The Northrop maintenance people were unable to correct the
problem, which apparently involved a computer glitch.

The F-5 had a drag chute that could be used to slow the plane down after landing. However, when I used it, it took a great deal of time and effort to get it repacked and installed for the next flight.

On one occasion, I landed and didn't use the drag chute because I had my airspeed right on the money. I touched down right on the end of the runway, kissed it on the numbers just perfectly, and slowed to about sixty knots.

It was raining and when I applied the brakes, the water built up in front of the tires (hydroplaning). I could feel the brakes becoming completely ineffective. It was almost like waterskiing. Instead of slowing down, the plane seemed to accelerate.

I could see the end of the runway coming up. If I went off the end, the gear was going to collapse, and I'd wreck the plane. I therefore locked the brakes and hoped that they would become effective before the tires blew.

It worked. I stopped on the far end of the runway away from the crowd when the tires blew. I added power and taxied off the runway where the airplane could not be seen by the spectators. No one knew the tires were blown.

Those tires blew because I caught a dry spot on the runway, which is exactly what I wanted to happen. It saved me from going off the runway. It was a bumpy ride clearing the runway because the tires were still on the wheels, banging up and down just like a flat tire on an automobile.

Besides mechanical concerns about the F-5E, I had to deal with the potential for blacking out in the airplane because of the sustained high-g forces. After about forty seconds at 8.5 g's, a pilot can begin involuntarily coughing when he's in an upright position as I was in the F-5E.

To handle the increase in g's, I anticipated my reaction time as I approached forty seconds. I found that for the first fifteen to twenty seconds, I was all right. Then I started going into what I call the choke mode. I would take a deep breath, then hold it. Tightening up all the muscles in my neck clamped down on the blood flow from the head. This kept my vision straight and I avoided blacking out. That method has always worked for me.

The last day of the Paris Air Show was called the Public Day. More than a million people were on hand to view the air displays.

On the Saturday night before Public Day, the French held a reception for all of the pilots flying in the show. Throughout the first ten days, there had been a fierce competition between the French Concorde and the Russian TU-144, both supersonic transports.

I believed the Russian pilot was exceeding his flying capabilities. On one landing, he overshot the runway and had to execute a go-around (aborted landing). On another he landed short.

At the reception, he boasted that on Sunday he would outfly the Concorde. That day, the Concorde went first, and after the pilot performed a high-speed flyby, he pulled up steeply and climbed to approximately ten thousand before leveling off.

When the TU-144 pilot performed the same maneuver, he pulled the nose up so steeply I didn't believe he could possibly recover without a whip stall. I was observing the flight from the deck of the Bendix chalet with members of the press. I yelled, "Get your cameras. He isn't going to recover."

When the pilot stalled, the nose of the plane pitched over violently into a steep dive. As he attempted to pull out of the dive, the airplane started breaking up, and pieces of burning debris rained down on a French village nearby. Miraculously, no one on the ground was hurt. All on board the TU-144 perished.

In my preflight preparation, I considered what specific maneuvers to perform in the F-5E. I decided to begin with a roll on takeoff. I would then head straight up and complete a half roll and pull over before coming straight down toward the ground. I felt doing all that from four thousand feet would be enough to make the plane look superior. It would give the appearance that the aircraft had more power than would ever be needed.

After I completed those preliminary maneuvers at the show, I then set up for four-, eight-, and sixteen-point rolls. After each roll, I went back to a vertical climb and transferred one form of energy, speed, into another, altitude. Those routines displayed the plane's high-speed maneuverability as well as its capabilities at slow speed.

The effort at the Paris Air Show was a success. Three thousand F-5Es were eventually sold, with each plane costing several million dollars.

Prior to my flying for them, Northrop asked what the price tag would be for my services. I told them that Gabe Disaway, a four-star general friend of mine, was advising me to "build a nest egg." He suggested if I charged anything less than $200,000, I was out of my mind.

However, I explained that I did not want to charge a fee. Even though I had flown the F-5E twice a day for ten straight days, the total flying time was less than ten hours.

Once the positive results were tallied, however, Tom Jones, president and CEO of Northrop, not only wrote me a nice letter, but enclosed a stock certificate as well. He thanked me and stated that "for a very short time, you worked for me. As a shareholder, I will now work for you."

In the early 1970s, I was introduced to yet another form of flying— helicopters.

They had always fascinated me. They could be flown backward, sideways, and straight up. I was always impressed with their hummingbird maneuverability, but I'd never flown one.

That changed when Bob Anderson and I became frustrated one day after being told that the weather was not good enough for our helicopter operation to fly us from the Los Angeles Airport offices to our plant in Downey. "Let's learn how to fly helicopters," I said to Bob, "then we won't have to depend on others."

That suited him fine. Although Bob never found time to take lessons, I signed up for a course in Santa Monica the next day. Before I finished the course, I received a call from my old friend famed attorney F. Lee Bailey. He was an avid aviator who had flown jets in the Marines. He also owned the Enstrom Helicopter Company.

Lee told me, "Bob, please continue your instructions, but do so in one of my helicopters. Then I'd like your help in promoting them."

Patty Bailey, Lee's wife, flew one of his helicopters to the Torrance airport. On the day I passed an FAA check ride to obtain my license, Lee staged a press conference during the annual helicopter convention in Anaheim. Later my friend Clay Lacey and I became dealers for him on the West Coast.

Flying a helicopter was a new dimension of flying for me. It's like rubbing your stomach and patting your head at the same time, requiring a different type of dexterity and discipline. After a while, though, I felt comfortable flying the rotary wings.

A few years before I tried my hand at helicopters, a fine aviator named Ben Abruzzo provided me the chance to fly a hot-air balloon. We had become friends at Reno when I agreed to have him fly with me in the P-51 when I started the unlimited air races.

He in turn invited me to fly with him in a balloon race at Flint, Michigan, where I was participating in an air show. The balloons were flown early in the morning or late in the afternoon because there was little wind during these times of day.

Ben invited me to fly after he finished a safety briefing to more than a hundred balloonists.

"I want you to fly my balloon. I'll coach you."

I said, "Ben, I don't know anything about balloons."

"You're just going to do what I tell you to do. You'll actually be operating the balloon from start to finish."

That meant I was in charge of blasting the flame that controlled the hot air that filled the balloon. That in itself was no easy task because I had to anticipate the lag between using the burner and getting lift from the heat. Before I knew it, most all of the other balloons were airborne. Ours was still on the ground.

With Ben's expert tutelage, I ended up placing third in the race—the first time I'd ever been in a hot-air balloon. I really enjoyed the flight except for the landing. By that time, the breeze had picked up at ground level.

The key to landing was to add just enough hot air from the burner to stop the rate of descent. The balloon was supposed to land near a marker set out on the runway of the airport. I found that to be tricky since hitting a definite point depended on just the right drift and rate of descent.

I was moving too quickly when the basket caught the ground. Ben and I and the television cameraman flying with us flopped over in the basket. We weren't hurt, but it was a pretty hard landing. That was enough ballooning for me.

There was no question I had learned from an expert. Ben Abruzzo and two companions were the first balloonists to cross the Atlantic and then the Pacific.

Flying those monstrous balloons requires a great deal of skill. As with most things, experience pays off. I saw that firsthand when I rode with a friend of mine who was a Navy captain. He could take the balloon kiss-close to a row of trees. We'd be right on the corn tassels, just moving along at a good pace. Then he would hit the burner pumping the hot air into the balloon. I was sure we were going to snag the trees, but he just eased up over them, then settled back down. His timing on lighting the burners had been just right.

I've also flown the Goodyear blimp a few times. Nowadays, it's not as difficult, since they have propellers that can be put in reverse. Prior to that feature, however, a pilot only had control of the blimp if he had wind over the control surfaces in the back of the aircraft. Nose-up and nose-down elevators back there gave the pilot pitch control. The rudder provided directional control. That's all that was needed in a blimp since it was always rightside up.

Taking off on a windy day in the blimp was easy. The pilot just rolled the wheel back, added the power, which forces the nose up, and away he went. As soon as he started getting some forward speed, the blimp could be controlled with the elevators. When there was wind, the trick to landing was to adjust the power properly. If the descent was too rapid, the controls had to be pulled back. That cushioned the blimp for landing. Then the power was backed off and it just settled in. Ground personnel grabbed the ropes and that was it.

On a calm day the rate of descent had to be set up while there was still some control from forward speed. Then the pilot had to guess at where he was going to run out of control without flying into the ground and crunching the gondola. On a go-around or landing abort with too much sink rate, adding power would pitch the nose up.

I've seen blimp pilots in past years make as many as ten approaches on a calm day, just trying to prevent a hard landing. However, with reverse propellers, it is a great deal easier.

I participated in a one-of-a-kind aviation extravaganza called Trans-Po '72, the largest air show and international exposition we have ever had in the United States. Held at Dulles Airport outside Washington, D.C., it was to be our version of the famous Paris Air Show.

The driving force behind Trans-Po '72 was Mendel Rivers, a congressman from South Carolina. He was also chairman of the Armed Services Committee. Through his efforts, our government allocated $6 million to underwrite the event.

During the expo, I performed three times a day for nine days in the P-51, the Aero Commander, and the OV-10 Bronco. Crowds were enthusiastic. And large.

Mendel Rivers wanted Trans-Po to become an every-other-year event in the United States. That never happened, but it certainly wasn't his fault.

Tragically, one pilot was killed on each of the first two days of the air show. On the third day, I had trouble in my P-51 when I couldn't get the left landing gear down. I circled for more than forty minutes to use up fuel. I then landed on one wheel, but not without substantial damage to the airplane.

In spite of the fatalities at Trans-Po, when the famous Thunderbirds took to the air, everyone was excited. But their excitement turned to horror when one of the wingmen in an F-4 suddenly lost his flight controls and pitched straight up from the formation with such a high-g acceleration that I figured he was incapacitated.

To his credit, the wingman somehow managed to eject. Meanwhile, the F-4 stalled and then plunged to the ground, exploding in a huge fireball.

The crowd gasped at the crash of the airplane. Then they cheered when they saw the pilot floating under his parachute. Just when everyone relaxed a bit, the parachute drifted and was drawn right into the fireball. That made the tragedy even worse.

Those unfortunate events doomed Trans-Po. Attempts to revive it over the years went nowhere. Mendel Rivers had a great idea, but multiple tragedies in the sky bedeviled him.

*   *   *

Many people have asked me what it's like to see a fellow pilot killed. Unfortunately, in my fifty-plus years in aviation, I've seen far too many. The shock is always the same.

Perhaps the worst situation I ever witnessed came at an air show and race at Cape May, New Jersey, in the mid-1970s. I was starting the races there with the P-51, acting as safety pilot, and performing my Aero Commander and P-51 aerobatic routines.

On the first day of the show, one of the pilots was killed when he hit a pylon with his wing and crashed with a huge fireball.

The second day, a good friend of mine almost killed me. He nearly pushed me into a row of trees when he got too close while I was attempting to start a race at a low altitude.

Unfortunately, the worst was yet to come. In a race, four T-6s were close to one another. The lead plane lost power, the second one flew into him, the third plane hit the second one, and the fourth flew into the ground trying to avoid the others. All the pilots were killed.

At that point, there was complete pandemonium among the stunned crowd. To settle everything down, promoters asked me if I would fly to divert attention away from the tragedy.

An air show performance demands maximum concentration. My sympathies were with the friends and families of those dead pilots, but I concentrated on giving the crowd something else on which to focus.

My flight went off without a hitch, but more tragedy was nearby. A dear friend of mine named Bill Fornoff was killed at an air show just a few miles up the road. He and his son Corky were flying two Grumman F-8-F Bearcats as a team in formation when Bill hit rough air and lost his wing.

My number almost came up a few months later even though I wasn't even airborne. At El Toro, California, a pilot was putting on a demonstration in an F-18. I was to follow him with a Shrike Commander performance, and so I taxied out and contacted the tower.

I wanted to taxi across the active main runway so I could be at the far end of the runway for my scheduled takeoff time after the F-18 Hornet had completed its act. The tower advised me to hold my position. I argued strenuously with them, but they were adamant.

For five minutes, I sat there fuming away in the cockpit, wondering why I was being held back. I then spied the F-18 up over my left-shoulder window. My first thought was, "He's never gonna make it!"

Sure enough, I watched the pilot pull the nose up, but he got it up so steep the plane was sinking toward a certain crash on the runway. The afterburners were at full blast. When he hit, they almost acted like a cushion. He hit on the tail, and the force slapped the nose of the airplane down with a horrible crash. The plane skidded almost a thousand feet, right across the path where I would have been if ground control had allowed me to taxi across the runway.

My escape from that near-tragic episode at El Toro was just one example of the good fortune that has followed me throughout my aviation career. My friend Leo Loudenslager, a great aerobatic champion who's no stranger to tempting fate, says I've been lucky and also made my own luck. He's right on both counts.

22

Honoring Charles Lindbergh

In 1969, I served my first term as president of a prestigious organization called the Society of Experimental Test Pilots. Later on, I would be honored to be the only man ever to hold the office of president twice.

Ironically, when I first wanted to join the organization, whose membership was exclusively pilots who had achieved acclaim in flying experimental aircraft, an executive at North American banned me from doing so. He told me, "You pilots are trying to organize a union. If you join, you can forget working for this company."

He did not understand the intent of the organization. All we wanted to do was begin an exchange of information that would educate people and help save lives. Nevertheless, my request to join was denied. Only many years later was I able to become a member.

When I took the office of president, I was aware that Charles Lindbergh wasn't a member. I talked this over with astronaut Wally Schirra, who was a vice president in the society. He informed me that the great aviator had been asked to be an honorary fellow several times, but always declined.

I had first met Mr. Lindbergh in Europe when I was demonstrating an F-86 for the Air Force. He also visited me from time to time at North American in the late 1960s. He was a member of the board of directors of Pan American Airlines and wanted to keep up-to-date on supersonic-transport research and development.

Charles Lindbergh was a shy and private man. He even used an assumed name for his visits so no one would know he was at the North

American plant. I'd get a phone call telling me "Mr. Schwartz" was coming, so I could prepare for his visit.

After a time, Mr. Lindbergh asked me to call him by his nickname, Slim, but I had trouble doing that. I addressed him as "Mr. Lindbergh" and then "General Lindbergh," but he kept insisting that I call him Slim. Finally I did, but I never felt comfortable doing so.

Many people don't realize that Charles Lindbergh flew combat missions during War II in P-38s and also lectured military pilots on long-range planning when fuel was low.

By that time, Charles Lindbergh had flown nearly every aircraft our country produced. Obviously, he commanded quite an audience. When he spoke, people listened.

He told me that while he was in the Pacific, he successfully guided a young pilot who was low on fuel back to base. He gave the pilot precise instructions about how to reduce the rpm (propeller pitch), keep the throttle wide open, pull the mixture control back until the engine quit, and then move it forward until the engine started again.

While those instructions ruined the engine, Lindbergh knew that was the only way to save the plane and the young pilot's life. When that pilot told people he was guided back to base by Charles Lindbergh, I'll bet no one believed him.

Of course, Mr. Lindbergh's finest hour was when he became the first aviator to fly across the Atlantic. It's an achievement that can never be overestimated. I consider that thirty-three-and-a-half-hour flight in the *Spirit of St. Louis* to be one of the great milestones of aviation. Chuck Yeager's breaking of the sound barrier and Neil Armstrong's moon landing are equally significant.

I once flew a replica of the *Spirit of St. Louis*. My flight only lasted an hour, but I was physically exhausted when I finally landed.

Lindbergh recognized the unresponsiveness of the plane. He once told me that he purposely wanted the plane to be difficult to fly. He said he was worried that if he didn't have to pay attention every second, he might fall asleep. I'm still in awe of how he physically handled the rough conditions during his historic flight.

Mr. Lindbergh's vivid account in his log of his voyage in 1927 always made me feel as if I were right there in the cockpit with him. His words were reprinted in *Aviation, a Smithsonian Guide:*

> The *Spirit of St. Louis* feels more like an overloaded truck than an airplane. My eyes feel dry and hard as stones. The lids pull down with pounds of weight against the muscles. Fog and clouds surround me. Everything is uniform blackness, except for the exhaust's flash on passing mist and the glowing dials in my cockpit, so different from all other lights. My world and life are compressed within these fabric walls.

* * *

Based on his accomplishments, I thought it important that the Society have Mr. Lindbergh as an honorary fellow. Wally and I received permission from the executive committee to again extend the invitation. Wally then contacted Mr. Lindbergh:

> I wrote General Lindbergh a very strong letter. I told him we were very impressed with his contributions to aviation and would like him to become a "fellow" in our organization. I went on to say that we would respect his desire for privacy and not schedule press conferences or permit interviews. Then I put in a final few words that meant business. I said, "This will be the final time we will ask you to become a fellow. If you don't wish to do so, the hell with you."
>
> I certainly meant no disrespect by those words. In keeping with the aviator's creed never to fawn over anyone, regardless of their accomplishments, I wanted him to know that he was just one of us. No more. No less.

Wally's straightforward letter did the trick. After Mr. Lindbergh accepted the invitation, he requested that his visit be organized without fanfare. Wally and I agreed to shield him as much as possible. We knew this would not be easy.

The timing of the annual meeting of the Society of Experimental Test Pilots in 1969 coincided with an important event in American aviation history.

Just days before the ceremony honoring Charles Lindbergh's fellowship in the Society was scheduled, astronauts Neil Armstrong, Buzz Aldrin, and Michael Collins had captivated the world with the first landing on the moon.

Over the years, many people have asked me if I yearned to be an astronaut. I never did for one simple reason: I wanted to be in control of my fate.

By design, the first astronauts were simply along for the ride. After a time, they started gaining some control by actually piloting the spacecraft. When that occurred, I would have been interested in becoming an astronaut, but by then any chance had passed.

Even though I didn't participate in the program, it took nothing away from the incredible admiration I had for the astronauts. I knew many of them when they were test pilots. I saw even more of them since North American Rockwell had been heavily involved in the Apollo program. For most of the launches, I would fly to Cape Canaveral and be a witness to history in the making.

The first American astronaut to be launched had been Alan Shep-

ard. We'd met on the carrier trials with the FJ-2. He was flying a Mc-
Donnell Banshee jet.

I could see right away that Alan was a first-class test pilot. It didn't
surprise me at all when he was chosen as one of the original seven
astronauts.

Astronaut Wally Schirra and I had first met in the early 1950s. I
was test-firing rockets from the F-86 at Inyo Kern Naval Air Station,
the base north of Muroc, where he was assigned as a Navy test pilot.
He was demonstrating the Sidewinder A-9, a heat-seeking missile designed to zoom into the hot tailpipe of enemy aircraft.

Wally is delightful company, a man with a quick laugh and a mem-
ory like an elephant. He always kidded me because I wasn't an ace in
War II. "You should be," he'd say. "Hell, you punched out at least five
Allied planes."

Neil Armstrong was a test pilot assigned by NASA (National Aeronautics and Space Administration) on the North American X-15 test
program when I first met him. On one occasion, he was in the X-15
when some confusion occurred as to where to release him from the
mother ship. That mix-up made it extremely difficult for him to land
safely on the lake bed at Muroc.

I listened to the deadly serious communications between Neil and
ground control from the control room. He was as cool as could be and
used his skill and cunning to maneuver the plane back to a safe landing
without incident.

I had been fortunate to be at Cape Canaveral when Neil and Buzz
Aldrin and Michael Collins headed Apollo XI to the moon. When Neil
stepped out on the surface of the moon and uttered his famous words,
I cheered on my friend like millions of others around the world.

When the three astronauts returned to earth after their historic
flight on July 24, 1969, they were immediately put into quarantine in
Houston. Our medics were taking no chances. They had no idea what
sort of contamination might be prevalent on the moon's surface.

Deke Slayton was running the astronaut program at the time. I also
knew him from flight-test days. I called him to see whether the three
astronauts, all members of the Society, might be released from quarantine in time for the annual awards banquet in Los Angeles.

I told Deke about the special ceremony for Charles Lindbergh. I
also informed him that I wanted to present a special award to the
Apollo XI crew. He promised he'd do everything he could to get them
to the dinner.

Even though it was scheduled one day after their release from quarantine, Deke came through. Neil Armstrong, Buzz Aldrin, and Michael
Collins would be permitted to make an appearance.

The Presidential Suite at the Beverly Hilton in Los Angeles was rented for a private reception in Lindbergh's and the Apollo XI crew's honor before everyone headed down to the main ballroom. Bob Hope and Conrad and Barron Hilton were among the invited guests.

While all of them waited in the suite, I stood by the front door of the hotel, watching for Mr. Lindbergh. At the appointed time, I saw him emerge from a nondescript sedan. "There are a few people who want to meet you, sir. They are at a reception up in a suite," I told him.

"Oh, no," he replied, "I just want to sit and read my speech to you."

"But they just want to be introduced and shake your hand."

"I told you I didn't want any publicity."

Recognizing that I had vowed to help him with that situation, I asked him what he had in mind.

"Is there a private place where I can read you my speech, Bob?" he asked.

"Of course, Mr. Lindbergh. There's a private bedroom in the suite. We'll go there."

Much to the disappointment of the guests, we did just that. To shield the sixty-seven-year-old Mr. Lindbergh as promised, I even blocked a photographer whom Bob Hope had invited from taking a picture.

In the bedroom, I listened patiently as Mr. Lindbergh read his speech. I realized his presence would electrify the audience of eighteen hundred and that what he said would make little or no difference. When he finished, I encouraged him since I knew he was nervous after not having appeared in public for so many years after the tragic kidnapping of his son.

Even though Neil Armstrong, Buzz Aldrin, and Michael Collins were at the dinner, the very moment I brought Charles Lindbergh into the ballroom, all eyes were on him. True to the nature of the test pilots, no one made a fuss, but the energy in that room was unmistakable.

I had positioned my wife, Colleen, to sit between Mr. Lindbergh and Neil Armstrong at our table. To this day, I assume she is the only person to have sat with the first man to cross the Atlantic in an airplane on one side and the first man to set foot on the moon on the other. A UPI cameraman took a picture of them. The next day that photo appeared in newspapers all over the world.

When Neil began signing his autograph for a few people, Mr. Lindbergh leaned over and whispered, "You're making a mistake by signing those." He apparently believed someone might slip in a blank check or sell the autographs to make a buck.

Colleen recognized the uncomfortable moment:

> Neil was taken aback by the comment, not realizing that Mr. Lindbergh was suspicious of everything after the kidnapping. The situation reminded me of when he had visited our home a few years earlier. Mr.

Lindbergh had wanted to come out near the beach because his mother had brought him there to find seashells when he was young.

After he arrived I was nervous, but our seven-year-old-daughter, Anita, didn't know anything about him. She brought a sheet of paper and said, "Mr. Lindbergh, would you please give me your autograph so I can show it at school tomorrow?"

Mr. Lindbergh paused before he answered. It was very quiet. I thought he was going to say no, but he took the piece of paper and signed his name. That incident crossed my mind since Neil was not sure how to reply to Mr. Lindbergh's warning about the autographs.

Finally, Neil looked squarely at him and said, "But you don't understand, these are my fellow aviators and my friends. They've all had high risks too." As we would find out after Mr. Lindbergh spoke, that comment had quite an effect on him.

Mr. Lindbergh's acceptance speech was hailed with an enthusiastic and prolonged standing ovation. He stood there as a symbol of all that was great about our profession.

After the speech, people began wandering up, wanting to shake Mr. Lindbergh's hand. When he reluctantly acquiesced, there was a wild rush to the stage, threatening chaos.

I suggested to him we set up a receiving line. He agreed. When he signed an autograph, that started another stampede. We had to sit him down at a table so that could be done in an orderly fashion.

I'm certain Mr. Lindbergh was deeply touched by the overwhelming response of the test pilots. I also reminded him that the people in that room had their rear ends out on the line just as he had. I believe he felt a real affinity with his fellow aviators and understood why Neil could not ignore the people requesting his autograph.

Shortly after the ceremony, I received a gracious letter from Mr. Lindbergh. His handwriting would confound hieroglyphic experts, but here is the text of the letter:

Hong Kong
October 22, 1969

Dear Bob:

Accumulated obligations and almost constant traveling have caused the lateness of this letter. I just haven't been able to find enough writing time. (It is now dawn, in Hong Kong, after a night that began with room searching—I had arrived at about 21:30, from Honolulu. "No hotel rooms in Hong Kong." I tried three and another that turned out to be a brothel—no luck there either, and then one close to the ferry. "No rooms anywhere, all full!" Finally a woman at the last hotel desk said she had a friend—, so I'm in a small bedroom of a small Chinese private apartment, wondering what I'll encounter after the sun rises and I open the door. (05:30 here; 10:30 Honolulu).

(I have written that I'm in Hong Kong. Actually, it's Kowloon; I haven't crossed the ferry).

But back to the reason for this letter:

Bob, I can't overemphasize my appreciation for the part you took in presenting me with the honorary membership in the Society of Experimental Test Pilots. But again for the most considerate, skillful, and effective way in which you directed all of the proceedings. In addition, to being extraordinarily interesting. The occasion resulted, I think, in the most perfect combination of formality and informality I have ever witnessed.

When I spoke to you by phone from Seattle (Bainbridge Island), you mentioned wanting to reprint my address and of course I was glad to give any authorization. You are welcome to, and to authorize such reprinting at your discretion; reprint it, or excerpts from it; and should you need any written authorization, this letter will constitute it.

Now, since I hear stirrings in the apartment outside of my room, I will dress and open the door. I hope thereafter carrying on as a good experimental test pilot.

Again thanks, and best wishes always.

Charles [R. Lindbergh]

A week later, Pres. Richard Nixon wanted to honor the three astronauts who had raced to the moon. I was invited to that gala affair at the Century Plaza Hotel in Los Angeles. I will never forget the excitement I experienced when Neil Armstrong brought the president from the head table to the table where Colleen and I were seated. Neil introduced the president to us and we shook hands. That was a very kind gesture on Neil's part, and I appreciated it very much.

Years later, in 1986, I was invited to a ceremony at the Smithsonian where I would receive the Lindbergh Medal for Lifetime Achievement. Prior to the ceremony, Anne Morrow Lindbergh, a very gracious lady, gave me permission to have read the letter that I had received from her husband.

I asked Wally Schirra if he would read it. He agreed. After I received the award, I introduced Wally. He read the letter and the audience gave him a generous round of applause. Looking back, I should have left well enough alone, but I decided to liven things up a bit by telling a humorous story involving Wally.

After one of Wally's space flights, he called me from Denver. "Bob," he said, "you know how when a reporter asks you a certain question and you can't answer it like you want to? Then you always wake up in the middle of the night and think of the answer you wish you had given?" I told him I knew exactly what he meant.

"Well, today at a press conference, I thought of it at just the right time," he said. "A reporter asked me, 'Captain Schirra, now that the decision has been made that there will be women in space, do you think there is a possibility of conception?' "

"And what did you say?" I asked him.

"I paused and then said, 'I don't know about conception, but there might be some outercourse.' "

Since I laughed like hell when Wally told me that story, I assumed the audience would have the same response. Apparently, I either didn't tell the story well or misjudged the audience. There was dead silence after I'd finished. I left the stage with no applause and under perhaps the most embarrassing conditions of my entire life.

Wally tried to console me by telling me Deke Slayton had experienced a similar fate when he messed up one of Wally's stories in front of a group of aviators. "The joke went like this," Wally said. "What do you call a prostitute's children?" After waiting for a second or two, Deke said, barely able to contain his own laughter, "Brussels sprouts." Dead silence. No laughter. Of course the real answer was "brothel's sprouts."

That glitch with Wally's story did not dampen one bit the tremendous satisfaction I felt about that evening at the Smithsonian. To receive the Lindbergh Medal was an incredible honor. I cherish it to this day.

23

Speed and More Speed

During my thirty-six-year career with North American and Rockwell, I had many adventures in the air. But none were more exciting than the times when I attempted to set speed records.

My first attempt at such a record was a most memorable one. It had occurred in 1946, just after I returned from World War II.

The challenge was to see how fast I could deliver the mail from Wright Field in Dayton, Ohio, to nearby Columbus. While my memory is a bit fuzzy regarding the particulars of that flight in a P-80 Shooting Star, I do recall one thing very clearly. A seventy-five-year-old gentleman named Orville Wright was there to see me off.

Even though I was just twenty-four, I still remember the thrill of meeting Mr. Wright. I don't remember what he said to me, but I will never forget shaking his hand before getting into the cockpit.

That fortunate meeting permits me to say proudly that I have known Mr. Wright, the man who made the first successful powered flight in a heavier-than-air machine; Charles Lindbergh, the first man to fly across the Atlantic; Chuck Yeager, the first man to fly faster than the speed of sound; Yuri Gagarin, the first man in space; and Neil Armstrong, the first astronaut to set foot on the moon.

Another attempt at a speed record occurred in the mid-1950s. That's when North American requested that I try to gain notoriety for the F-100 F, the first two-place (two-seater) F-100, by attempting to set a speed record from Los Angeles to Andrews Air Force Base in Washington, D.C.

In the backseat with me on that record-breaking attempt was my old friend Robby Risner. Our plan was to refuel the plane at Tinker Air Force Base in Oklahoma City with the engine running during our ten-minute ground time. Then we'd head straight for Andrews, where we would take up numerous high-level government people as part of the project to acquaint them with the F-100's capabilities.

About seventy-five miles from Oklahoma City, I told Robby that I didn't think the fuel was feeding properly. I reduced the power to idle and glided to the runway to save fuel. At Tinker, we refueled, and I had a member of the crew use a stethoscope to make sure all the fuel pumps were operating.

All appeared to be functioning, so off we went. We calculated that we would still break the record in spite of the lost time with power off approaching Oklahoma City.

About a hundred miles from Washington, however, I noticed that we were using fuel out of the main tank faster than it was being transferred from the other tanks. Despite my desire to break the speed record, I cut the power as a safety precaution.

When the plane finally reached Andrews, we had missed the record by just three minutes. I was very disappointed, but later on I would learn that my conservation paid off.

While in Washington, I took a number of military officials and civilian dignitaries for supersonic flights in the F-100. All the while, I was concerned that the fuel wasn't feeding properly.

One of my passengers was Gen. Curtis Le May, the Air Force chief of staff. He would later run for vice president on the American Independent Party ticket with George Wallace.

I was aware of the general's reputation as a harsh disciplinarian. When I finally met him, I found him to be far different from what I anticipated. He was certainly a strict, no-nonsense military officer, but he treated me with respect.

The Air Force pilots associated with this endeavor knew General Le May could put an end to careers if something went wrong during a flight with him. Since I was a civilian with no concern for my job security, I was asked to take him up in the F-100.

It was always pins-and-needles time when generals arrived for their flights. On one occasion, General Le May was forty minutes late for his flight, so I invited Leon Johnson, a four-star general, to take his place.

Just as General Johnson, who led the Ploesti oil-field raids in War II and received the Congressional Medal of Honor, had comfortably strapped himself in, General Le May showed up. I could tell he wasn't pleased that I'd replaced him. The perceptive General Johnson saved me from my dilemma. He climbed out of the cockpit immediately.

General Le May was very quiet for several minutes after we were airborne. When I turned over the controls of the plane to him, he finally opened up a bit.

The F-100 was easy to overcontrol when someone took the controls for the first time. The new pilot experienced a sensitivity that required a steady hand.

I advised General Le May to treat the F-100 like a sensitive woman. My suggestion didn't draw a chuckle, but he obviously understood what I was talking about. He smoothed out the flight in no time.

When I was at the controls, I took the general supersonic on that flight. We did a roll as well. He didn't know I was concerned about the accuracy of the fuel gauge on the main fuel tank even though the North American maintenance people had told me all the fuel pumps were operating. I didn't take any chances on not being near the airport at the completion of each demonstration.

I would later learn that somehow the aft fuel cell, which held 109 gallons of fuel, was never connected. The fuel was trapped and not usable even though the pump was operating. Everybody kept saying I was too conservative for worrying about a problem they thought didn't exist, but my instincts had told me the plane wasn't getting all the fuel on board.

I flew more than twenty flights with that malfunction during that project. Every time the fuel gauge got to a certain level, my wheels were on the ground. If I hadn't backed off and made certain I landed with an excess of fuel, disaster would have occurred.

The secretary of the air force and Sen. Barry Goldwater, himself an accomplished pilot and later an inductee into the Aviation Hall of Fame, were among the other passengers who accompanied me before the problem was corrected. None of them were ever at risk since I made certain that I always had enough fuel to return safely to Andrews.

In the mid-1970s, I was asked by Rockwell to break three time-to-climb altitude records in the 690B Turbo-Propeller Aero Commander. A new record would call attention to the airplane and hopefully increase sales. Attempts at ten thousand, twenty thousand, and thirty thousand feet were anticipated.

The prestigious international air show in Hannover, a city located in north-central Germany near the East German border, was to be our showcase. We anticipated extensive international press coverage. Preflight testing procedures began before dawn. French and German authorities were there and policed our every move.

To qualify to break the record, the plane had to be weighed with me in it. We started the weigh-in at dawn when the Commander was placed on the scales. I expected to be finished in short order. It took more than two hours with me scrunched in a sealed airplane dressed in a business suit.

That plane had been sitting outside all night at freezing temperatures getting cold-soaked. It was like sitting in a freezer since no upholstering or cabin interior was present, just bare metal, which was extremely cold to the touch. Everything that could be removed had been to save weight and permit greater performance.

The day's weather brought freezing cold and later heavy rain. Despite the conditions, I took off and was climbing through thirteen thousand feet when suddenly my instruments and radios went out. Apparently the cold had rendered them inoperable.

I continued on up to thirty-two thousand feet. What I didn't know was that while I was in the air, officials in the control room were going through a horrifying experience. Bob Cattoi, a vice president of engineering for Rockwell, recalls what happened:

> We lost communication with Bob, so all of our eyes were glued to the radar screen. We saw that the Commander was straying off course and actually over into East German airspace. All at once, one of the staff yelled, "Oh, my God."
> We all looked at the screen and saw what he had seen: three MiGs were headed straight in Bob's direction. Quickly, an attempt was made to contact Bob, but we still couldn't get through.

Confident that I had broken all three records, I began my descent. I glanced out to my left and there were three contrails across the sky. I instantly put two and two together. I got the hell out of there.

Bob Cattoi remembers the atmosphere in the control room:

> We were all transfixed. If Bob was shot down, this could cause an international incident. I just hoped somehow he would avoid the MiGs. All we could do was watch the radar screen. Failure of the recorders prohibited Bob from setting a time-to-climb record on that flight, but I guarantee you he set a record for descent.

The question now was whether to make another attempt. I asked for a day or so to thaw out. That wasn't possible, I was told. Bob Cattoi and others argued against my going back up, but I wanted to keep my promise to Rockwell.

I was now forced to make a difficult decision. As I mentioned, that plane was a bare-bones aircraft. It was not only uncomfortable, but I had frozen my butt off. In fact, when I landed my teeth were chattering uncontrollably. I was one cold fish.

After some thought, and assurances that the radios and navigation equipment checked out, I decided I had no choice but to try again. After several cups of coffee, I climbed back in the plane.

The second flight was fraught with as much anxiety as the first. At thirteen thousand feet, the radios and navigational equipment failed as before, so once again I was in terrible weather with only the most basic instruments: needle, ball, and airspeed.

Then I reached thirty-two thousand feet and saw that multiple contrails were converging on me. That meant the Russian MiGs had been alerted more quickly than before. Nevertheless, I entered the overcast weather at the red-line maximum speed with the hope that the radios and navigational equipment would become functional below thirteen thousand feet as they had on the previous flight. Fortunately, they did.

Adding to my worries was concern about fuel. Each of the flights had begun with only enough to attempt to set the record. There was practically no reserve. On this flight, my takeoff had been delayed by air traffic control, which had eroded my fuel supply. As a result, I was critically low on fuel after my rapid descent. The low-level fuel warning light was illuminated throughout the approach to landing.

Despite the problems, by nightfall we had three time-to-climb records. We'd put the Commander into the record books.

Attempting to set long-distance records in the P-51 Mustang presented a different set of challenges. Enough fuel had to be stored to enable the plane to fly the anticipated distance to establish a record.

The answer was to rebuild the wings with thicker aluminum skin so that they would be strong enough to handle the extra weight of the fuel. We retained the bulletproof bladders that were under the cockpit so I could have an escape from fire. Once this was accomplished, the airplane had comfortable coast-to-coast capability at high altitudes.

Sometimes too much fuel in an airplane can be just as big a problem as too little.

On one occasion, I was flying the P-51 cross-country to Pennsylvania from Bend, Oregon. Late at night over the Black Hills of South Dakota, I noticed the engine was running rough.

Aviators have a saying that if they're over rough terrain or water or flying on a dark night in a single-engine airplane, the engine always seems to run rougher than in the daylight hours. I therefore didn't know if it was my imagination or if I really did have trouble on my hands.

I decided to land just to play it safe. That proved wise even though ground engine checks proved normal.

About fifty miles after takeoff the next day, the engine started missing intermittently. I knew I needed to land as quickly as possible. The plane was so heavily loaded with fuel that I needed a long runway. It was also one big combustible fuel tank.

Air traffic control told me of an airport eleven miles away, but that runway was only four thousand feet long. I had never landed the P-51 with that much fuel. I knew the short runway could be a real problem.

My plan was to circle the airport and continue climbing to see if I could gain enough altitude to fly to the larger airport at Pierre, South Dakota, seventy miles away. While I was climbing, I was contacted by a fellow pilot in a Bonanza. He had heard my distress call. He informed me that when I passed him, he noticed I was smoking badly.

Suddenly, I heard an explosion. The engine had blown.

I radioed a Mayday. I was at fifteen thousand feet with no way to get rid of the excess fuel. I set up my approach, turned off all switches for the engine and fuel, and headed for the runway. I was going to be landing on that short runway with incredible speed just to keep control of the plane.

At this enormous weight, one hundred and fifty knots had to be maintained to keep the P-51 under control. Luck was in my favor and the P-51 touched down right on the numbers at the end of the runway. I was then able to turn off on a taxiway at the far end of the field.

To my amazement, not one single person other than me was at that airport. If I had experienced difficulty in landing, no emergency help would have been there to assist me.

The pilot in the Bonanza landed and flew me to Pierre, South Dakota. I left the airplane on the taxiway. I felt silly leaving a note on the windshield of the P-51, but that's what I did.

From then on, I decided that if I was going to carry that much fuel, I needed some way to jettison it. I talked to the mechanics and they solved the problem by adding an electrical pump the pilot could switch on to empty the fuel out of the wingtips.

That was in place when I attempted to set a cross-country speed record on a flight from Los Angeles to Daytona Beach, Florida, in March of 1985. I had just turned sixty-three. That flight was intended to provide publicity for my longtime friend Rick Grissom's Daytona Beach Air Show.

The morning of the proposed flight was dismal. Steady rain pelted the Los Angeles Airport from the moment I arrived at 5 A.M. The cockpit was unpressurized and unheated, so I wore ski clothes over my regular flying suit in anticipation of the fifty-degree-below-zero temperatures at altitude.

To make the ski clothes functional, I had a tailor alter them so they zipped on like cowboy chaps. A heavyweight parka and wool mittens completed the odd ensemble.

With all the preparation behind me, I was disgruntled when shortly after takeoff, I lost the generator (electrical system). I thought I would have to abort. Numerous attempts at resetting the switch were futile. Then the red light suddenly went off. I swerved back out over the coastline and told air traffic control to follow me on radar.

They hit their stopwatches when I tagged the coastline of California. Since I couldn't get a clearance through the missile range near White Sands, New Mexico, I headed in a direction just north of El Paso. My plan was to stay at about thirty-five thousand feet minimum to pick up the jet stream.

I experienced a lack of oxygen at about twenty-nine thousand feet. Then I started to get the bends, an excruciating condition that occurs when an air bubble locks up in a finger, a toe, or a knee. On this flight, I suffered the pain in the knuckle on my middle finger. It was unbelievably painful.

My oxygen mask was not sealed to my face properly, I was experiencing the bends, and the wind gave little assistance. This wasn't what I had in mind when I set out for Florida. The bends lasted almost three hours. The pain traveled like a steady, burning fuse from my finger to my elbow to my shoulder.

Fortunately, the winds began to assist me as I got closer to Florida. With all the problems, I still managed to cross the coastline in five hours and twenty minutes, setting a new record for a propeller-driven plane. Average speed was 409.83 mph. That record still stands for a propeller-driven reciprocating-engine airplane. If I hadn't experienced the oxygen-mask problem and could have flown at a higher altitude, I believe I could have achieved the projected time of four hours and thirty minutes.

Besides records set in the Aero Commander and the P-51 Mustang, I set speed records in the Sabreliner that are still on the books today. Just before my departure from Rockwell in 1986, my good friend and copilot Robert Morganthaler and I flew from St. Louis to Reading, Pennsylvania, at a speed of 572.46 mph. We also hold the record for flying from Kansas City to Reno, at more than 438 mph.

PART

VII

AIR-SHOW MAGIC

24

Air-Show Adventures

Air shows have been part of my life for over half a century. My participation began when I started demonstrating military aircraft in the early 1940s.

I then escalated my performances during my years with North American and Rockwell. I also continued to perform all over the world when I joined Del Smith's Evergreen International Aviation Company after I left Rockwell in 1986.

At an awards ceremony in 1995, my good friend Tom Poberezny said that I have flown in more air shows and performed in front of more spectators than anyone else in history. I jokingly told him that was because I had outlived all the other air-show performers.

While the number of air shows I've participated in continues to grow to this day, I believe I've flown in more than two thousand. Tom says it's more than that. My adventures have taken me around the globe and permitted me to see how the interest in air shows has grown over the twentieth century.

Today more than 26 million people attend air shows in North America each year. Except for major league baseball, more people watch air shows than any other spectator sport.

Flying combat is the greatest challenge for a pilot, but participating in air shows is on a par with testing experimental aircraft. Pilots who go into combat risk uncertainty, and their personal skills determine life or death.

Experimental test pilots require innate abilities to get them through a flight test program. If they are unfortunate, they might end up losing their lives and having streets named in their honor at Edwards Air Force Base, where most of the streets bear the names of dead experimental test pilots.

The air-show pilot must have the same alertness, preciseness, and instinctive abilities as the experimental test pilot. The pilot is also required to fly very low to the ground, something not normally done by the experimental test pilot.

For many years, flight testing was considered more dangerous than performing at air shows. Fortunately, advanced technologies have now dramatically reduced the number of fatalities in the experimental flying arena.

On the contrary, the loss rate for air-show pilots remains high. Performing close to the ground leaves little room for error. Conditions also vary at every air show location. A combination of the airfield elevation and outside temperature (density altitude) has a pronounced effect on both engine and aircraft performance. These variables affect every single performance, as does the velocity of the wind. Because of the combination of factors affecting safety, I have only the highest regard for all pilots who have ever been in this profession.

Air shows and races have a rich heritage in this country. From 1908 until the outbreak of World War I, "air meets" were held. Aviators and aircraft designers alike not only demonstrated their airplanes, but competed in aerobatics, altitude, endurance, and speed contests for cash prizes.

The early airplanes were built of wood and patched together with primitive wire connections and turnbuckles. They had no cockpits per se. The pilots sat out front in wicker-basket seats where they operated a control wheel and rudder pedals.

A large number of fatalities occurred when pilots were thrown from their planes. No safety belts existed. The pilots had to hold on for dear life during a forced landing.

Most air-show pilots wore flight goggles, a baseball hat turned backward, and the Norfolk jacket. Many of them became instant celebrities since the shows were heavily covered by the press.

Competition at the air shows played a leading role in promoting aviation. Early on, the aircraft designers' only purpose was to prove their planes could outrace automobiles. Once that was achieved, the fierce competition was between the aircraft companies to break speed records.

In 1910, Glenn Curtiss, a frequent competitor at the air shows, won $10,000 when he flew from Albany, New York, to New York City, a distance of 152 miles, in slightly less than three hours. One year later,

Calbraith Rodgers flew from Pasadena, California, to New York. He survived *fifteen* crashes and completed the trip in *forty-nine days*.

In the 1920s and 1930s, air shows and races were extremely popular in different parts of the country. This was in spite of numerous fatalities.

The air-show circuit in the United States has always been exciting. The season used to begin on the West Coast in the early part of the year. It then moved to Daytona Beach, Florida, in April. In the summer months, there were shows at Quad Cities, Iowa, Indianapolis, Denver, and over in Nebraska.

In July, Dayton, Ohio, would host a gala show, and I would reacquaint myself each year with old friends from the 1950s. Then in August, the circuit would hit Pittsburgh, Harrisburg, Reading, Binghamton, New York, and the Fly In extravaganza at Oshkosh, Wisconsin. The big finale for the year would be and still is the Reno Air Races and Air Show in mid to late September.

During my years participating at air shows, I have forged cherished friendships with skilled aviators with diverse expertise.

There is something for everyone at an air show. Performers attempt to thrill the crowd by flirting with danger at every turn.

Daredevil stuntman John Kazian is a perfect example. Over the years, I've watched in awe as he's ridden motorcycles through fire, hung on a ladder underneath an airplane, and been dragged through burning walls.

On one occasion, he broke his left arm, but he wouldn't quit long enough for it to mend. It's disfigured, but he's still got the strength of a lion. Talk about passion for what he does. He just hangs on while he performs all his stunts without the benefit of a safety cable.

Jim Franklin is another talented show performer. He can make his trademark black-and-silver War II UPF-7 WACO snap to attention. He pilots the plane through the sky with great skill while his colleague Lee Oman does the wing-walking.

During an air show in Portland one year, it was cold and damp. Lee lost his grip while hanging on the landing gear. When his hand slipped off, only the safety cable saved him.

He dangled from the end of the cable as Jim tried to figure out what to do. Both knew the plane couldn't be landed or Lee would be killed. Jim radioed the tower for help. Fortunately, nearby was airline pilot and fellow air-show performer Bud Granley. He and Jim devised a plan and Bud raced for a pickup truck.

While the spectators watched with nervous anticipation, Bud drove that pickup down the runway at almost one hundred miles per hour. Jim, who had experience in transferring stuntmen to other airplanes, motorcycles, and automobiles, flew overhead at the same speed and deposited Lee close enough to the bed of the pickup so that Bud's friend could use a machete to cut the cable and Lee dropped into the truck bed. Lee was spared to wing-walk another day.

Those wing-walkers are a mystery to me. I think they have a death wish. During my early years flying at air shows, I was performing in Bowling Green, Kentucky, when a young man approached me. He asked me if I would allow him to wing-walk on my Stearman. That seemed harmless enough, so I agreed.

During the flight, the fellow walked out toward the tip of the wing. When I signaled to him to return to the cockpit, he couldn't move. He was frozen with fright.

I knew I couldn't land with him out there on the wing. The added weight that far out on one side of the aircraft would tip the plane, causing me to lose control on landing.

"You're going to be killed if you stay out there," I yelled at him. "There's only one way to survive and that's to climb back here in the cockpit."

The glazed eyes on the man didn't give me much hope. Since the fuel gauge told me I'd better land, I increased the tone of my pleading.

Somehow, some way, he finally started moving toward the cockpit. At the last moment, he climbed back in the plane. I landed safely.

Many years later, my worst fears about wing-walking aerobatic stunts were confirmed during the Reno Air Races. A pilot who wouldn't listen to warnings came in over the airfield upside down. A wing-walker was precariously strapped on the upper wing. The plan was for him to grab a ribbon that was stretched between two poles when the pilot flew the plane near the ground.

My fear was that at the Reno altitude, one bobble from a gust of rough air could mean tragedy. That's what happened. The plane settled inverted into the runway and the wing-walker was decapitated. The headless torso, still attached to the plane by a safety line, thrashed about as it dangled from the wing.

Somehow the pilot rolled the plane rightside up and landed with the body swinging against the side of the cockpit. The crowd witnessed every second of this grotesque tragedy.

There are also skywriters at air shows. Aerobatic great Steve Oliver's wife, Suzanne, is one of the best. Her skill is something I really admire because the one time I tried it I was a miserable failure.

In the 1950s Chuck Yeager and I tried to impress our wives by writing their names in the sky. All we did was make a mess since nobody could have read anything we wrote.

Pyrotechnic expert Rick Gibson is another of the veterans who travel the air show circuit. He constructs a mile-long range of highly dangerous explosives and then simulates bomb drops when the warbirds fly by. At night, the wall of fire is spectacular.

People like John Kazian, Jim Franklin, Suzanne Oliver, and Rick Gibson are like family. We all care about each other and respect one another's abilities.

The feeling of fraternity between us does provide some fun times. On one occasion, I was flying at the Mt. Comfort Air Show outside Indianapolis. As I swooped down on a high-speed pass in the Shrike, I saw fifteen bare bottoms mooning me near the Gibsons' pyrotechnic area. Rick's wife, Sheri, had arranged the greeting for me. I was laughing so hard it was difficult to complete my aerobatic routine.

My own experience with a bit of unusual flying had nothing to do with an air show, but involved a glass of iced tea.

North American had designed the T-39 to carry military and civilian VIPs. I took up high-level people in Washington when we were trying to sell the airplane to different branches of the service.

On one occasion, I had Secretary of the Air Force Gene Zuckert on board. He was sitting in the right seat. George Kennison, a friend and former fellow test pilot, and three generals were in the back.

All at once, Gene asked me, "Will it roll?" I said, "Of course." We were on the speakers. The four men in the back, including one who was drinking a cup of coffee, could hear our discussion.

To prove the T-39's worth, I did a nice, easy barrel roll. The amount of force on our bodies was similar to that in an elevator. It caused none of us to move at all.

After we leveled off, George told me that the general with the cup of coffee hadn't spilled a drop. He was excited and said, "We ought to put that on film." So we did. That's how the Upside Down Iced Tea Maneuver was born.

I decided that if I could roll with a glass of iced tea, why couldn't I pour the tea? That seemed possible, so we mounted a camera to capture the action. Unfortunately, my elbow was in the way, so the camera couldn't record it. I therefore had to pour the liquid with my left hand. That was difficult since I am right-handed. I still had to fly the airplane.

I picked up the pitcher and poured the iced tea as the plane was rolling. When we were upside down, I had a steady stream of tea going into the clear glass. I never spilled a drop. Not even on the first try.

The maneuver became quite well known. I ended up not only doing a commercial, but also appeared on ABC's *That's Incredible!* and other television shows as well.

I had several other opportunities to work with the entertainment industry, but unfortunately, my experiences weren't always positive.

Many times, directors and producers of films asked me to perform routines I felt were unsafe. I was quick to draw the line when they wanted me to fly so low that I might cut people's heads off or kill myself. That made me a bit unpopular with the "creative types" who wanted a daredevil stunt to pep up their film or commercial.

On one occasion, I was hired to work on a commercial that featured Dorothy Stratton, the sultry centerfold for *Playboy* magazine. Production took place up in the Mojave Desert. We filmed until nearly midnight.

The scene called for me to fly the P-51, with landing lights on, right over the top of her head. She was standing in the middle of the runway wearing a flimsy silk negligee. I made several passes, trying to keep my mind on flying. That wasn't easy to do since Ms. Stratton's charms were difficult to ignore.

After each time I passed over her head, the director told me I wasn't low enough. Finally, I told him enough was enough. I refused to fly again.

Show business and air shows have a lot in common. One man who has the vision to combine the very best of both worlds in the coming years is Dave Fink. He's a former executive at Disney and Sony who's organized a concept called the Hollywood Air Force.

Together with experts in music, choreography, and computer technology, Dave plans to promote weekend air-show blockbuster events across the country. For three days, spectators will be treated to a "music concert" open-air atmosphere and spectacular aerial performances by aerobatic greats like Leo Loudenslager, Sean D. Tucker, Steve and Suzanne Oliver, Jim Franklin, and others of note.

I'll also be performing at these shows. Dave's idea is fabulous and will only serve to broaden the appeal of all air shows as we approach the twenty-first century.

My respect for the men and women who promote air shows is immense. They are the risk takers, never knowing if bad weather, competing sports events, or lack of promotion will kill attendance and produce red ink.

Rick Grissom, the organizer of the annual air show at Kissemmee near Orlando, is one of the best. He's survived all the obstacles thrown at him, lost money on occasion, and always come back for more. I was proud that my initial air-show performance in the United States after a successful three-year dogfight with FAA over my medical license (see epilogue for details) was at Rick's show in late 1995.

Another air-show promoter I have great respect for is Bob Cheffin, who ran the Latrobe, Pennsylvania, air show for many years. One year Bob told me he couldn't pay a guarantee up front. I told him, "I'll fly.

If you make money, I make money. Otherwise, I fly for free." Fortunately, we all came out ahead.

Over the years, the air-show promoters organized under an organization called ICAS (International Council of Air Shows). It assists organizers with marketing and promotion over North America.

At the 1995 ICAS convention, I was inducted as the first member of their Hall of Fame. That was a great honor, especially since three of the great aerobatic pilots of our time, Leo Loudenslager, Sean Tucker, and Steve Oliver, were in attendance.

Over the years, I've had a close relationship with all three of these men.

What separates them from many others is their ability to concentrate on precise routines that thrill air-show spectators while avoiding perilous situations from which they cannot recover.

Leo Loudenslager is a flat-out, first-class performer. He's also a talented aircraft designer. He worked his way through the ranks and drove himself to perfection.

Leo didn't become a seven-time National Aerobatic Champion and World Champion by accident. He set his goals and never lost sight of them until they were achieved.

I've always been proud that Leo feels I gave him some inspiration:

> I went to the first Reno Air Races in 1964 and watched Bob Hoover and thought, "Boy, you know if you could fly an airplane like that, there's nothing else." That's where the seed was planted. I watched Bob Hoover perform. I left that show and went back to work on my burning goal.

I'm pleased that I've been able to influence others to enter the aerobatic profession. I can think of no other profession that is as exciting and filled with so many rewarding experiences and wonderful people.

Leo has survived because he's dedicated to planning and flying his aerobatic routine flawlessly.

Former U.S. National Advanced Aerobatic Champion Sean D. Tucker is another great pilot. He has a routine where he cuts three ribbons (two thousand feet apart) in his Challenger Pitts S-25 biplane. He comes in and catches the first ribbon with his right wing on a knife edge. He rolls to the inverted and cuts the middle ribbon. Then he rolls to a left knife edge and cuts the third one. It's an exciting maneuver. It's also very dangerous.

Steve Oliver is another aerobatic pilot who's a champion. He performs a night act in his Chipmunk using pyrotechnics that brighten up the sky like Mardi Gras in New Orleans. The choreography is beautiful, and the image amazing to the eye.

* * *

Starting in 1983, I began flying both the P-51 and the Shrike. As the years went by, I increased my appearances.

With the P-51 Mustang, I completed precision aerobatic routines that included the roll on takeoff, four-, eight-, and sixteen-point hesitation rolls, one-wheel landings, touchdown, pull-up, roll, and touchdown, and the Cuban eight. I featured four complete loops: a round one, a square loop, an eight-sided loop, and a landing out of a loop (description of maneuvers in glossary).

The aerial show in the Shrike was probably the more dramatic of the two since it involved a larger plane. Audiences always enjoyed the Energy Management Maneuver, where I completed rolls and loops with the engines turned off. I also performed the roll on takeoff, one-wheel landings, eight-point hesitation slow rolls, and the loop and vertical climb in the Shrike (description of maneuvers in glossary).

Along with the Sabreliner, the Shrike is probably the most challenging of all the airplanes I have ever flown in air shows. That's because neither plane was designed for high-stress loads requiring constant attention to flying a sensitive and delicate profile.

My longtime friend and announcer Jim Driskell first met me shortly after I joined North American. In early 1973, Jim inquired about flying the Shrike to and from air shows for me. That still hadn't been decided when he met up with Colleen and me at an air show later that summer. After my performance, Colleen remarked, "I don't think that narrator does a very good job explaining what's happening." Jim said, "I don't either." Colleen replied, "Well, do you think you could do better?" Jim said, "I sure as hell think so." Colleen said, "Well, do it then."

From that point on, Jim not only flew the Shrike to air shows, but narrated all of my performances. One of Jim's typical narrations might go something like this:

> Ladies and gentlemen, on the takeoff roll from your right, the incomparable Robert A. "Bob" Hoover flying the Shrike Commander.
>
> What you're going to see today, ladies and gentlemen, will be a series of maneuvers that you probably won't even believe after you see them. As most of you know, the Shrike Commander is not an aerobatic aircraft. Instead, it's an executive airplane that's designed to take people from point A to point B. But Bob is going to put it through a series of maneuvers like you've never seen before.
>
> As he nears the right-hand portion of the viewing area, watch for the sharp pull-up of the nose as he begins his roll to the left, a signature maneuver for Bob Hoover.
>
> As Bob comes downhill now from your right, ladies and gentlemen, watch for the two curls of smoke as he takes the airplane to the maximum permitted 287 miles an hour. As he nears midfield, watch for the sharp pull-up as Bob brings the aircraft to the vertical with both en-

gines running full power. As the aircraft absolutely stops flying, watch how straight over the nose goes.

Now, ladies and gentlemen, Bob is going to the left-hand portion of the viewing area and will again climb to about twenty-five hundred feet above the airport. This time, you're going to see the same maneuver, but as Bob comes downhill, I want you to watch the two trails of smoke as he reaches 287 miles an hour. Suddenly, you will see that there is no smoke since Bob has shut off the engines. Now it's quiet. Very quiet. In fact, just listen to the quiet. Shhh! Just listen.

A number of precision maneuvers follow. Jim then describes the finale:

Following the sixteen-point roll, Bob now climbs to about twenty-five hundred feet above the surface, high to the right. Now watch as Bob circles, getting ready to perform a series of maneuvers *after* he has shut off the engines in the Shrike. First, he'll do an inside barnstormer's loop, followed by an eight-point roll and a 180-degree turn before he lands and taxis right in front of me without ever restarting the engines on the Shrike Commander.

High to your right now, the nose is coming up. That's the signal that Bob is going to be starting downhill. Watch for a one-turn spin to his left. You'll be able to tell by that telltale pigtail in the sky as Bob comes downhill from your right. Just about now, watch the two trails of . . . whoops . . . there's no smoke. He's cut the engines.

Okay, ladies and gentlemen, watch the nose come up, there's the loop. He has to watch his airspeed very, very carefully as he comes down the back side of the loop. Bob has to store enough energy for the eight-point roll, 180-degree turn, and the landing. So watch. If the nose comes up, that means Bob's going to roll the airplane. Yes! He's going to roll the airplane. We'll count the points . . . one, two, three, four . . . Here's a 180-degree turn, a . . . n . . . d touchdown.

Many times, if we're performing at an airport at ground level, Jim will take off his visor and throw it out on the runway and say, "Bob's supposed to taxi up in front of me, but I don't think he favors the wind just right today, so he's not going to be able to get all the way up here." Of course I do, and the nosewheel runs right over his visor.

Jim completes the show by saying, "Ladies and gentlemen, Bob's got a couple of switches to shut off. Then we'll see him." I then step out of the airplane, and Jim says, "From Los Angeles, California, Robert A. 'Bob' Hoover."

25

Thrills and Spills

Ninety-nine percent of the flying I've done at air shows or to and from them has gone off without a hitch. Over the years, though, I've had my share of thrills and spills.

The Reading Air Show has always been a favorite stop for me on the circuit. In the early 1970s, I'd drop into a riverbed that curves around the south and east side of the airport to add to the drama of the routine. Then I'd make my pass by touching down on one wheel, pull up and roll, and then touch down on the other wheel. I'd add power and go down in the riverbed where no one could see me. The dip off the end of the runway made it appear that the P-51 had crashed into an area that is not visible to the spectators.

I knew the geography around the river well. Every year, to intensify the suspense and the crowd's excitement, a fire truck would head for that area.

After disappearing, I would follow the riverbed. Then I'd reappear from the opposite direction the crowd was looking.

On one occasion, someone forgot to tell me a forty-thousand-volt unmarked power line had been strung across the river the year before. The shows at that time were always held at dusk, so I never saw the wire since it had no marking, no balloons.

I was thus totally surprised when my plane lurched to the left with a violent yawing motion. A big, blinding fireball appeared down in the river. I knew I'd hit a power line. I believed I had severely damaged the scoop and radiator. If so, I knew I had little time left in the air since without coolant the engine would overheat and catch fire.

I looked for a place to land and spotted a field to the right. I was prepared to land if the coolant (radiator) temperature increased, but the P-51 Rolls-Royce engine continued to run normally and all the instruments were in the green normal readings.

When I looked out to my left, I saw the damage inflicted by the cable. The outer section of the wing was pointed straight up, but it hadn't affected the performance of the airplane.

Since I didn't have much left to do in the routine, I finished it. The landing was smooth and we patched up the wing so I could perform the next day.

My name was not very popular in Reading that evening. The clipping of the cable created a power outage in a large section of the city.

At a future show in Reading, Jim Driskell ran into Jerry Ennis, my compatriot who escaped with me from Stalag I. I'd never told my family or Jim the story, and he was amazed to hear Jerry tell about our stealing the FW-190 and my flying it to freedom.

Absolutely no one has witnessed more wide-eyed rides with me than Jim Driskell. He remembers a hair-raising escapade in 1986.

> Fortunately, it was a beautiful clear day as Bob and I lifted off the runway at Medford, Oregon, in his newly acquired T-28B. It was Sunday afternoon, August 3, 1986, and we had both been participating in the air show, but we had to leave for Portland to catch the airliner home so we could make our tight schedule. It was to be Bob Hoover night in the "Theatre in the Woods" at Oshkosh the next night. On the previous Friday, Bob had started my "checkouts" in the T-28B, giving me "stick time" going from Medford, Oregon, to McMinnville, Oregon, and return, explaining to be very careful with the power settings and especially in power reductions. But back to the flight. As we were climbing through about 4,500 agl, I noticed a surge and fluctuations in the rpm gauge, indicating a runaway prop. We were twenty-five miles north of the Medford airport. Bob said, "Jimbo, we got us a real problem." I replied, "Yes, I know, I have a gauge too."
>
> Bob immediately made a climbing 180-degree turn, declared a Mayday. As we were still on the Medford radio frequency, we expected them to reply—as the air show was still in progress. Bob told me how we would handle the canopy and I would be expected to exit the aircraft on impact (we had no parachutes).
>
> From the way the aircraft was acting, it did not appear we would be able to make it back to the airport—and between our position and flight path back to the airport were only huge rocks in the mountainous terrain, very few open areas. Bob's continuing "Mayday, Mayday" brought no response, which was strange. As Bob tried to hold on to what little precious altitude we had to try to make it back to the airport, our troubles worsened as a fire developed in the lower engine. A

thought that had flashed through my mind at the start of the incident was, "If we had to make an off-airport landing, I was sure glad it was the Hoov in the front cockpit."

Somehow, calling on his past experiences and airmanship, he nursed the T-28B back so that we just barely made the runway at Medford. Immediately at touchdown the engine froze, and miraculously the fire blew itself out as we both scrambled to safety.

While there is something memorable about all of the air shows, the one at Reno stands out.

The Reno Air Races and Air Show began in 1964. The founder, Bill Stead, asked me to assist him in getting it started.

He was backed by several of the wealthy gambling-casino owners in the popular Nevada city. With their support, the event became very successful.

In addition to helping them in the early days, I began a thirty-year tradition of being the official starter for the races. Each one was begun with the words, "Gentlemen, you have a race." Then I would peel off and the competitors would go at it. It's a beautiful sight to see.

I performed aerobatic routines at Reno long before the races started and cherish the many friends I have made there over the years. Describing the excitement that goes on at Reno isn't easy, but my friend Richard Sands summed up his feelings about that event and one of my performances there in an article he wrote in the late 1980s:

> The scene at the Reno Air Races is truly an American portrait. If you're an air show aficionado, you are perched on top of your camper alongside the pit area adjacent to the east-west runway at Reno-Stead.
>
> You are sporting your aviator-type sunglasses, a B-17 baseball cap, and you have a cold drink in hand. . . . Bob Hoover's announcer, the ever-faithful Jim Driskell, has told you the Shrike was not designed to fly aerobatics and he warns other pilots of that fact. So for the last fifteen minutes you've been watching a pilot performing the forbidden.
>
> Now as Hoover finishes his third loop in the Shrike, you notice the unusual quiet. . . .
>
> All you can hear is the air rushing over the aluminum skin of the aircraft. Hoover pulls up at the east end of the runway holding two times the pull of gravity. For an instant, the aircraft just seems to hang in the sky as he goes over the top of the last loop, then the plane's nose slowly points toward the ground.
>
> The Shrike is coming downhill now and the powerless aircraft is screaming as it disappears from view on top of the sagebrush in the middle of the field, and everybody stands up to view the carnage. "Well," you say, "he's bought the farm on this one," and you wait for the telltale cloud of dust and smoke and noise of the fire engine and ambulance as they go to pick up what's left of the best pilot in the world.
>
> But there's no explosion, no ball of black smoke; just the Shrike

climbing out of the desert like a scared magpie flying out of the sage-brush. Hoover executes an eight-point roll before extending the landing gear beneath the aircraft. One more sweeping turn to the left after the roll and he aligns the aircraft with the taxiway for the landing.

Bob Hoover now touches the left wheel on the taxiway, the right wheel, lands the aircraft, exits on the high-speed taxiway and pulls up right in front of the cheering crowd—all without the aid of the engines. The last of the true barnstormers springs from the aircraft, tips the Hoover trademark—a wide-brimmed hat—and throws it to the crowd.

But wait a minute—this guy doesn't look like a hot stick and rudder-jamming, after-burning throttle jockey. Look at him! He's dressed in a Nomex fireproof flying suit. Until 1984, it had been a business suit and tie, but a near-catastrophic fire brought a change of attire.

Just look at him! There's the thick glasses and sun reflecting off that bald pate. He's over six feet tall and so thin you could snap him like a string bean. Tennessee Ernie Ford described him at one air show as a 2-iron with an Adam's apple. Maybe this guy's a college professor or a lawyer but certainly not a pilot. Where's the flowing black Clark Gable hair and the white scarf? Could this be the pilot they call the very best?

I appreciate Dick Sands's comments, but I don't think he needed to include the part about Clark Gable and the string bean.

I've had my share of close calls at Reno. One year I had a spine-tingling incident in the P-51.

I was performing a knife-edge-to-knife-edge routine prior to start-ing a race. Normally pilots perform a knife edge and then roll out and go over the top and do a knife edge on the other side. That means they are flying with all the lift coming off the fuselage during knife edge. The wings aren't assisting at all.

It's a difficult maneuver because the pilot has the controls crossed. They're pushing almost full rudder. That's a heavy force in an airplane like the Mustang.

To make it even more difficult, instead of rolling over the top, I'd roll underneath. That put negative loads on my body and on the air-plane.

On this occasion, I went from knife edge, underneath, upside down, and back to knife edge in the opposite direction. Just as I inverted and felt the negative loads, the seat belt snapped. I was thrown right into the canopy.

I was out of the seat. My buttocks were up against the canopy, face pressed against the windshield, and feet inverted up in the air. I was approximately one hundred feet above the runway. I was living a night-mare.

When I reached for the throttle and stick, I could barely reach them. My feet were a long way from the rudder pedals. Without their use for directional control, I knew changes in power would have to be applied gently. If I added too much power, the plane would get away from me because of the engine torque.

I managed to push the stick forward. All the while I had been worried whether the engine would quit from fuel starvation from being upside down.

When I felt I had enough power and airspeed, I eased the nose up. The plane kept yawing without rudder control. When I got the nose up high enough, I rolled and got the plane rightside up. I immediately flopped back in the seat and on the controls.

Puzzled looks greeted me when I landed. Trying to explain what happened was of great interest.

From that day on, I've had two safety belts in the Mustang. One is bolted to the floor so that if the seat breaks off its mounts, I'm still hanging in there. The other is connected to the seat.

After the incident, a strange thought came to mind. Had I not been so lucky to recover, it would have been easy for an accident investigator to have concluded that I was too old to be doing that type of flying and had had a heart attack.

Many years later, I experienced sabotage at Reno. In the early 1980s, I had just gotten airborne in the P-51, planning to start an unlimited race, when I noticed that I had dangerously low oil pressure. The race plane next to me did not hear my call of a Mayday and stayed in close formation. I was concerned that he would fly into me since I had no choice but to turn into him to make the runway. Fortunately, that didn't happen and I managed to land the plane safely with no damage.

To my disbelief, when the mechanics inspected the plane, they found mechanic's rags stuffed into the oil system. The crew reported this to an air-safety inspector. The FBI began an investigation.

Two suspects were identified. Then someone blew up a casino in Tahoe a few days later. The investigation got sidetracked, and I heard little about it from then on.

The Reno Air Races have not been without their deaths or dangerous incidents. Over the years, many pilots have been killed and many others have experienced near-disaster situations.

In September of 1988, a P-51 piloted by a Los Angeles attorney named David Price was competing in the unlimited Gold Race at Reno. His engine failed. He was set up to land on runway 14 and was handling the emergency quite well. Unfortunately, he had too much speed.

I sensed the problem, which is basically a judgment call I had had to make at Reno many times. At that speed, David had a chance to go right off the deep drop-off we call the "cliff" at the end of the runway. If that occurred, his P-51 would have flipped upside down.

Realizing the potential for real disaster, I called out, "Ground loop now, boot full right rudder, full right rudder." David heeded my instructions, and while the plane was damaged, he lived to fly another day.

Shortly after the incident, I received a letter from David that was most appreciated. It read in part:

> Dear Bob:
>
> I have had time to reflect upon the occurrence of last Saturday. I know that because of your personality and air show performances, the whole country has an affection for you, and all the people I know admire your accomplishments and attitude and politeness. . . .
>
> I realize now that without your calm guidance, I wouldn't be here to write this letter. The reason I say that is I have never ground-looped an airplane before (we were taught to avoid that). I also wasn't thinking of the cliff at the end of 14. I was only thinking about getting the airplane down. So for both reasons, the odds were very good that if you weren't up there taking care of your chickens, I would have sailed over that cliff with disastrous consequences.
>
> The damage to the airplane can be fixed and will take three to six months. I think the experience of the air racing and the emergency will make me a better pilot in the future.
>
> Obviously, it is not easy to thank somebody for saving your life. You saved mine and I certainly stand by to help you in any way that I can in the future. I hope you are not too timid to ask me when you need to.

In the late 1970s, I had performed at an air show at an SAC (Strategic Air Command) base in Grand Forks, North Dakota. I was flying the P-51 when I discovered a massive oil leak.

The tachometer had failed, which in itself is not a big problem. When I landed, however, I found out that a bunch of gears in the drive indicator had failed as well.

I told the commanding general there that I needed to get the plane fixed, since I was scheduled to depart for Calgary, Canada, right after my final performance. I would be performing there the next day.

Fortunately, the ground crew could fix the problem, but the general asked if I could spend the night and leave early the next morning. The mayor and the governor were coming to a dinner at which I was to be the guest of honor. As it turned out, I was lucky I didn't fly that night.

I left at the crack of daylight the next day for the two-hour flight across the Canadian plains to Calgary. There had been a great deal of rain, and the wheat fields below looked like swamps.

Thirty-five miles from Calgary, my engine started backfiring and shaking so violently that pieces of cowling blew off. The engine started emitting black smoke and firing intermittently. I couldn't land in the fields because of the water.

As I viewed the terrain, I noticed a country road, a turtleback containing two narrow lanes. The road wasn't wide enough for both wheels. Having no other choice, I landed on one wheel, and as the speed decreased, I eased the other main wheel down. I had shut off all the engine switches and sat there just short of a bridge, straddling the road in the middle of nowhere.

A few minutes went by before a car came over the hill toward me. I couldn't put on the parking brake to get out of the plane. The brakes were so hot they would weld together from the excessive heat from the heavy braking that was necessary to get stopped before hitting the bridge.

The driver of the car took one look at the big, smoking airplane sitting in the middle of the road. He must have thought he'd slipped into a *Twilight Zone* episode. He raced back to his car and took off.

A short time later, someone drove up in back of me. A petite woman emerged from a van full of school children. She briskly approached the cockpit as if an airplane blocking the road were a daily occurrence. She said in a calm but firm tone, "You get that thing off the highway; I have to take these children to school in Strathmore!"

Despite her demands, I had to sit there for some time before a farmer arrived who told me he was a pilot and understood my problem. By this time, several cars were waiting to get by. He got them to back up so I could let the airplane roll backward down a bank, which permitted one lane of traffic to get by.

After about an hour, two Royal Canadian policemen arrived in a police car and advised me that I was under arrest for entering the country without clearing customs. They advised me that they were taking me to the police station in Strathmore where I would be detained until the customs official arrived.

The police were very cordial. One of the officers asked if I knew Milt Harrandence, a Canadian who once owned two P-51s. I told him I'd met Milt at an air show in Las Vegas. I asked if he knew how I could reach him by phone.

I called Milt in Alberta to find out if he knew where I could locate an engine. When I got through to him, he said he'd fly down to Calgary that morning. "I will take care of customs for you," he said. "I'll get Roy Moore, who has an airplane dealership at the airport, to take care of your airplane. You will be my houseguest, and I'll have a car for your use until the airplane is ready to fly."

The P-51 was towed with a police escort thirty-five miles down the Trans-Canadian Highway to the airport. The only engine available was a spare that was being used to pump oil at an oil field. I had never considered that an aircraft engine could be used in an oil rig.

The pump engine was installed, and I made a short flight to check it out since it was not certified for flight. Before departing for Abbotsford near Vancouver, British Columbia, I climbed to thirty thousand feet above the Calgary airport before heading over the Rockies. Just in case the oil-pump engine gave me a problem, I would be able to glide a long way. Fortunately, that wasn't required and I made it safely to Abbotsford.

Through Milt, I would later meet a great man named Sir Douglas Bader.

Prior to World War II, Sir Douglas had been in a crash of a Bristol Bulldog fighter. He lost both legs. Doctors told him he'd never fly again, but he became so skilled at walking with his prostheses that they couldn't keep him out of the war.

During the Battle of Britain, Sir Douglas was shot down in a Spitfire and captured by the Germans, losing his artificial legs. His captors were so impressed with him that they permitted a British cargo plane to enter the war zone free from fire to drop new ones.

Sir Douglas immediately used those new legs to escape. He was captured again. His legs were taken away. They only gave them back after he gave his word he wouldn't try again. He didn't.

The queen of England knighted Douglas. Later, an inspiring book describing his exploits was published. I used to give it to any aviator friends who had lost a limb.

In 1988, I was participating in the Fort Worth Air Show with both the Sabreliner and the Shrike Commander. During the Shrike demonstration, I entered a planned five-turn spin prior to the energy-management dead-stick maneuver.

Suddenly, the nose sliced out to the left into a flat spin. The nose would not drop below the horizon. I instantly placed the flight controls into a recovery application, to no effect. The wings were almost level. The engine power was at idle for the first two turns. On the third turn, I applied maximum power to the left engine and idled the right engine. No change. I couldn't seem to break the gyroscopic effect.

At this point, I realized I was in a life-threatening spot. I decided to pull the throttles to idle, then apply full power on both engines. Normally this would speed up the rotation of the flat spin. I was hoping that at full power with the elevator control full forward, I would get enough wind under the down elevators to dump the nose.

It worked. Within two turns, I had a full recovery from the spin— just soon enough for a safe recovery on the pullout to level flight.

The chance I took in adding full power on both engines was the only option available since I do not wear a parachute. Even with a parachute, I would have gone right into the propeller as I exited the door. I had been performing spins in the Shrike for twenty years and would have bet anything that it would not spin flat. That experience taught me differently. I omitted the spins from my performance.

The P-51 and I have a long history of adventure. Jim Driskell says besides that shaky episode in the Shrike at Fort Worth, the most frightened he's ever been for my welfare happened over the skies of Marysville, Ohio:

> Hoov had just about completed his routine in the Mustang. He had just done a landing out of a loop and taken off.
>
> All at once I heard his voice on the radio: "Jim, I have a problem. I don't think I can make it back to the field."
>
> Bob was headed across my view from left to right. As he pulled up, I scrambled the crash trucks, the fire trucks, and the ambulance.
>
> Hoov continued downwind. As far as I could tell, the flight looked normal. What I didn't know was that he didn't have any airspeed, and he was already on fire internally.
>
> When the plane came in straight at me, I saw the hundred-foot flames and yelled, "Fire in the bottom of your right wing." Finally, he got the plane on the ground on that short two-thousand-foot runway with trees at the end and ran for safety. He was wearing only a crash helmet, but no other safety equipment. He set a speed record as he ran from the plane.

While most people believe I'm competent to take an airplane through risky maneuvers at an air show, one man will always question my ability to drive near one.

In 1984, I was participating in the Abbotsford Air Show east of Vancouver. Unfortunately, bumper-to-bumper traffic from the freeway to the airfield put me behind schedule. To get a bead on how close I was to my launch time, I kept peering out the window of the rental car to see who was performing.

While concentrating on the planes in the air, I smacked the car ahead of me, which had abruptly stopped. Before I could get out to assess the damage, the driver raced to my open window.

"Damn it, I just bought this brand-new Lincoln for my wife," he exclaimed. "Worse than that, now I'm gonna miss seeing Bob Hoover fly."

I was embarrassed to have to tell him who I was, but it helped alleviate the man's concern that he would miss my flight. He parked his car over by the curb and he and his wife hopped in with me. I took them through the VIP gate and right up to the P-51 and the Shrike that I would be flying that day.

Another bout with an automobile at the Kissimmee Air Show in Florida earned me a spot on famed radio personality, fellow aviator, and longtime friend Paul Harvey's famous "Rest of the Story" segment in October of 1988.

Paul began his broadcast with the words, "Bob Hoover has crashed." He went on to tell the listener of my aviation achievements and the fact that he had flown with the man he called the "pilot's pilot."

Once he had his audience expecting my demise in some tragic plane crash, Paul told them the "rest of the story." I had been broadsided by another car while driving from the annual Kissimmee Air Show. Five broken ribs and a punctured lung put me in the hospital.

One of the more frightening experiences I've had occurred after an air show in 1989 at San Diego. It was held at Brown Field, which is located just a few miles from the Mexican border.

I had completed my performances in the P-51 and the Shrike Commander. I told the line boy who drove the fuel truck to service the Shrike quickly so I could leave right after the show was completed.

The young man asked how much fuel I needed. I told him I wanted precisely sixty gallons. I added, "That's hundred octane."

After my performance, I went to the manager's office, where he received a phone call from the same young man. The manager told me the boy wanted to know if 100 LL (low lead) was all right for my airplane. I told him it was. He relayed the message.

Normally I like to be present when the airplane is being serviced, but I was held up when I came out of the airport manager's office. By the time I got to the airplane, the truck was pulling away. I said, "Fueling done?" The boy replied, "Yes, sir. It was sixty gallons precisely."

When I taxied out, probably at least a hundred airplanes were waiting for takeoff. But as soon as I called in, the tower said, "Mr. Hoover, we want you to taxi to the head of the line."

I did not like to leapfrog ahead of other pilots. However, since time was scarce that day for me and my two passengers, I accepted the tower's kind offer.

The takeoff was smooth. Everything was normal and checked out perfectly. All of a sudden, at about three hundred feet, I realized I didn't have any power in the Shrike. I started losing airspeed.

I dumped the nose, but I couldn't understand what was happening. Everything checked out. The manifold pressure was right where it was supposed to be. The rpm were at the right setting. The fuel pressure and oil pressure were in good shape.

Even though the gauges indicated that nothing was wrong, I knew something was. I started looking for a place to land. That would not be easy.

Brown Field is located on a plateau. To the north where I was headed, there were deep ravines. I could try to recover and head back to the airport, but I knew I wouldn't make it.

My two passengers tried to remain calm, but they were obviously frightened. Both thought we were going to crash and die. "Mr. Hoover," they asked more than once, "are we going to make it?" I assured them we would.

As I have mentioned before, each time potential disaster strikes, I rely on my experience of anticipating trouble to help me out. I had flown the P-51 cross-country for many years. I'd often considered what might happen if I had to put it down over the Rockies.

Recalling those thoughts, I dumped the nose of the Shrike. I kept my best glide speed until I reached the very end of the ravine. Landing in the bottom of the canyon meant no survival. Our only chance was to pull up and land on the side of the ravine.

As my airspeed bled off, I dropped the landing gear and flaps. I wanted to be at a minimum forward speed on impact. The landing gear would cushion the impact along with the tires and struts before the impact hit us square on.

I was down in a V-shaped ravine. A thousand feet wide at the top, it narrowed down to nothing at the bottom. I went right to the bottom to maintain the best glide speed. I then pulled the plane up and landed into the side of the ravine. I didn't travel very far at all before I hit a rock pile that caved in the nose. The instrument panel was torn out of its mounts and dropped down on my shins.

Neither of my passengers was hurt, but there was one fatality. We ran over a rattlesnake with the belly of the airplane when the gear tore out from under it.

We sat there awaiting rescue. I considered what had caused the lack of power. Only one thing was possible: the plane had been serviced with jet fuel instead of gasoline.

To confirm my suspicions, I went around to the side of the airplane and opened the drain valve. I leaned down and took a whiff. Sure enough, it was jet fuel.

My mind flashed at once to the young man I had asked to service the airplane. He must have known by then what had happened as I had informed the tower of the emergency.

Within minutes, rescue helicopters were on the scene. My passengers and I climbed up the ravine and were transported back to Brown Field.

After making sure the Shrike would be protected from theft, I asked, "Where is the line boy who serviced the plane?"

Everyone seemed reluctant to tell me, apparently afraid that I wanted to chew him out or be unkind to him. Finally, someone said, "He's outside."

An article in the *Fullerton* (Calif.) *News-Tribune* the next day quoted me regarding what happened next:

> When I got back to the field, I saw the boy standing by the fence with tears in his eyes.
>
> I went over and put my arm around him and said, "There isn't a man alive who hasn't made a mistake. But I'm positive you'll never make this mistake again. That's why I want to make sure that you're the only one to refuel my plane tomorrow. I won't let anyone else on the field touch it."

Just as I said, I had the boy refuel my P-51 for the final two days of the air show. Needless to say, there were no further incidents.

Shortly after that, I received a wonderful letter from a doctor in Palos Verdes named William Snow. He wrote:

> I wanted you to know that I was quite touched by the apparent casual way in which you treated your unfortunate incident. Thank goodness it was just that and nothing more! However, what really impressed me was your genuine concern for the young man who had serviced your plane.
>
> It is rare to find a person who has just experienced such a close brush with death and yet feels such compassion for his fellow man. God surely must be your copilot!

As I look back, my participation in air shows has been a wonderful experience.

When people ask what it's like to perform aerobatic maneuvers, I go back to the words I used to describe my first solo flight more than fifty years ago. Every time I fly, I experience another dimension of existence, no longer tied to the earth. I feel free—free of gravity, free of everything. It's the greatest feeling in the world.

EPILOGUE

Dogfighting with the FAA

During more than fifty years of flying, safety has always been my main consideration. I have never flown when I didn't feel that I had the capacity to do so or that I might in any way endanger others. Through my behavior, I have tried to set an example for other pilots.

Over the years, I was cited for minor violations by the FAA, but I could never have anticipated entering into a three-year-plus battle with them to save the medical certificate that is required to keep a pilot's license. Despite my safety record and handling of countless emergencies and mechanical failures, my collision course with FAA over whether it was safe for me to fly finally grounded me from flying solo in the United States.

The whole brouhaha began after I performed my usual aerobatic routine in the Shrike Commander during the 1992 Aerospace America Air Show in Oklahoma City. I felt that my flight demonstrations met the high standards I have always set for myself. Expert aerobatic champions Leo Loudenslager, Sean D. Tucker, and Steve Oliver, all members of ACE (Aerobatic Competency Evaluators—appointed by the FAA) who witnessed the performance, agreed.

Nevertheless, more than two months after the performance at Oklahoma City, two FAA inspectors named Clint Boehler and James Kelln arbitrarily filed a report stating that, based on their observations at that show, my flying skills had deteriorated. They concluded that, at seventy years of age, it was time for me to hang up my wings and retire from air show performances.

I didn't know either of these two men. Later I was told that they saw this as an opportunity to make a reputation for themselves by being the ones who grounded Bob Hoover. One of them referred to me as the "old bastard" and said that "[Hoover] has been around a long time, and he is not what he once was. He has never been violated because of who he is. It's time he has to stand accountable like everyone else."

Based on their report, official word soon reached me that I would be required to take a battery of tests designed to check my mental and physical competence. Still believing the allegations of impropriety to be some sort of mix-up, I volunteered to take the tests. They were administered by an FAA-appointed psychiatrist, who pronounced me fit. This was no surprise since I always prided myself in being in top physical and mental condition.

Based on this evaluation and other tests that were performed, I assumed my worries were over. It was then that I discovered what governmental bureaucracy can do if it decides to flex its muscle. This slap in the face occurred when the FAA, apparently bowing to internal pressure, informed me and my personal physician, Bert Puskus, that I was unfit to fly and should surrender my medical certificate. I had no idea that I was not required to do so without further findings of fact.

Before April 13, 1994, the only time I had been grounded for any length of time during my years in aviation was when I was captured by the Germans during War II. On that date, however, the almighty FAA, flush in the face of my aviation record, my service to my country, and a mountain of evidence in my favor, informed me that I could no longer fly solo.

The amazing thing about this arbitrary action, done without a hearing or other due process, was that it disregarded the fact that I had flown thirty-three demonstrations since the investigation had begun without incident. Realizing this and bowing to pressure from colleagues and supporters who championed my cause, the FAA agreed to let me undergo a new, independent series of tests.

For the next eighteen months, the battle would involve further physical and mental examinations and legal maneuvers by my attorney, F. Lee Bailey, and his colleague John Yodice. Prior to an administrative law hearing scheduled for Oklahoma City, Lee suggested that I videotape my aerobatic routine so that I could demonstrate to the court that my abilities had not deteriorated.

I secured an ex-Navy T-28B Trainer NX171BA for this purpose from Bob Grant, owner of Great American Aircraft, who maintained my P-51. He also linked me up with Ray Hughes, a pilot who holds a commercial license and letter of authorization in the T-28. He agreed to videotape the demonstration from the backseat of the aircraft.

Ray and I could never have anticipated what was in store for us.

After I landed the T-28 on January 5, 1994, the following flight report was filed:

> Prior to takeoff, the engine was warmed up until the oil temperature and pressure were in the green. The engine run-up and magneto check were normal without a drop in rpm. After takeoff clearance was received, the power application was smooth with a normal takeoff and climb over the top of the Torrance airport at 2,500 feet. The airplane was continued in a climb toward Catalina Island. The engine operation was normal through a series of maneuvers, a four-point roll to the right, then an eight-point roll to the left, followed by a sixteen-point roll to the left. Two loops and one-half of a Cuban eight were performed. Upon recovering from this maneuver, the Chip warning red light illuminated, indicating a detection of metal in the oil system. This warrants landing the airplane as soon as possible.
>
> Immediately following the illumination of the Chip light, the propeller governor control failed to hold the engine and propeller rpm, causing an excessive overspeed condition. This resulted in an increase on the oil temperature gauge and decrease in oil pressure. The engine was kept running intermittently by constantly manipulating the engine controls, throttle, mixture, and propeller lever, as well as the engine cooling flaps. Each time the engine would stop running or backfire, an adjustment was made to get it running again. When the engine was running, it was so rough that it felt as if it would shake the airplane apart. The airplane was headed on a straight line to the Torrance airport immediately after the Chip warning light came on.
>
> The control tower was advised of the Mayday with a request for a straight-in approach. The T-28B was landed without power on the end of runway 29. Right at touchdown, the engine froze, shaking the airplane so severely as to break the fittings, attach points to the fuselage to the wings, and twist the engine from its mount. The bolts holding the engine mounts were sheared and the engine twisted the fuselage.

Handling of this emergency should have convinced the FAA that my capabilities were as good as ever. They had alleged that my "cognitive abilities" were deficient, but their medical consultants admitted that someone with such deficiencies should not have been able to handle a novel or emergency situation such as the one experienced in the T-28.

Prior to the hearing, my friend Bill Rheinschild, an unlimited air-racing pilot, introduced me to Dr. Brent Hisey, a neurosurgeon and owner/pilot of the *Miss America* P-51 unlimited racer. He agreed to put me through the most thorough exams possible at no cost. I passed those tests, and Brent and his colleague Dr. David Johnson agreed to testify for me in court. Based on the videotape of the T-28 flight, my safety record, and the doctor's potential testimony, Lee Bailey, who had represented me at no cost during the entire legal process, felt we had a good chance in front of administrative law judge William R. Mullins.

We were successful at the hearing, but all of the evidence was completely ignored by the National Transportation Safety Board when they reversed the judge's decision. Unsuccessful appeals all the way to the U.S. Supreme Court followed.

Since air show performances had been my main source of income for many years, the grounding had not only restricted me from doing what I enjoyed most, but left me without needed sponsorships. If not for a wonderful group of aviators headed up by Tom Poberezny, Chuck Yeager, Leo Loudenslager, Sean Tucker, Steve Oliver, and Jim Brown, who formed a financial-help group called Friends of Bob Hoover to aid my legal defense, I could not have continued to fight to retrieve my medical certificate.

I will always be appreciative to those who contributed to that fund. I received letters of support containing donations from all over the world. One boy, a ten-year-old, wrote a letter and sent a $5 bill in the envelope. Of course, when money came in like that, I sent it back, but it was heartwarming all the same.

I also had wonderful encouragement from my family. My wife, Colleen; son, Rob; and daughter, Anita, wanted me to fight back no matter the cost.

Prior to the grounding, I had met with Margeret and Terry Mulholland, residents of Tasmania, Australia. They were planning Sky Race '94, the first-ever pylon air race there. Our discussions resulted in a signed contract whereby I would start their races and perform every day in a Shrike and a T-28.

The cooperation I received from everyone in Australia was incredible. Steve Nott, who owns General Aviation Maintenance in Melbourne, provided use of a Shrike that I had flown in the United States before he bought it. He and his chief pilot, Gary Trench, generously flew the plane to locations so I could fly it. Don Kendell, founder of Kendell Air Lines, let me use his T-28.

The Mulhollands contacted Dr. Rob Liddell, director of aviation medicine for the CAA (Civil Aviation Authority) in Australia. Made aware of the FAA action, Rob suggested I take an Australian First Class medical examination from Dr. Larry Marinelli. After I passed that test, Rob told me that he would set it up for me to take a CPL (commercial pilot's license) written exam and flight check.

When Colleen and I arrived in Australia, we were treated royally. Terry and Margeret Mulholland and Di and Hugh Targett, the director of Sky Race '94, were most helpful. Hugh made arrangements with the Launceton Aero Club to assist me in preparation for the CPL test. Three members acted as coaches through my study period. Hugh even lent me his law office so I could sort out the differences between the FAA and CAA air regulations.

I was flight-checked by Barry Diamond, a former Australian Navy fighter pilot and the CAA flight operations manager. He told me that the check ride would be even more thorough than normal since he anticipated close scrutiny of the results. After our flight, Barry told the Australian publication *Aeroplane Monthly*, "In a smooth and precise routine, Bob Hoover proved that age has had no obvious effect on his awesome ability with two-engines . . . one-engine . . . no-engines aerobatic routine."

After completion of all of the tests and the flight check, I was given a first-class commercial airline pilot rating, which qualified me to fly anywhere in the world *except* the United States.

I will always be thankful to Rob Liddell and all the many Australian friends who supported me. They gave me back the dignity that had been denied by the FAA.

To show my appreciation, I had the Australian flag sewn on one shoulder of my flight suit. The American flag is on the other.

Despite my pleasant experiences in Australia, reinstatement of my medical certificate in the United States was still foremost in my mind. Loss at the court level had been very discouraging. When that occurred, I had seen little hope for success. Many people thought I should give up.

One who didn't was my great friend Rob Liddell. In the spring of 1995, he suggested I attempt to set up a meeting with Dr. Jon Jordan, the FAA federal air surgeon. Rob felt that there had been many misunderstandings and bureaucratic mistakes. He thought that perhaps if Dr. Jordan and I talked face-to-face, things might be cleared up.

Rob organized the meeting with Dr. Jordan, which took place in May of 1995 in Anaheim, California. Rob and one of Dr. Jordan's associates, Dr. Bob Poole, joined us.

That meeting resulted in my agreeing to pursue my rights without further legal representation. I also agreed to submit to additional neurological, psychological, and physical tests that were to be coordinated by Dr. Garry Ferris, a friend of both Jon Jordan and Rob Liddell.

Dr. Jordon told me he would personally review the results and, if favorable, reinstate my medical immediately. Time dragged on as I awaited the results. When the report was in my favor, I was certain I would be reinstated. I was sadly disappointed when Dr. Jordan informed me that would not be the case, but he did agree to have the test results reviewed by independent consultants not on the FAA payroll.

I doubt Dr. Jordan's decision would have been changed had it not been for the continuing pressure being applied by my friends and supporters. Thousands of letters and repeated complaints to FAA officials kept the heat on. FAA administrator David Hinson found out how strong the support was at the EAA Annual Fly In at Oshkosh in July of 1995. Beside seeing thousands of flyers that read "Let Bob Fly" posted everywhere, he was asked many questions about the status of the case. His answer that my test results were being reviewed by independent consultants to the FAA did not bode well with the audience.

Several months went by without any decision. I would wake up in the night and think about what had gone wrong. I asked myself, "How could this happen in a great country like ours?" I couldn't comprehend how such an injustice could be set up without basis.

I had just about given up hope when the telephone rang on October 19, 1995. The caller was Dr. Bob Poole, and he informed me that my medical was being reinstated.

What caused Jon Jordan and the FAA to change their decision I do not know for certain. I have to believe that continued pressure by those who supported me and some sense of regret for the arbitrary manner in which the medical certificate was taken finally prevailed. After eighteen months, I would be able to fly solo once again in the United States of America.

The whole episode with the FAA has been a nightmare. Hopefully, my success in fighting the system will prevent something like this from occurring in the future to other pilots.

Through this episode, I learned many things. None more than what true friendship means. Colleen and I will never forget the thousands of aviators and friends who stood with us in the fight to win. To all of them, I say thank you.

My first chance to fly solo in the United States came at the Skyfest Daytona '95 air show in Florida in November of 1995. Promoter Rick Grissom's event was a most memorable one. Air Force captain Scott O'Grady, who spent four days eluding hostile forces after his F-16 fighter was shot down over Bosnia, was the grand marshal. The show also marked the final performance by Charlie Hillard, Tom Poberezny, and Gene Soucy, all members for twenty-five years of the famous Eagles Aerobatic Team. In my travels around the world, they were considered to be the best.

While I had been used to performing in the Shrike Commander, Palm Beach Roamer, an aviation company owned by F. Lee Bailey (and operated by his son, Scott), invited me to fly their new *Hoover Hornet* at Skyfest. It's an Aero Commander aircraft that has been remanufactured and completely modified with the latest technological advances in avionics and environmental systems. Because of aerodynamic cleanup, the rate of climb has been greatly increased.

Flying the *Hornet* with the new electric air-conditioning system made my flight in the Florida humidity a true pleasure.

The reception by the spectators and the news media interest and coverage at the air show was heartwarming. I'm certain 1996 will be a banner year since I will have the opportunity to thank the many thousands of people who supported me in the fight with the FAA.

I hope to continue performing into the next century unless I feel my capacity to do so has diminished. If so, I will be the first one to throw in the towel. Until then, I'll continue on, forever flying.

GLOSSARY

Bob Hoover Aerobatic Maneuvers

I. The Roll after Takeoff

Synopsis: To begin an air show, Bob Hoover lifts off with sufficient speed so as to gain enough altitude and then roll the plane on its longitudinal axis 360 degrees.

Bob Hoover on the Roll after Takeoff: "Aviators need to gain sufficient speed to get the nose well above the horizon so they can roll it and recover at a comfortable height."

2. Point Roll

Bob Hoover describing the slow Roll on the Point: "If a pilot were to see a very tall smokestack from a few miles distance and wanted to roll on a point, he would picture the top of the smokestack and roll toward it and never change altitude. The nose is pointed in that direction and toward the object all the way through."

3. The Knife Edge to Knife Edge

Synopsis: Instead of the aircraft's being horizontal to the earth, Bob Hoover tilts the plane sideways to make it perpendicular gaining lift from the fuselage (body of the aircraft rather than the wings). Going over the top is not difficult, but he rotates underneath and back up on the other side.

Bob Hoover on the Knife Edge to Knife Edge: "The pilot rolls the plane up on its side perpendicular to the earth. All that is lifting the plane is the fuselage. Then the pilot goes underneath [upside down] and back up on the other side. It wouldn't be as difficult if the pilot went over the top, but by going underneath it's more difficult to hold the nose up. I used to do it over the top, but then I decided to test my skill and go underneath. The danger is that if the pilot lets it dish, he's dead."

4. Four-, Eight-, and Sixteen-Point Hesitation Rolls

Synopsis: To perform the four-point hesitation roll, the aircraft is taken from a level position and rolled to ninety degrees, paused, then rolled another ninety degrees until upside down, paused, then rolled ninety degrees to the knife edge, paused, then rolled the final ninety degrees to right side up.

To attempt the more difficult routines, the pie is sliced eight times, then sixteen.

Bob Hoover on the Hesitation Roll: "The hesitation slow roll can be described as slicing a pie sitting flat on the table. By cutting from one side of the pie through the middle to the other side, and then cutting that one more time, that would be four equal slices of pie. Now think about taking that pie and setting it up on its edge and then starting at the middle and making each slice separate and equal. It becomes a lot more difficult because it's more difficult to start at the middle. But that is required when pilots do a point roll or hesitation slow roll. They're on a point like the smokestack I described before, and they roll like this [waves hands in rolling motion] and stay on that point.

"The eight-point roll is the same except they're chopping the pie now into eight slices and then into sixteen. I have on several occasions in years gone by done as many as thirty-two. Nobody can appreciate the thirty-two-point roll because the hesitations are so brief the pilot and plane are out of sight in a fighter. But a sixteen-point roll can be completed over a five-thousand-foot runway with an average fighter.

"I've always referred to the sixteen-point roll as the grandaddy of preciseness."

5. Loops

Synopsis: Loops are common in any aerobatic routine, but the key is not asking the plane to perform any tasks for which it is overmatched. Round loops close to the ground are more tricky if the pilot doesn't have plenty of power or speed to be able to climb high enough for a safe recovery.

Bob Hoover on performing loops: "Every aerobatic pilot has a loop incorporated in his sequence of events. It's not a difficult maneuver. But when pilots start adding derivatives of a basic loop, it can become more difficult or require more skill in executing the maneuver accurately. If the airplane has the proper performance, and most all of the current aerobatic airplanes do, pilots have sufficient power to do a number of things with a given loop. For instance, I developed a maneuver many years ago with some of the fighters where I come around and just do a level roll a couple hundred feet above the ground, then execute the pull-up of ninety degrees to the vertical. Then I execute a roll going straight up on the vertical, recover, and then pull the nose down to parallel with the horizon, then another roll across the top of the loop. This would be a square loop—four sides—but instead of straight up, straight across the top, and straight down, you have to do a roll on the vertical, a roll across the top, and a roll coming straight down, and then pull out of the dive, then another roll on the level two hundred feet above the ground."

6. Cuban Eight

Synopsis: An American aerobatic pilot in the late 1920s or early 1930s performed this maneuver down in Cuba. The Cuban eight is slightly more than a half loop, and when the plane comes over the top, it is pulled through until the nose is forty-five degrees downhill from the horizon, then rolled right side up, and the dive is continued until you are ready to pull up for the second half of the maneuver. What you have is the numeral eight laid on its side. It's easy as pie to do even for an amateur aerobatic pilot.

Bob Hoover on the Cuban eight: "Now they can make it tough, and many performers do these days. If they put twists in there, it makes it much more difficult. For example, they can come in, and as they start up on the loop, they can do it inverted if they have an airplane designed to fly inverted. The aerobatic airplanes are all designed for that kind of flying. So they can come in and do this inverted. They come in flat, roll upside down, and then do their Cuban eight, roll, and come back out, go all the way around, and they can still be upside down. Then they do a series of rolls coming down, and they can do them inverted. They can do any number of things. These are the innovations to the same horizontal figure eight."

7. Tennessee Waltz

Synopsis: Bob Hoover's most graceful maneuver, the Tennessee Waltz is a series of side slips that cause the plane to rock back and forth in perfect sync while appearing never to lose a step.

Bob Hoover on the Tennessee Waltz: "This is not a difficult maneuver, but it is certainly a graceful one. An announcer at an air show dubbed it the Tennessee Waltz since I'm from Nashville. I enjoy doing the maneuver because it is so graceful."

8. Vertical Flight to Zero Airspeed

Synopsis: The Aero Commander is not designed to go backward, but in this routine the plane goes straight up until it runs out of speed. Just before the airspeed reaches zero, the controls are pushed forward to start the nose back to level flight. The timing is critical because if the plane went into a whip stall, it could be catastrophic.

9. Five-Turn Spin

Synopsis: The controls are positioned to make the plane spin in a gyroscopic effect. If the spin goes flat, the plane's attitude is almost level with the horizon. A normal spin would have a nose-down attitude of approximately forty-five degrees. In the Shrike, recovery from a flat spin is marginal.

10. Touchdown with One Wheel and Then the Other

Synopsis: After the plane has been run through its array of maneuvers, a Bob Hoover performance culminates in a touchdown with one wheel, then a touchdown with the other.

11. The Upside-Down Iced Tea

Synopsis: This routine, which features Hoover pouring iced tea into a glass while upside down in a Sabreliner or Shrike, is done strictly for television and promotional purposes since it is not visible from the ground.

Bob Hoover on the Iced Tea Maneuver: "To show how smooth I could roll the new Sabreliner, I mounted a piece of Styrofoam out from the instrument panel. I put the glass up there and then held a full pitcher of iced tea in my right hand. I flew the plane with my left and poured the tea into the glass in a kind of backhanded way as the plane rolled. I poured iced tea as the world went around and amazingly enough didn't spill a drop."

I2. The Dead Engine Energy Management Maneuver

Synopsis: From thirty-five hundred feet above the ground, the plane is dived to ground level with both engines shut off and propellers feathered. The nose is pulled up into a loop. This is followed by an eight-point hesitation slow roll. Upon recovery, the plane is maneuvered through a 180-degree turn before heading toward the runway. A touchdown on one wheel is followed by a touch-down on the other one.

Hoover on the Dead Engine Energy Management Maneuver: "The Aero Commander, and the War II Lockheed P-38 Lightning, are the only planes that I have used for this maneuver. This routine really leaves no margin for error. It is a matter of converting altitude into airspeed and airspeed into the maneu-vers, dissipating the airspeed with each maneuver yet maintaining enough to get to the runway.

"In major international air shows such as Paris that run for eleven consecu-tive days, each flight is a challenge because there are no instruments to aid me. It is a constant assessment of positioning and timing because the wind and temperature have a tremendous effect on the profile.

"Even though I have repeated this maneuver thousands of times, I remind myself before each flight that the slightest error in judgment cannot be toler-ated."

APPENDIX

Auth __CG. 3AF__
Init _____
Date __11-18-42__
G-21

HEADQUARTERS ARMY AIR BASE DREW FIELD
Office of the Base Commander

Tampa, Florida.
Nov 13, 1942.

SPECIAL ORDERS)
               :   E X T R A C T
NUMBER   322)

       *   *   *   *   *   *

     22. Pursuant to authority contained in IA Secret ltr, Hq Third Air
Force, file 3AF 370 (11-17-42) AFB-056, Sub: "Movement Orders, Shipment AFB-056-
C & D", dtd Nov 17, 1942; the following EM and O, Hq 337th Ftr Gp, are reld fr
asgd thereto and trfd and reasgd to Shipment AFB-056-C:

2nd Lt EDWIN F. FULLER	0664174	2nd Lt. CHARLES A. RAWLS	0663561
2nd Lt CHARLES R. WOMACK	0664231	2nd Lt. RAY A. SAMUEL	0664243
2nd Lt WALTER O. WEST	0792085	2nd Lt. ALFRED A. ESPOSITE	0664165
2nd Lt BURL L. CREECH	0664143	2nd Lt. THOMAS E. SMITH	0792168
2nd Lt TAYLOR MALONE, JR.	0792044	2nd Lt. JAMES L. HOLLINGSWORTH, JR.	0792121

#In Charge
*S/Sgt. ROBERT A. HOOVER	20443029	S/Sgt. GEORGE A. BOLGER	20758523
" CHARLES A. GARRETT	18040868	" ROBERT C. ALLEN	14039755
" GEORGE Q. HOESCHER	15053914	" THOMAS E. WATTS	18043873
" ROY T. CARTER, JR.	6914404	" DEWEY L. GOSSETT	14030424
" WILLIAM R. JOY	14026267	" LESLIE M. CARPENTER. JR.	14060621
" URBAN F. STAHL	6995583	" WALTER J. MACKEY	20517864
" THOMAS W. GRAY	20443240	" THAD K. JOHNSON	14027171

    Shipment AFB-056-C, WP fr this sta to Ft. Hamilton, N. Y., de-
parting this sta in time to arrive thereat not later than 0400 Z, Nov 21, 1942,
RUA thereat to CO for duty pending movement overseas. PCS.
    Personnel will be equipped for extended field service in a mod-
erate climate with the following additional equipment:

        1 each compass, pocket
        1 each knife, hunting, 5" blade with leather sheath.
        1 each set of amber lens for goggles.
        1 each kit, jungle, emergency.
        1 each headset, HS-38 or HS-33 (HS-23 or HS-18 until exhausted).
        1 each flashlight, TL-122 A.
    IGF, while traveling, Govt will furnish party meal ticket (4 meals,
14 men), rate not to exceed $0.75 per meal, or $1.00 per meal, per men
when taken in dining car. (AR 30-2215). TOT journey going.
    Provisions of Third Air Force Memoranda 75-24, 75-25, and 65-3, as
amended, will be complied with.
    TDN: FD 31 P 431-01-02-03-04-05-07-08 A 0425-23.

- 1 -

289

S E C R E T

SECRET EX SO No 322, Hq AAB, Drew Field, Tampa, Fla., Nov 18, 1942 (Cont'd)

23. Pursuant to authority contained in IA Secret ltr, Hq Third Air
Force, file 3AF 370 (11-17-42) AFB-056, Sub: "Movement Orders, Shipment AFB-056-
C & D", dtd Nov 17, 1942; the following EM and O, Hq 337th Ftr Gp, are reld fr
asgd thereto and trfd and reasgd to Shipment AFB-056-D:

2nd Lt DAVID C. CRUM	0792686	2nd Lt HARRY W. BALDWIN	0792672
2nd Lt VERE M. BOHMAN	0792948	2nd Lt WARREN H. CHAPMAN	0792803
2nd Lt JAMES F. CASEY	0792959	2nd Lt ROBERT C. CONGDON	0792964
2nd Lt NEIL F. WASHER	0792889	2nd Lt ROBERT N. BARNETT	0792946
2nd Lt RICHARD J. DRAYTON	0792972	2nd Lt JEROME ENNIS	0792699
2nd Lt WILLIAM H. ELMER	0792351	2nd Lt HERMAN S. SOLEM	0792886
2nd Lt GEORGE T. FITZGIBBON	0792823	2nd Lt LEROY V. DODD	0792816
2nd Lt STANLEY S. HAND	0792830	2nd Lt ROBERT L. BURNETT III	0792955
2nd Lt FAY W. HEADIS	0792951	2nd Lt QUENTIN CHARLTON	0792805
2nd Lt GORDON W. FISHER	0664170	2nd Lt BRYANT Y. ANDERSON	0792943
2nd Lt ROBERT F. BELOVICH	0792794	2nd Lt JOHN R. BERTRAND	0792795
2nd Lt HOWELL B. COATES	0792962	2nd Lt LLOYD K. COVELLE, JR.	0792806
2nd Lt CLAUDE G. GODARD, JR.	0792983	2nd Lt RAYMOND E. SMITH	0662685
2nd Lt WILLIAM F. MEEL	0793014	2nd Lt WILLIAM S. SWANSON	0793026
2nd Lt WILLIAM A. MARANGELLO	0792722	2nd Lt ARTHUR E. SCARTORE, JR.	0792687
2nd Lt. WARREN G. STRALEY	01699065	2nd Lt HARRY A. COLEMAN	0792684
2nd Lt AUGUST V. DEGENARO	0792814	2nd Lt GEORGE S. DIETZ	0792815
2nd Lt GEORGE T. HARTMAN	0792024	2nd Lt HOMER J. BEATTY	0792674

S/Sgt LAWRENCE W. DYE	20619436	S/Sgt KIRBY E. SMITH	15056218
" ROBERT A. NICHOLSON	13023251	" ROBERT P. SPAULDING	11014129
" FREDERICK N. SMITH JR.	19006384	" KENNETH B. SMITH	6914277
" LEONARD H. JEFFRION JR.	14039859	" KENNETH W. McCARTHY	20349505
" ROGER V. HEARN	13001241	" JOHN J. KLEIN	16029151
" HOWARD S. ASKELSON	20717048	" HAROLD T. BARNABY	18007358
" JOSEPH L. SHANNON	20443196	" JAMES C. SMITH	13034544

Shipment AFB-056-D, WP fr this sta to Ft Hamilton, N.Y., departing
this sta in time to arrive thereat not later than 0400 Z, Nov 21, 1942, RUA
thereat to CO for duty pending movement overseas. PCS.
Personnel will be equipped for extended field service in a moderate
climate with the following additional equipment:

1 each compass, pocket.
1 each knife, hunting, 5" blade with leather sheath.
1 each set of amber lens for goggles.
1 each kit, jungle, emergency
1 each headset, HS-38 or HS-33 (HS-23 or HS-18 until exhausted)
1 each flashlight, TL-122 A.

IGF, while traveling, Govt will furnish party meal ticket (4 meals,
14 men), rate not to exceed $0.75 per meal, per man, or $1.00 per meal, per man
when taken in dining car. (AR 30-2215). TOT journey going.
Provisions of Third Air Force Memoranda 75-24, 75-25, and 65-8, as
amended, will be complied with.
TDN: FD 31 P 431-02-03-04-05-07-08 A 0425-23.
S E C R E T

-2-

S E C R E T

SECRET EX SO No 322, Hq AAB, Drew Field, Tampa, Fla.; Nov 18, 1942 (Cont'd)

*   *   *   *   *   *

By order of Colonel ASP:

A. W. LEWIS,
1st Lt., Air Corps,
Adjutant.

OFFICIAL:

F. W. Lewis

A. W. LEWIS,
1st Lt., Air Corps,
Adjutant.

SYMBOLS: WP - will proceed
RUA - reporting upon arrival
TOT - transportation officer will furnish transportation
IGF - it being impractical for the Govt to furn facilities for
cooking rations
TDN - travel directed is necessary in the military service

DISTRIBUTION: 5 cys CG, AAF
2 cys CG, Third Air Force
2 cys CG, III Fighter Command
2 cys CO, Hq 337th Ftr Gp
2 cys each O and EM involved (% CO, Hq 337th Ftr Gp-total 148 cys
2 cys Base Postal O
2 cys Base S-3
2 cys Base S-1
2 cys CG, NY P of E, Brooklyn, N. Y. (Attn: Operations Division)
2 cys Base Ord O
2 cys Base Finance O
10 cys File (Adj)

S E C R E T
-3-